D1236594

Tea

by the same author

The Great Hedge of India

Tea

**Addiction, Exploitation
and Empire**

ROY MOXHAM

CONSTABLE • LONDON

Constable & Robinson Ltd
3 The Lanchesters
162 Fulham Palace Road
London, W6 9ER
www.constablerobinson.com

First published in Great Britain by Constable,
an imprint of Constable & Robinson Ltd, 2003

Copyright © Roy Moxham 2003

The right of Roy Moxham to be identified as
the author of this work has been asserted by him in accordance
with the Copyright, Designs and Patents Act 1988

All rights reserved. This book is sold subject to the condition
that it shall not, by way of trade or otherwise, be lent, re-sold,
hired out or otherwise circulated in any form of binding or cover
other than that in which it is published and without a similar condition
including this condition being imposed on the subsequent purchaser.

A copy of the British Library Cataloguing in Publication Data is
available from the British Library

ISBN 1-84119-569-3

Printed and bound in the EU

For my mother – for many things,
including keeping the numerous letters that
I wrote to her when I was a tea planter.

Contents

Illustrations and Maps

Illustrations and Maps

Maps

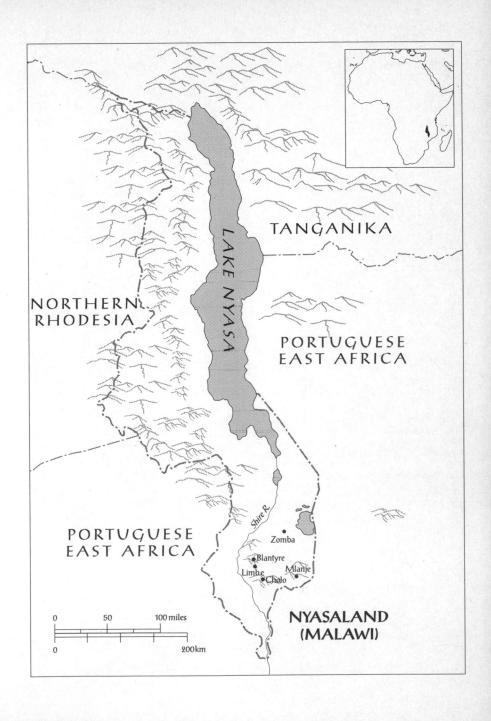

TANGANIKA

NORTHERN
RHODESIA

LAKE NYASA

PORTUGUESE
EAST AFRICA

PORTUGUESE
EAST AFRICA

Shire R.

Zomba

Blantyre

Limbe
Cholo

Mlanje

NYASALAND
(MALAWI)

0   50   100 miles

0   200km

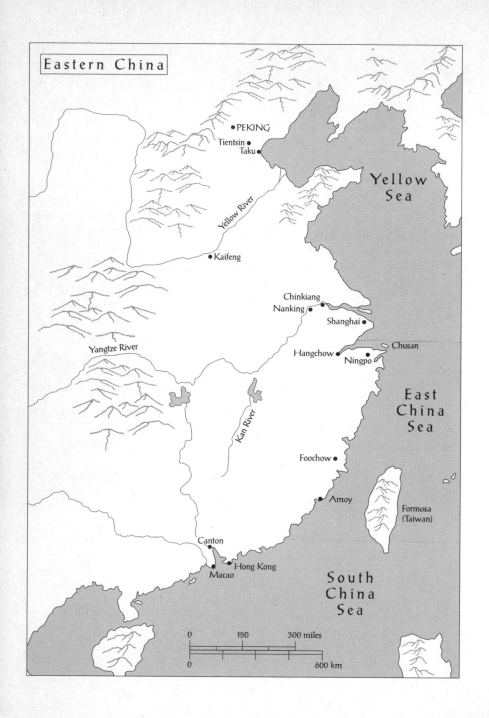

Eastern China

PEKING
Tientsin
Taku

Yellow
Sea

Yellow River

Kaifeng

Chinkiang
Nanking
Shanghai
Chusan

Hangchow
Ningpo

East
China
Sea

Yangtze River

Kan River

Foochow

Amoy

Formosa
(Taiwan)

Canton
Hong Kong
Macao

South
China
Sea

0   150   300 miles

0   600 km

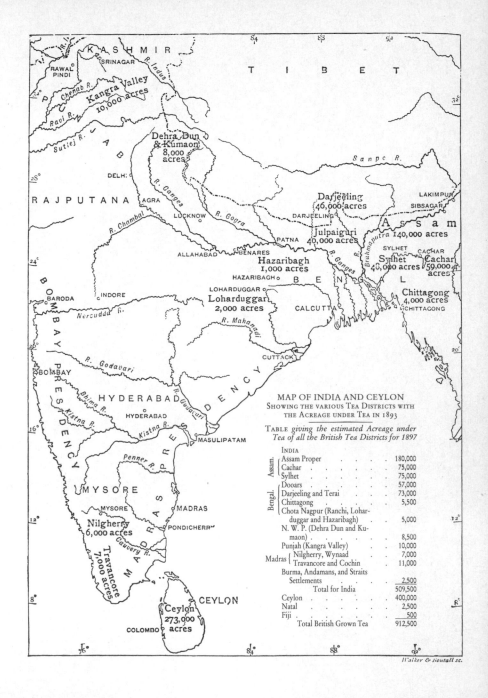

MAP OF INDIA AND CEYLON

SHOWING THE VARIOUS TEA DISTRICTS WITH THE ACREAGE UNDER TEA IN 1893

TABLE giving the estimated Acreage under Tea of all the British Tea Districts for 1897

A Job in Tea

In November 1960, thwarted in my attempts to get to university and tired of living in Britain, I placed an advertisement in the Personal Column of *The Times*:

> TOBACCO or Tea Estate ; young man (21), good A levels (Science), now fruit farming, seeks position, v.cw management.—Write Box Y.1901, The Times, E.C.4.

I only had one reply. A Mr Maclean Kay wrote to say that he owned a tea estate in Nyasaland (now Malawi) and was in Britain looking for an assistant manager. If I was interested, I should arrange an appointment to meet him at his London agent's office in Plantation House, Mincing Lane.

Mr Kay was short and stocky and, although in his seventies, his hair was still black. He was pleasant and direct, and sympathetic to a young man who wanted to see the world. He himself had been in the navy in the First World War and afterwards had been a planter in Malaya before he bought the estate in Nyasaland. He liked that I knew about fruit farming, and thought my grammar school education fine, even though most tea estates took men from public school.

He proposed what was, he said, a standard three-and-a-half-year contract. My passage out would be paid, and also my

1

passage back at the end of the contract, after which I would get six months' paid leave. In addition I would have a fortnight's local leave each year. I would be given a free house with basic furnishing, free water and free electricity. If we suited each other my contract would be renewed. My salary would be £600 a year.

The single fare to Nyasaland by air was over half a year's salary, so I was taking a big risk. I had no money, and my mother was a poor widow. If things went wrong I should not be able to afford the return fare. I needed to be sure that I was making the right decision.

When I had received Mr Kay's reply to my advertisement, I had only the vaguest idea about Nyasaland. I had gone to a public library to look up details. It was a small country by African standards, slightly smaller than England. Located in east-central Africa, it was in the tropics, south of the equator, and completely landlocked – bordered by Portuguese East Africa (now Mozambique) in the south, and by Northern Rhodesia (Zambia) and Tanganyika (Tanzania) in the north. The long narrow colony was mountainous and had a lake running almost its entire length. There were 3 million Africans and less than 10,000 Europeans. Although British, it was part of the Federation of Rhodesia and Nyasaland, which had a measure of self-government.

Mr Kay seemed very straight to me. I had no real idea whether the conditions he was offering were good or not, for I had no knowledge of tea planters or of Africa. He told me that my salary would be adequate to meet the cost of living, indeed more than most new 'assistants' received, and I believed him. The interview was over in half an hour. He promised that as soon as my references were checked, his agents would draw up a contract. I would then need to be interviewed by the British Immigrants Selection Board to obtain a residence permit for the Federation of Rhodesia and Nyasaland. If that all went smoothly, he wanted me to fly out mid January, as the estate was very short-staffed and it was the height of the plucking season.

'One thing,' he said. 'We like all our young men to join the Colonial Police Reserve – in case of trouble. Will that be all right with you?'

'Yes,' I said. 'I was in the cadets at school, so I should be able to manage that.'

'Good.' He shook my hand, and I was almost out of the door when he added, 'And, of course, you can drive?'

'Yes,' I lied without hesitation. I thought that once I was in Africa I could easily learn, and that in any case it would be too expensive for him just to send me home.

I flew into Blantyre airport on Wednesday, 18 January 1961. Earlier that morning the plane had stopped at Salisbury, where I had officially immigrated into the Federation of Rhodesia and Nyasaland. It had been cold and damp – a great disappointment to me – but in Blantyre it was warm and humid. I was met by the general manager of Satemwa Tea Estates, George Holden. He was fortyish, short and sunburnt, with a brusque military manner – it was no surprise to learn later that he had finished the war as a major in the Indian army. It was a pleasant surprise, however, to be asked to call him 'George', for back in Britain managers were 'Mr'. We drove for half an hour or so to a small town. There were only a few people on the streets – mostly Africans in shabby European clothes. The town had blotched white ramshackle buildings and virtually no traffic. At a small bistro we had an excellent *steak à la Portugaise*.

'I had no idea what to expect,' I said to George. 'I hadn't thought there would be such a good restaurant in Cholo.'

'Cholo!' He looked startled. I could see him thinking that recruiting me might have been a mistake. 'This is Blantyre, the country's commerical capital and biggest town. Cholo's an hour's drive away. And there are no restaurants there – good or bad.'

We drove out of Blantyre, and the adjoining town of Limbe, into open country. The landscape was generally flat and it was difficult to realize that we were on a plateau 3,600 feet above sea level, higher than anywhere in England. It was pleasantly hot.

Interested as I was in the landscape, my main attention was elsewhere. It was quickly becoming clear to me that my not being able to drive was going to cause difficulties. Why, I wondered, had I lied to Mr Kay; why had I imagined I could deceive everyone? Already George had spoken apologetically about the delivery of my vehicle being delayed. He hoped, however, that it would arrive in a fortnight's time. Could I pick up the elements of driving, just by watching others, so as to perform adequately when the time came? What would happen if I were found out? I watched surreptitiously as George, who drove aggressively, changed through the gears. The road was tarmacked, but only twelve feet wide, so that George had to take the far-side wheels of the Morris 1000 pick-up off the tar when we met oncoming traffic, or tried to overtake. This was a tricky manoeuvre, since the earth verge had washed away and was corrugated like a washboard, so that we rattled along at a precarious angle. Fortunately traffic was scarce.

We soon came to tea gardens. The road was flanked by great expanses of brilliant green, dotted with tall shade trees. Some of the fields were perfectly flat; others were contoured with rising tables of tea bushes. Gangs of Africans, surrounded, waist-high, by the tightly planted flat-topped bushes, plucked leaves into big wicker baskets slung across their backs. Occasionally there were large thatched open sheds, where the leaf was being weighed and taken away by tractors and trailers. We passed a huge rock by the side of the road.

'The Mwalanthunzi rock,' George said. 'The Africans walk

4

round it for good luck before they go off on a journey. The name is Chinyanja for "smoking stone" – in the hot weather, when the rain evaporates off the surface, it looks like smoke. Your estate is named after it. And here we are.'

We turned right, on to a dirt road. Flat fields of tea stretched into the distance. In front of us, several miles away, there was a tall hill covered with dark forest.

'How far does our land stretch?' I asked.

'To the top of Cholo mountain there. We've several square miles of land in all. Mwalanthunzi here, where you'll be, is about 2,500 acres all told. Much of it's not been cleared yet, but there's 500 acres of tea.'

We reached the end of the neatly tabled tea, and drove alongside a wilderness of weeds, five or six feet tall.

'What's happening there?' I asked.

'That's young tea, completely overgrown.' He laughed. 'Your workers have just been on strike. They're a difficult lot.'

Before I had time to respond to this alarming news, we arrived at the factory perimeter fence. A uniformed watchman at the gate saluted and let us in. The factory was a large rambling two-storeyed building, clad in corrugated iron. Gangs of men were unloading tractors and trailers, piled high with bulging sacks of freshly plucked tea.

'It's the season,' George said. 'The factory's working day and night, seven days a week. But I'll come back to check things later – you'll want to get unpacked and cleaned up. Let's go on up to the bungalow.'

We drove out of the far gate, through some tea fields, up on to the lower slope of Cholo Mountain, to a large white bungalow. It was surrounded by a very green lawn dotted with red frangipanis and bordered by beds of luxuriant orange cannas. On the verandah we were greeted by an African servant in immaculate white coat and trousers, tied at the waist with a red sash. George ordered tea.

'The *memsahib's* away in Rhodesia,' he said, using the Indian title rather than the more common, Portuguese-derived, *Dona*. 'Seeing doctors. We'll have to fend for ourselves.'

As he had a cook, an assistant cook, and two 'houseboys', plus two gardeners and a watchman, this turned out not to be a problem.

Later that evening, we had supper on the verandah. The air was balmy, and full of sound – croaking frogs and screeching cicadas. An occasional mosquito buzzed in my ear. Over large whiskies with plenty of water, George told me what was happening.

There were three estates on Satemwa, each with about 500 acres of tea, grouped around the factory, and there was a fourth estate a few miles away. George ran one estate, as well as keeping an eye on the others and the factory. There was a factory manager, two estate managers, me, and George – that was five of us, all British. Because the factory was currently working twenty-four hours a day, George had to spend a lot of time there, so he had little to spare to induct me. I could stay in his house and travel round with him for a while to learn the ropes. After that, I would move into the Mwalanthunzi Estate bungalow and manage that estate. He had in mind, he said, that I could take over the running of Mwalanthunzi in about a fortnight's time. I took a sip of whisky. My mind was spinning. I knew nothing about growing tea; I knew nothing of the language. I saw George looking for my reaction.

'Good,' I said. 'I'm sure I'll cope.'

It was an extraordinary proposition. It was, however, not nearly so strange as it appears today. I had been brought up in an era of empire, and inculcated with the idea that for the British to go out and run colonies and tropical enterprises was perfectly normal. I had read the short stories of Somerset Maugham, and from his acute observations had a surprisingly good idea of how planters behaved. I had read a good deal about young men who worked in the tropics. The job was challenging but not daunting. I knew nothing about tea, but I could learn.

ONE

Addiction and Taxation; Smuggling and Revolution

To what a height of folly must a nation be arrived,
when common people are not satisfied with wholesome
food at home, but must go to the remotest regions
to please a vicious palate!

JONAS HANWAY, 1757

On 22 September 1747, the privateer *Swift*, captained by William Johnson, lay off the coast of Poole in Dorset on watch for smugglers. His Majesty's customs had taken to licensing privateers to do their work for them, an innovation that would often backfire as the privateers took to smuggling themselves. At five in the afternoon, seeing a suspicious boat, the *Three Brothers*, to the east, the *Swift* moved to intercept it. The *Three Brothers* put about to take advantage of the wind, and then sailed away at top speed. The *Swift* followed in pursuit. It took her six hours to draw level. The *Three Brothers* ignored instructions to stop, but after several shots from the privateer, finally surrendered.

Captain Johnson and his men went aboard the *Three Brothers* to find it carried a crew of seven. They also found it was carrying thirty-nine casks of brandy and rum. These casks were slung with ropes, ready for them to be loaded on horseback. More importantly, inside canvas bags and wrapped in oilskin, were eighty-two parcels. These were later weighed, and they totalled almost two tons. They contained tea.

The *Three Brothers*, which had taken its illicit cargo on board at Guernsey, was escorted into Poole harbour. Pending legal proceedings, the tea was lodged on the quay in the customs house.

A fortnight later, sixty smugglers gathered in Charlton Forest, close to Poole. Most were members of the Hawkhurst Gang, from the village of that name in Kent, which lay well inland, midway between Hastings and Maidstone. It was they who had arranged for the contraband found on the *Three Brothers*. They arrived on horseback, armed with guns and other weapons. Half of them were positioned to keep a lookout over the roads approaching Poole. In the early hours, the remainder rode into the town, where they smashed open the doors of the customs house. Inside was thirty-seven hundredweight of tea, which they loaded on to their horses, leaving the rum and brandy behind. Then, unhurriedly, they rode off north.

Halfway towards Salisbury they came to the small Hampshire town of Fordingbridge. The townspeople came out to gawp. A shoemaker, Daniel Chater, recognized one of the smugglers, John Diamond, for they had once worked together at harvest time. The two shook hands, and Chater was given a small bag of tea before the smugglers rode on. At the next village the raiders stopped and divided their booty. There was some argument over splitting the tea fairly, since some had been spilt at the customs house. The smugglers re-weighed the bags on scales, apportioned the tea parcels, and went their separate ways.

Many other such incidents concerning tea smugglers had occurred in the 1740s. In 1744 a customs officer had been wounded and captured at Shoreham. The two informers with him had been tied to trees, flogged, and dumped on the coast of France, with whom the British were at war. In 1745 three customs officers were wounded at a pub at Grinstead Green, and then robbed. In 1746 an altercation between the Hawkhurst and Wingham gangs at Sandwich, while off-loading eleven and a half

'The smugglers breaking open the King's Custom House at Poole Oct 7 1747

tons of tea on to 350 horses, left nine wounded. In 1747 the smugglers shot four soldiers at Maidstone.

Raiding the king's customs house at Poole, however, was a new type of outrage, which had serious implications for the Exchequer. The authorities were determined to act forcibly. Accordingly, a proclamation was issued offering immunity from prosecution and large rewards for information leading to a conviction. John Diamond was arrested on suspicion at Chichester.

The shoemaker of Fordingbridge, Daniel Chater, was a talkative man, and the gift of tea he had received came to the attention of the customs. He was brought before a magistrate, and under pressure agreed for a fee to identify Diamond. The penalty would be death by hanging.

On 14 February 1748, Daniel Chater, together with a customs officer, William Galley, rode towards Chichester. They broke their journey at the White Hart in Rowlands Castle. The landlady there had sons who were smugglers, and she was suspicious of the pair. She sent out for assistance. Several local smugglers arrived. They separated the two travellers, and got Chater to admit what he was doing. They then plied the pair with liquor, and while they were in a drunken sleep, searched their pockets and found incriminating letters. Chater and Galley might have been punished fairly lightly, perhaps dumped in France, except that two of the wives were determined on revenge. 'Hang the dogs,' they said. 'They came here to hang us.' And so it was agreed that the smugglers would hold the couple until they knew John Diamond's fate, and then would do to them what was done to Diamond. The smugglers – William Jackson, William Carter, and five others – agreed to put up threepence a week each to cover the expense.

Jackson awakened the captured pair by climbing on to their bed and driving his spurs into their foreheads. They were then horsewhipped until they bled. Galley and Chater were mounted on one horse, with their feet tied together under the belly, and then whipped all the way north, through several villages, to the Sussex village of Rake. On the fifteen-mile journey, the couple turned upside down several times, so that the horse's hooves repeatedly struck their faces. At first they had been righted, but later, as they grew too weak to stay upright, they were transferred to sit before a mounted smuggler. Occasionally, one of the smugglers would crush the customs officer's testicles.

At the Red Lion in Rake, the landlord showed the smugglers a place where people buried smuggled tea. First, they chained Chater up under guard in a turf house, then, by the light of lanterns and candles, they buried Galley. Much later, when the body was disinterred, the customs officer was found in an upright position, with his hands in front of his eyes. He had been buried alive.

The smugglers returned to their own homes, to establish alibis. Two days later, with more of their associates, they returned to Rake determined to finish off Chater. Initially, they had the idea of putting a gun to the informer's head, and then all of them pulling a string attached to the trigger, so that they would be equally implicated. This was rejected as being too humane.

Chater was constantly assaulted by one or other of the smugglers. Terrified, he knelt to say his prayers, whereupon John Cobby cut off his nose with a clasp knife. He was mounted on horseback and taken to a well. Five of the smugglers rigged up a noose, and tried to hang Chater by suspending him over the water. After a quarter of an hour, he was still alive, so they cut him loose and threw him head first down the well shaft. He continued to groan, however, and was finally despatched by hurling down rails, gate posts and rocks.

Even by the standards of the time, all this was considered excessively barbaric. The Press made much of the bodies when they were discovered, and especially of Galley who had been buried alive. Large rewards were offered, and some of the smugglers, fearing the death penalty, offered themselves as witnesses. Eight of the ringleaders were captured.

The trial opened at Chichester on 16 January 1749. Two days later, Jackson and Carter were convicted of the murder of William Galley; Tapner, Cobby and Hammond of the murder of Daniel Chater. One of the others was found not guilty, and two only guilty as accessories to the murders. The accessories were treated more leniently than the others. They were sentenced merely to be hanged and then buried. The others were to be hanged, and then – a punishment hugely feared – to be chained and left hanging in the open as a warning to all. It was illegal to take down and bury anyone exhibited in this manner. Cobby and Hammond were displayed on the beach where they had landed smuggled goods. Jackson died before he could be hanged, but his dead body was still put in chains and suspended for all to see.

In April of that year another five of the Hawkhurst Gang were tried for the lesser crime of breaking into the customs house at Poole. They were brought to the Old Bailey, and treated no less severely than those who had committed murder. Though one was acquitted, and one was later pardoned, the other three were sentenced to be executed at Tyburn. After the execution one was to be buried, and the other two hanged and displayed in chains. One of these, William Fairole, on the night before the execution sought to reassure his visitors. He told them with a smile, 'We shall be hanging up in the sweet air, when you are rotting in your grave.'

Perhaps what was most extraordinary about the risks smugglers took in the first half of the eighteenth century was that such formidable effort should have been concentrated on a commodity

'*Tapner & Cobby & the Smugglers going to hang Chater the Custom House officer in a well*'

that only a century before had been entirely unknown to the British.

It was on 13 May 1662 that fourteen British warships had sailed into Portsmouth harbour. They had left Lisbon three weeks earlier, but been blown off course and forced by stormy weather to shelter in Mount's Bay in Cornwall. This gave an opportunity to those along that coast to welcome the flotilla with artillery salutes and displays of fireworks. The lead ship was the *Royal Charles*, and its honoured passenger was the daughter of King Juan IV of Portugal, Catherine of Braganza. Soon after landing she wrote a letter announcing her arrival, which was sent by hand to London for her husband-to-be, King Charles II. That night, all the bells in London rang out and bonfires were lit outside the doors of the houses. That night also, Charles II dined at the home of his mistress, the heavily pregnant Lady Castlemaine. There was no bonfire outside her door.

Charles managed to reach Portsmouth six days later. The couple were married that morning, in a secret Catholic ceremony. Later that day they were married a second time, on this occasion by the Protestant Bishop of London.

Charles had been tempted into the marriage by the prospect of a large dowry. He had been promised £500,000 in cash – money desperately needed to pay off the debts that he had inherited from the Commonwealth administration, and further new debts he had run up himself. The marriage had nearly been called off when the Portuguese only provided half the agreed sum to accompany Catherine, and even that not in ready money, but as sugar and spices and other items to be sold off when the ships reached England. There were other goods in Catherine's dowry. One of them was a chest of tea – for Catherine was a tea addict.

Tea had come to Europe surprisingly late, many centuries after it became the common drink of the Chinese. The first known mention of tea as a drink in Europe is found in a Venetian book of 1559, *Navigatione et Viaggi*. The author, Giambattista Ramusio, related what he had been told by a Persian of 'chai catai':

> They take of that herb, whether dry or fresh, and boil it well in water. One or two cups of this decoction taken on an empty stomach removes fever, headache, stomach-ache, pain in the side or in the joints, and it should be taken as hot as you can bear it.

In the following decades of the sixteenth century, several other brief accounts of tea came back from Europeans travelling in the East, mostly from the Portuguese who were there as traders and missionaries. A Dutchman, Jan Huygen van Linschoten, however, first inspired the transportation of tea to Europe. His *Discours of Voyages* was published in 1595, with an English edition three years later. In it he described the vast colonial empire of the Portuguese in the East, gave detailed maps and charts, and accounts of the wonderful goods available. The Dutch and others followed the Portuguese. One of the commodities van Linschoten had mentioned as being used by the Chinese and Japanese was 'chaona': 'They use a certaine drink, which is a pot with hote water, which they drinke as hote as ever they may indure, whether it be Winter or Summer.'

In 1596 the Dutch began trading in Java. In addition to local produce, goods from China and Japan were transhipped back to Europe. Around 1606 the first consignment of tea was sent to Holland. Although it is possible that individuals, particularly Portuguese, returned from the East with earlier samples of tea, this is believed to be the first commercial importation into Europe.

Over the next decades, aided by their domination of the eastern trade, the Dutch became the premier tea drinkers of Europe. Nevertheless, because of its exorbitant price, tea remained the preserve of the wealthy. Use soon spread to fashionable circles in adjacent countries, and also to Portugal, which had its own independent trading network. In France by 1650, tea had become very fashionable, having been taken up by Cardinal Mazarin, chief minister to Louis XIII. Later, Louis XIV himself became an addict. His teapot was made of gold.

The British were very slow to discover tea. We have no record of its use before the 1650s. The first dated reference is an advertisement in a London newspaper, *Mercurius Politicus*, of 23 September 1658:

> That Excellent, and by all Physicians approved, China Drink, called by the Chinease, Tcha, by other Nations Tay alias Tee, is sold at the Sultaness-head, a Cophee-house in Sweetings Rents by the Royal Exchange, London.

The first London coffee house had been established in 1652. By the end of the decade there were several; by the end of the century several hundred – at least one for every thousand of the population. They were places for men to transact business and to discuss politics. At first they sold only coffee, but later added chocolate and tea. Where the first teas came from is not known – perhaps from the continent, perhaps from people returning from the East.

The coffee houses, it seems, also offered a take-away service, for Samuel Pepys in his diary entry for 25 September 1660 wrote: 'And afterwards did send for a Cupp of Tee (a China drink) of which I had never drank before.' That Pepys, who spent a good deal of his time in taverns and coffee houses, had never previously taken tea would suggest that it was still a curiosity in 1660.

It was Catherine of Braganza with her dowry tea, who made tea a fad at court. From the court its use rippled out across fashionable society. At first it was the drink of the wealthy, only later of the middle classes. For Catherine's birthday in the year after she became queen, Edmund Waller wrote a poem:

> Venus her Myrtle, Phoebus has his bays;
> Tea both excels, which she vouchsafes to praise.
> The best of Queens, the best of herbs, we owe
> To that bold nation which the way did show.

There were other presents in the queen's dowry, too. There was the gift of the African trading enclave of Tangier; there was the right to trade freely to Brazil and to the East Indies – rights previously regarded by the Portuguese as exclusively theirs; and there was the gift of Bombay (Mumbai). This last gift was to be of great assistance when Britain strove to dominate the tea trade.

The Portuguese had first landed on the islands of Bombay in 1509: 'Our men captured some cows and some blacks who were hiding among the bushes, and of whom the good were kept and the rest were killed.' After repeated attacks, the local sultan ceded the seven islands in 1534 to the King of Portugal. Local fishermen and farmers continued their business much as before. Missionaries built churches, had temples closed, and persuaded or forced many of the islanders to adopt Christianity. A wealthy Portuguese built a manor house, which he equipped with a few cannon. It seemed a poor gift for a royal marriage, but the British were to join together the islands, which lay just off the coast, and develop a harbour which would become one of the greatest port cities in the world. The East India Company had already petitioned Cromwell for another base on the west coast of India, now the restored king, Charles II, provided it. He made over Bombay to the Company 'in fee and common soccage, as of the manor of East Greenwich, upon payment of an annual rent of £10 in gold on the 30th of September in each year'.

The East India Company had been founded as a commercial enterprise in 1600 under a royal charter from Queen Elizabeth I.

It was given a monopoly over all trade with the 'Indies' – that portion of the globe which lay east of Africa and west of South America. Almost immediately its ships sailed to what is now called Indonesia to buy vastly profitable cargoes of spices. They established trading posts there, known as 'factories'.

In 1608 the Company reached Surat in western India, where the bazaars were crammed with exotic produce – pearls and diamonds, gold and ivory, perfumes and opium. Most desirable of all, there was an enormous array of Indian textiles. The only commodity the Indians lacked, as did the British, was spices. Soon the Company was buying huge quantities of cloth, both to export back to Britain, and also to take further east to exchange for spices. Some of these spices were sold in India to pay for the cloth, and the rest were sent on to Europe. In 1619 the Company established a factory at Surat, its first in India.

The East India Company had been put in an awkward position when Charles II was restored to his throne. Under the Commonwealth it had replaced its royal charters with a new charter from Cromwell, and so placed the legality of the Company in doubt. Gifts were needed. Accordingly, £3,210 was spent on plate for the king, plus another £1,062 on gifts for his brother. These presents proved acceptable, and in 1661 the king granted the Governor and Company of Merchants of London trading into the East Indies 'for ever hereafter . . . the whole entire and only trade and traffick . . . to and from the said East Indies'.

Charles II must have been especially grateful, for he also gave the Company new and extraordinary powers. It was given the right to send out its own ships of war, men and ammunition, and to authorize their commanders to 'continue or make peace or war with any Prince or People (that are not Christians) in any place of their trade, as shall be most for the advantage and benefit of the said Governor and Company: also to erect and garrison fortifications at any of their settlements.' With these privileges the East India Company was set to become the most powerful multinational corporation the world has yet seen, and would dominate the international trade in tea.

For the remainder of the seventeenth century the importation of tea into Britain was small. In 1664 the Company placed its first order – for 100lbs of China tea to be shipped from Java. Annual imports remained in three figures until 1678, when 4,713lbs were imported. This glutted the market for a number of years, until in 1685 12,070lbs were brought in, which saturated the market again. This pattern of larger and larger imports, interspersed with stagnant years of oversupply, continued until the end of the century. In 1690, 38,390lbs of tea were imported, but in 1699 only 13,082lbs.

The company sold its tea at auction 'by the candle'. A candle was lit, and bids taken until an inch of it had burnt away. As a consequence of the pattern of alternate oversupply then shortage, the auction price of tea fluctuated widely. In 1673 it averaged £1.19 a pound (for simplicity, the shillings and old pence used in British currency until 1971 have usually been decimalized), whereas in 1679, following the big imports of 1678, it was only 7p a pound. By 1699 fluctuations were narrower, and tea was auctioning at an average of 74p a pound.

Sales of tea were restricted by the manner in which it was taxed. From 1660 to 1689, tea sold in coffee houses was taxed as a liquid, at 3p a gallon. Not only was this inconvenient, but it was disastrous to its flavour, for the excise men would only visit once or twice a day to inspect the new brew. Meanwhile the tea for sale was kept in barrels and reheated. From 1689 the tax was shifted to tea in the leaf. At first, however, this new tax was so high, at 25p a pound, that it almost stopped sales. In 1692 it was reduced to 5p a pound, but the need to fund various wars resulted in it gradually climbing again to the old rate by 1711.

The retail price of tea was, of course, much affected by these changes in the auction price and the tax, as well as by the quality of the leaf. Such records as exist suggest that at the beginning of the second half of the seventeenth century tea retailed at about £3 per lb and that by the end of the century the price was nearer £1 per lb. This confined significant consumption to the wealthy, since at that time a skilled craftsman would have been lucky to have made £1 a week, and a labourer 40p.

Even so, more people probably tried tea than the high price would suggest. This was because, besides being sold as a beverage, tea was also being sold as a medicine. Pepys, who has been quoted earlier as taking tea as a beverage, records coming home in 1667 to find his wife making tea 'which Mr Pelling the potticary, tells her is good for her cold and defluxions'.

Thomas Garraway sold tea as a drink, and also in leaf form, from his coffee house in Exchange Alley off Lombard Street. It stayed in business for over 200 years. The site is now marked with a stone commemorative plaque together with a carving of its grasshopper sign. In a broadside of about 1660, *An Exact Description of the Growth, Quality and Vertues of the Leaf TEA*, Garraway extols the benefits of tea at extraordinary length:

It maketh the body active and lusty.

It helpeth the head-ach, giddiness and heavyness thereof.

It removeth the obstructions of the spleen.

It is very good against the stone and gravel, cleansing the kidneys and uritets being drank with virgin's honey instead of sugar.

It takeeth away the difficulty of breathing, opening obstructions.

It is good against lipitude distillations, and cleareth the sight.

It removeth lasiatude, and cleaneth and purifieth adult humours and hot livers.

It is good against crudities, strengthening the weakness of the ventricle or stomack, causing good appetite and digestion, and particularly for men of corpulent body, or such as are great eaters of flesh.

It vanquith heavy dreams, easeth the brain, and strengtheneth the memory.

It overcometh superflous sleep, and prevents sleepiness in general, a draught of the infusion being taken, so that without trouble whole nights may be spent in study without hurt to the body, in that it moderately heateth and bindeth the mouth of the stomach.

It prevents and cures agues, surfets and feavers, by intaking a fit quantity of the leaf provoking a most gentle vomit and breathing of the pores, and hath been given with wonderful success.

It (being prepared and drank with milk and water) strengtheneth the inward parts, and prevents consumption, and powerfully asswageth the pains of the bowels, or griping of the guts and looseness.

It is good for colds dropsies and scurvies, if properly infused, purging the blood by sweat and urine, and expeleth infection.

It drives away all pains in the collick proceeding from wind, and purgeth safely the gall.

John Chamberlayne's *The Natural History of Coffee, Thee, Chocolate, Tobacco* of 1682 quotes several similar champions of tea drinking, and dismisses a critic who describes it as 'a great dryer, and promoter of old age, and foreign to the European complexions'. Chamberlayne also focuses on tea as a stimulant – 'that it makes us active and lively, and drives off sleep, every drinker of it cannot be but sensible.' The effects of caffeine, and disputes as to the medical benefit or harm done by tea, would excite more passion in the next century.

By 1699 John Ovington could write of tea – 'the drinking of it has of late obtain'd here so unusually, as to be affected by both the scholar and the tradesman, to become both a private regale at court, and to be made use of in places of publick entertainment.' Nevertheless, the national import total of 13,082lbs for that last year of the seventeenth century shows that, in reality, the drinking of tea was still very much a novelty.

The next century was very different. The rise in demand for tea in eighteenth-century Britain was phenomenal. Why it should have been so is not easy to fathom, but the British took to tea with more zeal than any other major western country. Only the Dutch ran them close. Countries such as France, where tea had been briefly fashionable, soon reverted to coffee or wine. Fernand Braudel, the eminent French historian, has observed that tea only become really popular in those countries that did not produce wine.

Recorded imports into Britain rose from 13,082lbs in 1699 to 1,241,629lbs in 1721. By 1750 the total was 4,727,992lbs. These figures, however, only told part of the story, for much tea did not pass through customs. Many of the British wanted to drink tea, but the price was too high. The combination of a monopoly by the East India Company with the extremely high duties levied by the government made tea too expensive. The population's spending power could only be matched by large-scale smuggling and by adulteration.

Smuggling of tea was very considerable in the first half of the eighteenth century. There were outfits like the Hawkhurst Gang all over the country. Sometimes they appalled people with their excessive brutality. As *The Gentleman's Magazine* reported in 1740 from 'a market-town in the country': ·

> Almost every young lady related how she was frighted by the smugglers, and declared they'd go to London next winter, so that young ladies will be very scarce and we country batchelors shall be left to despair and dye.

In the main, however, the smugglers had the support of a population who wanted tea and other goods without paying what they regarded as an exorbitant tax. Millions of Britons connived with an illegal trade, and usually kept quiet about what they knew. There are many similarities with the present-day trade in cannabis, another drug, where millions of Britons buy and consume a substance which they know is illegally imported.

At that time, few smugglers were so well organized as the Hawkhurst Gang. More generally they ran a relatively small business. They had little capital, and could not raise credit. Their boats ranged from sailing cutters, similar to the *Three Brothers*, down to rowing-boats. They rarely carried more than two or three tons of tea. If armed at all, they only had light personal weapons – cudgels, swords, and the odd firearm. These smugglers usually sold to personal contacts, shopkeepers, or through hawkers who dealt in *dollops* of only 2½lbs.

Most of this tea was originally brought into Europe by French, Dutch, Swedish and Danish companies. Much was transhipped via the Channel Islands and the Isle of Man. A significant amount was brought in on the East India Company's own ships, by the crews, who transferred it to smugglers on the journey home. Another major source was from tea that had been exported from Britain in order to obtain a drawback on the duty, and then re-imported by smugglers. It is, of course, impossible to know exactly how much tea was smuggled into Britain during this time. However, legal imports, which had reached 1.2 million lbs in

1721, fluctuated at around that level until 1747, after which, following a dramatic reduction in the tea tax, they rose to over 3 million lbs. Contemporary estimates were that in the three years before the tax was slashed illegal imports were worth £3 million a year.

Lower taxes, and a shortage of tea on the continent due to various wars, seemed to restrict tea smuggling in the mid eighteenth century, but then it took off with a vengeance. More and more people had tried tea and taken to it, creating an extraordinary demand – a demand that could not be satisfied with taxed tea that was beyond their means. As happens when an illegal practice has the broad blessing of society and a huge turnover, organized crime took over. Individual smugglers still operated, but the major transactions were handled in what customs officers dubbed the 'new mode'. By the 1770s these new smugglers were using large, heavily armed vessels. Several hundred of these operated along the entire coastline of England, Wales and Scotland. Some were as big as 300 tons, with crews of eighty and armed with twenty-four guns. These carried 4,000 or 5,000 gallons of rum or brandy, together with 40,000 or 50,000lbs of tea. It was big business, with continental suppliers offering three or even six months' credit, and insurance being secured at Lloyd's.

Once the tea had been landed, distribution was handled in new and sophisticated ways. Some of the old smuggling gangs still moved tea around the country with armed men, but larger consignments required subtler methods. By law, each consignment of tea of over 6lbs required an excise permit, and a dealer risked severe penalties without it. Various ways of circumventing this regulation were employed. A considerable quantity of tea was broken down into packages of less than 6lbs. Even more was sanitized by bogus transfers between outlets, and the mixing together of contraband and legitimate teas. It became almost impossible for the excise to identify teas that had been smuggled.

In the 1770s annual consumption of legal tea was 4 or 5 million lbs. It is difficult to quantify the amount of smuggled tea but, by looking at total exports from China to Europe, and then deducting continental consumption, historians have made estimates. These suggest that the amount of smuggled tea was equal to that legally imported and possibly even more – somewhere between 4 and 7½ million lbs.

Legitimate dealers protested loudly of these abuses. Everyone knew smuggling was rampant. Throughout the kingdom people were drinking more and more tea, yet official imports showed no increase. The number of licensed tea dealers dropped significantly. One dealer complained that it was 'almost impossible to do any business within 30 miles of the sea coast'. The East India Company, which supposedly had a monopoly over imports, was greatly concerned, for continental rivals were usurping its business. It had a powerful lobby in Parliament, with many MPs as shareholders.

William Pitt the Younger became Prime Minister in 1783. Although only twenty-four, he had a deep interest in fiscal policy, having been Chancellor of the Exchequer when he was twenty-one. He decided to make a massive increase in the tax on windows, which had been introduced in 1696 and which was relatively easy to collect. This enabled him to slash the tax on tea. The tax on tea in 1784 was 119 per cent, and had been roughly at that level for most of the century. The Commutation Act of 1784 reduced it to 12½ per cent. At a stroke, this virtually stopped the smuggling of tea.

The exchequer benefited in the long term from the reduction in the tax. Within ten years of the passing of the Commutation Act, consumption of taxed tea rose so sharply as to restore the amount of tax collected. Confirmation that huge quantities of tea had previously been smuggled in from the continent can be seen in the estimated exports from China:

For the 10 years prior to the passing of the Commutation
Act –
 By the Dutch, Danes, Swedes,
  French, etc.   134,698,900lbs
 By the East India Company   54,506,144lbs

For the 10 years, 1790–1800 –
 By the Dutch, Danes, Swedes,
  French, etc.   38,506,646lbs
 By the East India Company 228,826,616lbs

Second only to smuggling, the desire for cheap tea was met
by adulteration. To some extent, indeed, they went hand in
hand, for it was difficult for the customs and excise to look for
adulteration in tea that was being sold clandestinely as smuggled
and therefore cheap. Tea could be adulterated with leaves from
plants other than tea, or with leaves that had already been
brewed.

Some of the 'tea' made from plants other than *Camellia
sinensis* was sold without much deception as 'British Tea'. In
1710 tea 'not much inferior to the best foreign Bohea tea' was
being advertised. In many cases, however, *ersatz* tea was used
surreptitiously to debase the genuine leaf, with fraudulent intent.
In 1725 it was found necessary to pass an Act of Parliament,
imposing a fine of £100 on

> the dealer in tea, or manufacturer or dyer thereof, who shall
> alter fabricate or manufacture with *terra japonica* [tannin from
> an acacia tree] or with any other drug or drugs whatsoever,
> or shall mix with Tea any leaves other than the leaves of tea.

In 1730 the fine was increased to £10 for every pound adulterated;
in 1766 imprisonment was brought in as a penalty.

The favourite leaves used for adulteration were hawthorn for green teas, and sloe for black teas; but birch, ash and elder were also used. Of course, the leaves of these trees did not make a convincing liquor, so it was necessary to add various colouring agents. In addition to the *terra japonica* mentioned above, additives included verdigris, ferrous sulphate, Prussian blue, Dutch pink, copper carbonate, and even sheep's dung. Of these, sheep's dung was probably the least harmful.

Used tea leaves were purchased from servants or from the poor, or even as a regular business from the coffee houses. They were then dried on hotplates and, in the case of green teas, augmented with copper compounds.

The scale of adulteration is difficult to quantify. Some accounts suggest an annual output of tens of thousands of pounds' weight; others of millions of pounds' weight. It was certainly on a considerable scale, for it had provoked Parliament into passing prohibitory legislation, and there are many contemporary accounts of seizures and trials. For example, in the *London Magazine* of November 1736:

> Came on the trial of a noted Jew, dealer in tea in the Minories, for selling, at several times, in parcels, to a dealer in Fore-street, to the amount of 175 lb. of dy'd tea, under the denomination of British Tea, at 9s. 9d. per lb. which the said dealer mix'd with good tea for sale. The exciseman coming to take account of his stock, seiz'd the said mix'd tea, amounting to 1020 lb. and gave information against the said dealer, who immediately discover'd who he had had the tea of, and the said Jew was found guilty. For every pound of dy'd tea, so sold, he forfeits £10 which is £1750 for the whole.

The publicity given to the adulteration of tea, and the understandable public concern about the use of poisonous copper dyes in green teas, in particular, seems to have brought about

THE
HISTORY

OF THE

TEA PLANT;

FROM THE

SOWING OF THE SEED, TO ITS PACKAGE

FOR THE

European Market,

INCLUDING

EVERY INTERESTING PARTICULAR OF THIS ADMIRED EXOTIC.

TO WHICH ARE ADDED,

REMARKS ON IMITATION TEA,

EXTENT OF THE FRAUD,

LEGAL ENACTMENTS AGAINST IT,

AND THE

BEST MEANS OF DETECTION.

Embellished with a descriptive Frontispiece.

LONDON:

Published by

LACKINGTON, HUGHES, HARDING, MAVOR, AND JONES,
FINSBURY-SQUARE,

For the London Genuine Tea Company,

AND SOLD AT

23, Ludgate-Hill; 148, Oxford-Street; and 8, Charing-Cross; by their
Agents in the Country; and by all Booksellers.

PRICE 1s. 6d.

the shift in consumption from green to black teas. When tea was introduced into Britain in the middle of the seventeenth century most tea was green; by the end of the eighteenth century green teas were still popular but black teas were selling slightly better.

The increasing popularity of black teas also accelerated the addition of milk. Milk was added to tea by some in the seventeenth century. The Marquise de Sevigné was early to use it in France. However, it was not until well into the eighteenth century that the use of milk in tea became common.

Sugar was added to tea in Britain from the beginning. In China, tea was taken without sugar. In Tibet, it was taken with salt. In India, where sugar had been in general use for many hundreds of years, tea was usually sweetened. As early imports of tea came from China via Surat in western India, it may be that seeing how it was drunk there influenced the ships' crews who brought it back to Britain, and subsequently the British at home. It was the huge increase in consumption of tea in the eighteenth century that fuelled the parallel increase in the consumption of sugar. So interlinked were tea and sugar, that some in the eighteenth century used the figures for sugar consumption to calculate total tea consumption, and then estimated the amount of contraband tea being imported. It has even been suggested that for many Britons tea was merely a vehicle to indulge their passion for sugar. In 1700 Britain imported 10,000 tons of sugar a year; by 1800 it was importing 150,000 tons.

Throughout the eighteenth century, and well into the nineteenth, there was impassioned debate as to whether tea drinking was good or bad for the health. As early as 1722 it was being tested for ill effects by giving it to animals. James Lacy, who considered tea as dangerous as opium, conducted a bizarre experiment:

I injected into a dog about three ounces of a strong decoction of bohea tea, which I found made very little alteration in the dog. After this I received an ounce of venous blood into a cup, in which was about half an ounce of the strong decoction of bohea tea: this blood was not congealed in three days ... From these experiments we may find that tea abounds with a lixiviate salt, by whose assistance it attenuates the blood, or renders it more fluid; but that its operation is not very strong.

This may not have been very enlightening, but he did note correctly that tea was both diuretic and a stimulant. However, he also wrote that it induced in the 'tender sex, a diminuation of their prolifick energy, a proneness to miscarry, and an insufficientcy to nourish the child'.

The debate may have been somewhat skewed by the effects of adulteration with poisonous dyes. Otherwise it is difficult to explain the virulence of the attacks on such an innocuous drink. No doubt, also, some of the ranting was due to the sudden craze for a drink so unlike what had preceded it. For many centuries the common drink of the British had been beer. Many regarded the switch to tea as un-British, and for men effeminate. 'Observations on the effects of tea' in *The Gentleman's Magazine* of 1737 is typical:

> Tea is utterly improper for food, hitherto useless in physick, and therefore to be arranged among the poysonous vegetables. Were it entirely wholesome as balm or mint, it were yet mischief enough to have our whole populace used to sip warm water in a mincing effeminate manner once or twice a day ... In this manner the bold and brave become dastardly, the strong become weak, the women become barren; or if they breed, their blood is made so poor that they have not the strength to suckle, and if they do, the child dies of the gripes. The poor people's children which are bred with it, as

they really are in the cities and towns, are only fit for footmen and chambermaids . . . I leave any one to judge what soldiers we are like to have. The Spaniards very likely had felt the force of English beer within this last 20 years, if the use of it had not been exchanged for warm water bewitch'd with Indian poyson.

This provoked an equally exaggerated response from 'a well-wisher for the health of Great Britain':

Tea is the preserver of beauty, makes the old look young, fills the body with life and spirit, good blood, and makes the barren fruitful: there is hardly a virtue it does not possess . . .

Perhaps the most venomous attack on tea ever written came in 1757 from Jonas Hanway (a noted philanthropist, and famous for introducing the umbrella to London, which eventually triumphed over the jeers of the coachmen and sedan carriers) in *An Essay on Tea Considered as Pernicious to Health, Obstructing Industry, and Impoverishing the Nation*:

To what a height of folly must a nation be arrived, when common people are not satisfied with wholesome food at home, but must go to the remotest regions to please a vicious palate! There is a certain lane near Richmond, where beggars are often seen, in the summer season, drinking their tea. You may see laborers who are mending the roads drinking their tea; it is even drank in cinder-carts; and what is not less absurd, sold out in cups to haymakers. He who should be able to drive three Frenchmen before him, or she who might be a breeder of such a race of men, are to be seen sipping their tea! . . . Were they the sons of tea-sippers, who won the fields of Cressy and Agincourt, or dyed the Danube's streams with Gallic blood? What will be the end of such effeminate customs extended to those persons, who must get their bread by labors of the field!

Unfortunately for Hanway his essay was reviewed in *The Literary Magazine* by Samuel Johnson, who admitted that it was likely

> to expect little justice from . . . a hardened and shameless tea-drinker, who has for twenty years diluted his meals with only the infusion of this fascinating plant, whose kettle has scarcely time to cool, who with tea amuses the evening, with tea solaces the midnight, and with tea welcomes the morning.

Dr Johnson duly savaged Hanway's essay, although he graciously admitted 'that tea is a liquor not proper for the lower classes of the people . . . Its proper use is to amuse the idle, and relax the studious, and dilute the full meals of those who cannot use exercise, and will not use abstinence.'

John Wesley, the founder of Methodism, was another who went into print against tea, to which he ascribed his 'paralytick disorders', and shaking of the hand. He urged his followers to pray to God for the strength to abstain, and to give the money saved to the poor. In later life, however, he recanted, and acquired a gallon teapot from Josiah Wedgwood.

One feature of tea that everyone seemed to agree on was that it was a stimulant. They were right, for tea contains the drug caffeine, and caffeine is indeed a stimulant. Leaf tea contains about 2–4 per cent caffeine. This is twice as much as in coffee beans, but a smaller weight of tea is needed to make a cup. The amount of caffeine in a cup of tea will, of course, vary with the amount of leaf used, but it is more affected by how long the liquor is left to brew. Typically, a cup of tea will contain 10–40 mg. of caffeine if brewed for one minute, but as much as 100 mg. if plenty of leaf is used and then it is brewed for five minutes. A cup of coffee might have 75–180 mg. of caffeine.

Caffeine somehow stimulates the central nervous system. There are many theories as to how it does this, but none of them is conclusive. Individuals react very differently to caffeine, and beyond a certain quantity more caffeine has no stimulative effect. Body weight is another factor, for smaller people need less caffeine to affect them – and this is particularly true of children. The time it takes for the caffeine to take effect and the length of time the stimulation lasts vary widely. Smoking and drinking alcohol also modify the effects of caffeine.

Whether or not caffeine is an addictive drug is controversial. Regular ingestion of caffeine cushions its stimulative effect. A non-caffeine drinker will usually get a hefty 'kick' from a strong cup of coffee, whereas a regular imbiber may be able to drink safely just before an evening's sleep. Most people seem to be able to adjust to moderate use of caffeine, and find it useful to stimulate the body at various times in the day. Withdrawal from caffeine produces symptoms similar to those experienced when deprived of stronger drugs, but milder. These symptoms include headaches, irritability, muscle aches and, as might be expected, drowsiness. Most people revert to normal in a few days or weeks. A few people react badly to caffeine, developing palpitations, increased heart rate, rapid breathing and anxiety attacks. In general, however, only excessive use triggers these symptoms and, indeed, non-caffeine users seem to be more disposed to nervous problems.

Caffeine has been the subject of a great number of health scares and clinical investigations in recent years. Many of these centre on concerns originally voiced in earlier times. The effects of caffeine on cancer, fertility, birth defects, cholesterol, the heart and respiration have all been investigated, and research is still continuing.

One famous experiment was conducted by the United States Aeronautics and Space Administration, NASA. Scientists assessed the ability of spiders to weave their webs after taking various psychoactive drugs, on the premise that the more toxic the drug was, the more deformed the web would be. Marijuana made the spiders lose concentration and forget the web pattern; Benzedrine speeded them up to leave gaping holes. Caffeine rendered the spiders totally incapable of spinning more than a few random wisps. Whether these results can be extrapolated to humans is doubtful. It is probable that caffeine is particularly damaging to spiders because the plants that produce it, such as coffee and tea, produce it as an insecticide.

All in all, therefore, current research indicates that caffeine can be seen as not particularly harmful if taken in moderation. The use of tea, which generally has a lower caffeine content than coffee, tends to minimize any ill effects.

Apart from caffeine, there are many other substances in tea, which may affect health. A good deal of recent research has concentrated on flavonoids. These occur in fruit and vegetables, red wine, and most of all in tea. In Britain tea contributes about 90 per cent of average flavonoid intake. Studies indicate that these antioxidants may inhibit development of heart disease, strokes and cancers.

A number of articles in reputable journals such as *The Lancet* have appeared in recent years, which seem to confirm the beneficial effects of drinking tea. The Zutphen Elderly Study tracked the progress of hundreds of elderly people in the Netherlands – analysing their diet, and relating it to coronary heart disease and strokes. This was shown to be related to flavonoid intake, the main source of which was black tea. A typical tea drinker reduced the risk of dying from heart disease by 68 per cent, and of having a first stroke by over 50 per cent.

Most of the clinical trials held to quantify the beneficial effects of tea drinking on the incidence of cancer have taken place in far-eastern countries, where people drink green tea. A detailed analysis of cancer mortality in Japan, for example, has shown that areas with high tea consumption have a lower incidence of cancer in general, and particularly of gastrointestinal cancers such as those of the stomach, oesophagus and liver. Trials that have been conducted on black tea drinkers seem to confirm that black tea inhibits cancers too.

Throughout the eighteenth century, the coffee houses continued to be a major provider of tea. In appearance the eighteenth-century coffee house was not unlike a small pub in a town of today. There would be large tables to sit at, perhaps smaller high ones to stand against, and an open fire with coffee, chocolate and teapots ranged in front. Many customers took snuff or smoked pipes of tobacco. There would also probably be a bar dispensing alcoholic beverages. Indeed, as the century progressed, with the coffee houses serving copious quantities of liquor, and the taverns selling much coffee and tea, it became hard to distinguish between the two.

For the man of substance the coffee house was an essential venue. A visitor to London in 1714, possibly Daniel Defoe, wrote:

> I am lodged in the street called Pall Mall, the ordinary residence of all strangers, because of its vicinity to the Queen's Palace, the park, the parliament house, the theatres and the chocolate or coffee-houses where the best company frequent. If you would know our manner of living, 'tis thus: We rise by Nine, and those that frequent men's levees find entertainment at them til eleven, or, as in Holland go to tea tables. At twelve the beau monde assemble in several coffee or chocolate houses; the best of which are the Cocoa Tree and White's Chocolate houses, St James's, The Smyyrna, Mrs

Rochford's and the British coffee-houses; and all these so near one another, that in less than an hour you see the company of them all. We are carried to these places in chairs (or Sedans) which are here very cheap, a guinea a week or a shilling per hour, and your chairmen serve you for porters to run on errands, as your gondoliers do at Venice.

If it be fine weather, we take a turn into the Park till two, when we go to dinner; and if it be dirty, you are entertained at picquet or basset at White's, or you may go and talk politics at the Smyrna or St James's.

I must not forget to tell you that the parties have their different places, where, however, a stranger is always well received, but a Whig will no more go to the Cocoa Tree, than a Tory will be seen at the Coffee-house St James.

The Scots go generally to the British, and a mixture of all sorts to the Smyrna. There are other little coffee-houses much frequented in this neighbourhood – Young Man's for officers; Old Man's for stockjobbers, paymasters and courtiers, and Little Man's for sharpers . . .

At two we generally go for dinner; ordinaries [à la carte meals] are not so common here as abroad, yet the French have set up two or three good ones for the convenience of foreigners in Suffolk street, where one is tolerably well served, but the general way here is to make up a party at the coffee-house to go to dine at the tavern.

This was the situation in the West End, where fashionable society had been drifting east from the City of London. The Great Fire of 1666 had destroyed most of the coffee houses already established in the City, but many were rebuilt and a multitude of new ones opened. In the West End, the City, and the streets between the two, the coffee houses became indispensable to upper- and middle-class men.

The Penny Post had been established in London in the 1680s, and used coffee houses for the collection and delivery of mail.

The great trading companies – the East India Company, the Hudson's Bay Company, the Levant Company – used the coffee houses for meetings and functions. Doctors and quacks advertised in the coffee houses and pedalled their cures. Thomas Smith, 'the first master corn-cutter of England' did a daily round of twenty-one coffee houses. The Freemasons used them for their meetings. Many of the coffee houses had a specialist clientele. As Bryant Lillywhite has recorded in his *London Coffee Houses*:

> The class and type of frequenter varied according to the locality of the coffee-house. The followers of the Court, the Whigs and the Tories, used the houses in Westminster, Whitehall, St. James's and Pall Mall. The Navy, Army, 'the Gentlemen of the Law', the doctors and clergy, and 'other professional gentlemen' were to be found in Charing Cross, Strand, Fleet Street, St. Martin's Lane, Holborn, and round St. Paul's. The news-writers and the quacks visited the lot. Booksellers and publishers made full use of those round St Paul's and on Ludgate Hill; the 'chap-books' derive their name from Chapter Coffee-house Paternoster Row. The literary, the intelligentsia, the wits, and men of science, all tended to congregate in a few houses, which changed according to the ebb and flow of fashion and other reasons. The dandies and fops, the playboys of the age, the gamblers and idlefolk, as well as dubious characters, all found a common interest in the coffee-house of their choice. Almost every phase of public activity, including prostitution found expression or an outlet in the life of a coffee-house. Swindles and robberies were planned, spoils divided, and not a few coffee-houses witnessed a prisoner being apprehended. The character of a house was sometimes denoted by its Sign. In the 18th century it is said that the Sign of the Star indicated 'every lewd purpose'.

The coffee houses were the preserve of men. A few of them, no doubt, took home a little leaf tea to be enjoyed by their families, but the tea drinking of the middle class in the seventeenth century must have been largely done by men. This would have been less so among the upper classes, for the tea rituals introduced by Catherine of Braganza had taken hold. It was the advent of the tea garden in the eighteenth century, however, that took the public consumption of tea to women.

Some of these gardens had been founded in the seventeenth century, in the pursuit of pleasure following the Restoration of Charles II, and some had survived from earlier times. At first, entry was free, but gradually a charge became usual. This often provided free tea, and many of the pleasure gardens began to style themselves 'tea gardens'.

London, of course, was much smaller than it is now, and gardens in Kentish Town or Islington were surrounded by fields. There was an inner collection of gardens around Clerkenwell and central London, and outlying groups at Marylebone, Chelsea, South London, North London and Hampstead. Some were renowned for their extensive ornamental gardens, while others were mainly spas. Some were small family businesses, while others were vast enterprises with elaborate facilities and entertainments.

Possibly the best known of all the pleasure gardens was Vauxhall, often called Spring Gardens, 'laid out in so grand a taste that they are frequented in the three summer months by most of the nobility and gentry then in and near London'. However, there does not seem much evidence to associate Vauxhall Gardens with serious tea drinking. An advertisement of 1762 lists champagne, burgundy, claret, hock, port, sherry, cider and beer, but no tea. The other famous garden, and principal rival to Vauxhall, was Ranelagh at Chelsea. Ranelagh Rotunda and Gardens were opened in 1742. Here the standard admission charge was half a crown (£⅛), which included tea, coffee, bread and butter. A lot of these must have been consumed for, except on special occasions, no other refreshments were available.

Ranelagh had a formal garden, with flowers and gravel walks lined with yews and elms. The main attraction, however, was a vast rotunda – very similar in shape to the round reading room in the British Museum – 150 feet in diameter, with a circle of fifty-two boxes inside, surmounted by a gallery with more boxes, and sixty windows – all beneath a huge dome hung with crystal chandeliers lit by thousands of candles. The most extraordinary feature, however, was the roof support in the centre of the room. This elaborately decorated concoction of columns and arches, was a giant chimney and fireplace, which in winter housed a huge open fire. Throughout the rotunda there was much painting, gilding and carving, so that Dr Johnson was able to declare it 'the finest thing he had ever seen'. There were regular concerts and fireworks at Ranelagh but the main attraction was to dress up and promenade round and round the interior of the rotunda.

The smaller spas and gardens merely offered tea and gossip. A 1778 print of Bagnigge Wells Gardens is nicely captioned:

> All innocent within the shade you see
> This little Party sip salubrious Tea,
> Soft Tittle-Tattle rises from the stream
> Sweaten'd each word with Sugar and with Cream.

As the eighteenth century wore on, the pleasure gardens lost their novelty and became less popular. A number became haunts of the disreputable. Since after 1752 they needed a licence for music and dancing, this often led to their closure, or conversion to being merely a place to sit and have tea. Ranelagh finally closed down in 1803; a number of others carried on until the 1830s or 1840s; Bagnigge Wells closed in 1841; Vauxhall limped on until 1859.

'The inside view of the Rotunda in Ranelagh Gardens with the company at breakfast'

The retail and wholesale tea trade developed out of the coffee houses. Often the East India Company would conduct their auctions in a coffee house. The coffee houses would buy their tea, usually via a broker, keep some for their own use, and then perhaps sell some on to their customers. They would also supply provincial coffee houses, as well as apothecaries and milliners – for until the middle of the eighteenth century it was apothecaries and milliners rather than grocers who retailed tea.

Twinings, in Deveraux Court opposite the Law Courts in the Strand, has a classic history. Thomas Twining, who had been employed by an East India merchant, set up Tom's Coffee House in 1706. He soon established a thriving retail business, selling coffee, chocolate, sugar, arrack and brandy as well as tea. However, perhaps because of his East India trade experience, he began to specialize in tea, and this became his main business. In 1711, Queen Anne appointed Thomas Twining her purveyor of teas, an honour that has been renewed by every monarch since. In 1717 he was able to buy an adjoining house, which he named the 'Golden Lion', especially for the sale of loose coffee and tea. By 1720 he was retailing and wholesaling eighteen varieties of tea. Individual customers included a host of lawyers, doctors and clergy. Seventy-eight of them had titles. He supplied a number of coffee houses, both in London and in the provinces, as well as inns in London, Winchester and Chester. Wholesaling was conducted through apothecaries, in London, Devizes and Northampton; cloth merchants and milliners in Marlborough and Preston.

Thomas Twining bought his teas either at the East India Company's public sales, which were usually held at the Marine Coffee House in Birchin Lane, or through a broker, Obed Smith. By 1721 Mr Smith had supplied him with goods totalling the huge sum of £100,000.

Thomas Twining was succeeded in 1741 by his son, Daniel. On Daniel's death in 1762 the business passed to his widow Mary, and then in 1783 to their son, Richard. Throughout this time the business continued to operate successfully. The demand for tea rose inexorably. However, the huge amounts of tea being smuggled into Britain over this period made it increasingly difficult to sell legitimate tea. Richard Twining was at the forefront of efforts to curtail smuggling by reducing the tax on tea. He published several pamphlets, and became chairman of the dealers in tea. As an adviser to William Pitt, he was a prime force behind the Commutation Act of 1784, which dramatically reduced the tax, and which brought to an end the serious smuggling of tea.

The Twinings thrived. In 1787 they were able to work their way forward through Deveraux Court, so that they had a frontage on the Strand. They built a grand new tea warehouse, with a delightful entrance surmounted by a golden lion that was flanked by two life-size pig-tailed Chinamen in colourful costume. These are still there today, and the Twinings still sell their fine teas. They have left the supply of ordinary teas to the great international tea companies, but they have a substantial business wholesaling and retailing specialist teas.

Grocers began to take over from apothecaries as retailers of tea during the second half of the eighteenth century. This reflected the transition from drug to beverage. The tax laws imposed stringent regulations on dealers or sellers of tea. They needed licences and a sign over the shop entrance. To prepare for the Commutation Act the excise men compiled detailed surveys. In 1783 there were 33,778 licensed tea dealers. About two-thirds of the tea they sold was black, and one-third green. By 1801, following the reduction in the tax, there were 62,065 tea dealers – one for every 174 of the population.

In the 1790s Sir Frederic Morton Eden toured Britain to research *The State of the Poor*. He recorded in detail the diet of poor people all over the country, and it is notable how many regularly bought tea and sugar. Typically, a labourer and his family used two ounces of tea a week, which together with the sugar that accompanied it, took 5–10 per cent of their income. By the end of the

John Richardson
Grocer
at the Canister and three Sugar Loaves
against Hatton Garden Holborn
London.
Sells Fine Teas, Coffee, Chocolate, Snuffs, Sago,
Hartshorn, Vermichelly, Starch, Stone & Powder Blues
With all sorts of Grocery & Confectionary Wares.
Wholesale and Retail

eighteenth century, for the British as a whole, rich or poor, a regular supply of tea had become essential.

For much of the eighteenth century tea had also been avidly consumed in Britain's American colonies. The Dutch had introduced tea into New Amsterdam, later renamed New York, where it had become popular even before it took hold in London. The other states on the eastern seaboard also took to tea with enthusiasm. During the first half of the eighteenth century the East India Company was barred from exporting tea to America. Their teas were auctioned in London and then shipped to America by London merchants. Since this tea carried the duty paid on import into Britain it was expensive, and liable to be undercut by smugglers. A large trade in smuggled tea was run out of Sweden and Holland. It is estimated that out of American total imports of 1 million lbs in 1760, three quarters of it was smuggled. To counteract this, legislation was enacted in 1767 to allow the import duty into Britain to be repaid if the tea was sent on to America. This largely eliminated smuggling, and British tea exports in 1768 rose to 900,000lbs.

This change was good for the profits of the East India Company, but it soon had other, more serious, financial problems. The Company had always kept a large stock of tea in store, but the rise in smuggling into Britain during the 1760s and early 1770s had both reduced their sales in Britain and simultaneously increased their stocks of tea. By 1772, this resulted in them having a huge surplus of 21 million lbs – four years' stock. They were in deep trouble, for they owed the government, including unpaid tea duty, a total of £1 million. The company approached the government for permission to export direct to America. This was granted by the Tea Act of 1773. The tea would carry a duty of 3*d*. (£ ¹⁄₈₀) per lb.

Addiction and Taxation

To the Americans this threepenny tax was extremely objection-able. They had been in a long-running dispute with the British Parliament over whether they should be taxed at all by the British. Parliament had imposed a tax on the colony's newspapers, bills and legal documents in the Stamp Act of 1765. This had been seen as an attempt to control a rebellious Press, and infuriated vocifer-ous lawyers. The Act was repealed the following year, but had already consolidated opposition to any British imposed tax.

In 1767 a new Chancellor of the Exchequer, Charles Townsend, imposed a tax on lead, paint, paper, glass and tea. The money raised would be used to fund the colonial administration. The colonists saw that this would make the administrators the creatures of the British Parliament rather than, if they raised a tax themselves and used it to fund the administration, the servants of the American legislatures. The Americans turned to self-sufficiency to nullify Townsend's Act. Smuggling was resumed, and legal imports of tea dropped dramatically. The Americans even took to making their very own 'Labradore tea' from a local root. Customs officers became symbols of British oppression, and had to be protected with British troops. In 1770 a party of these troops opened fire on a Boston mob, and killed a man. This sparked a series of protests, and the setting up of Committees of Correspondence to co-ordinate resistance.

Over the next three years, however, things had returned to a degree of normality. The wealthier colonists had been alarmed by the activities of the mob and, fearing for their own privileged positions, toned down their opposition to the British Parliament. The Tea Act of 1773 reignited their anger. Not only were they incensed by the threepenny tax, but they also saw the East India Company as a threat to their commercial interests. The Company not only had a monopoly on the importation of tea, but it also intended to distribute its tea in America, not through the estab-lished tea merchants, but through agents who were supporters of the British administration. Radical groups also urged resistance:

'Do not suffer yourself to sip the accursed stuff, for if you do the devil will immediately enter into you, and you will instantly become a traitor to your country.' Americans of all classes united to resist the tax on tea.

Meanwhile, the East India Company went ahead with arrangements to export its teas to America. The *Polly* was loaded for Philadelphia, the *Nancy* for New York, and four ships – the *William*, the *Dartmouth*, the *Eleanor*, and the *Beaver* – for Boston. The ships sailed in September and early October on a journey that could be expected to take, depending on the weather, from four to eight weeks. During that time, they would of course be out of communication, and unaware of developments in America. And there were developments, for agitation against the importation of taxed tea grew inexorably – public meetings became riots, and the warehouses the tea was destined for were attacked.

On 28 November 1773, the first tea ship arrived. The *Dartmouth* anchored at Castle William, a British garrisoned fort, near Boston. The townspeople called mass meetings, where they resolved that the tea must not be landed or the duty paid, and posted guards to ensure this. The businessmen who had agreed to market the tea refused to meet the rebels and were forced to take shelter in Castle William. Under orders from the townspeople, the *Dartmouth* left anchor and tied up at Griffin's Wharf, where its cargo, other than tea, was offloaded. On 2 December it was joined by the *Eleanor*. The *William* ran aground on Cape Cod; the *Beaver* arrived safely but temporarily had to go into quarantine offshore because of an outbreak of smallpox.

On 8 December the Governor ordered the navy to block off the harbour, so as to prevent any tea ship absconding without paying duty. On 14 December, the townspeople forced the owner of the *Dartmouth* to apply to the customs for its tea to be cleared without paying duty. The next day this was officially refused. On 16 December 1773, a mass meeting resolved to ask the Governor to allow the tea ships to leave port, which he refused to do. Then, as Alexander Hodgdon the *Dartmouth's* mate recorded in the ship's journal:

> Between six and seven o'clock this evening came down to the wharf a body of about one thousand people. Among them were a number dressed and whooping like Indians. They came on board the ship, and after warning myself and the Customs-House officer to get out of the way, they unlaid the hatches and went down the hold, where there were eighty whole and thirty-four half chests of Tea, which they hoisted on deck, and cut the chests to pieces, and hove the tea all overboard, where it was damaged and lost.

'The Boston Tea Party' lasted three hours, and every ounce of tea aboard all three ships was thrown into the sea.

The tea destined for Charleston was offloaded, but no merchant dared to take it, and it eventually rotted. The tea sent to New York and Philadelphia was sent back to London. It was the violent events in Boston, however, which most enraged the British Parliament. An Act was passed to close the port of Boston until reparations had been paid. In addition, Coercive Acts imposed direct rule. General Gage, Commander-in-Chief of the British forces in North America, was made Governor of Massachusetts. The colonists organized resistance, and the British army clashed with local militias. Finally, in 1775, the war began that ended in American independence. An anonymous poet of the time summed it up neatly:

> What discontents, what dire events,
> From trifling things proceed?
> A little Tea, thrown in the sea,
> Has thousands caused to bleed.

Despite the loss of America, the East India Company became ever more successful in making money from tea. It made huge sums from a monopoly that enabled it to add a mark-up of at least a third. However, it also made enemies in the process. The public wanted cheaper tea, and this brought calls for the abolition of the Company's monopoly. The rise in British consumption of tea in the late eighteenth century was truly remarkable. In the first year of the eighteenth century British consumption, even allowing for some smuggling, had probably been less than 100,000lbs; by the last year of the century it had increased over twenty-fold to 23 million lbs. Imports were so large that finding enough silver to pay the Chinese had become a major concern.

TWO

Keeping the Chinese in Order

*The time is fast coming when we shall be obliged to
strike another blow in China . . . these half-civilised
governments such as those in China, Portugal and
Spanish America, all require a dressing every eight
or ten years to keep them in order.*

LORD PALMERSTON, British Foreign Secretary, 1850

The Chinese have numerous legends about the origins of tea
drinking. Popular mythology credits discovery to the Emperor
Shen Nung in the third millennium BC. The founder of Tao, Lao
Tzu, is supposed to have been offered tea when he travelled
through Szechwan in the sixth century BC. Confucius is said to
have taken tea, and the Buddha is believed by some to have
introduced tea to China. Accounts of these episodes were, however, written later, and there is little hard evidence to support
these claims. A particular difficulty is that the Chinese character
t'u used in early references to a beverage that might be tea is also
used to describe infusions from other plants. It was only in the
third century AD that the character *ch'a*, which has very similar
calligraphy to *t'u*, came into use specifically to represent tea. It is
clear, however, that tea was used in China from well before then.

Early accounts of the use of tea focus on its properties as a
medicine to alleviate digestive or nervous conditions, and there
are also references to its use as a stimulant. It was only gradually
during the early centuries of the first millennium that it also

51

became a beverage. The first detailed account of tea cultivation, processing and preparation as a beverage was written by Zhang Yi in the third century AD. He describes tea cultivation in Szechwan and Hubei, where individual farmers produced tea from pruned, waist-high bushes. The leaves were compressed into cakes. Zhang Yi gives instructions for preparing the liquor – 'First bake the cake of tea until reddish in colour then pound it into tiny pieces and put these into a porcelain pot. Pour boiling water over the leaves and add onion, ginger and orange to flavour.' It was the shift from being a bitter medicine to being a pleasant drink which fuelled the increase in consumption of tea in China during the fifth and sixth centuries, together perhaps with the other benefits described by Zhang Yi: 'the brew sobers one after drinking and keeps one awake.'

Tea has been unearthed from several Han Dynasty (206 BC–AD 220) tombs. In one a celadon tea container is clearly labelled with the character *ch'a*. Emperor Qi Wudi (AD 479–502) stipulated in his will that he should receive posthumous offerings of tea. To this day tea is used by some Chinese as a gift to the dead – a ball of red paper containing leaf tea is left between the corpse's lips.

Tea became the undisputed national drink of China under the Tang Dynasty, AD 618–906. It was a time of greatly increased prosperity for China, with a consequent growth in the consumption of luxury goods. The empire was expanding, and foreign trade blossomed. Education and learning prospered, with important developments in mathematics, astronomy, medicine and printing. Poetry and painting flourished. Many Chinese consider it the golden age.

The drinking of tea was already established in Chinese court circles, and from there it spread to all sections of society. Better communications made it easier to transport goods across the huge country. Tea began to be moved across China and, as it became popular, plantations were established in the new tea-

Chinese watering a tea garden

Chinese sorting and sifting tea after drying

consuming areas. It was found that if the tea leaves were steamed before being pressed into cakes they lost their unpleasant 'green odour'. Improvements were also made in the way the cakes were compressed, perforated, strung together and baked. The compressed cakes were resistant to deterioration and highly transportable, and so they became popular with nomads living well beyond the borders of China.

Inevitably, with tea being widely consumed, people with money began to look for teas of a 'superior' flavour. As always happens with the taste for luxury, virtue was discovered in that which was most difficult to produce or obtain. Teas that were grown at high altitude began to acquire a cachet, for they were difficult to cultivate and yields were low. There is little doubt that many high grown teas have a more delicate taste, but the sophisticated took to searching for teas grown in the most remote and inaccessible places. (This desire for the almost unattainable is a recurring motif in Chinese tea history. A tea from Mount Meng in Szechwan was reputedly so rare that it came from only seven trees, and only ninety leaves a year were harvested.) Social status became dependent on the quality and price of tea. The making of tea became extremely complicated – it needed to be boiled in the right water; heated over the right charcoal; brewed in the right utensils; served in the right cups. Any error led to loss of face. In court circles the taking of tea became a ceremony. To ensure that all was done correctly, the emperor and important officials began to employ 'Tea Masters'.

The greatest of all the Chinese authorities on tea was Lu Yu. He was born sometime in the second quarter of the eighth century and died in 804. His book, *The Classic of Tea*, became the most important manual for tea drinkers in Tang China, and has remained so ever since. The book gives advice on the tools needed to harvest and process tea, the equipment needed to brew tea, and a list of the tea-producing districts graded by quality. The most striking features of the book, however, are the

Keeping the Chinese in Order

poetic and reverential descriptions of tea making and drinking. For Lu Yu tea was much more than a beverage:

> When the water is boiling it must look like fishes' eyes and give off but the hint of a sound. When at the edges it chatters like a bubbling spring and looks like innumerable pearls strung together, it has reached the second stage. When it leaps like majestic breakers and resounds like a swelling wave it is at its peak. Any more and the water will be over-boiled and should not be used.

The whole act of making and drinking tea, Lu Yu insisted, had to be accompanied by beauty – it was an art. The brazier should be decorated with ornamental designs and inscriptions; the roller should be made from the wood of the orange tree; the water filter should be of jade-green silk decorated with kingfisher feathers or silver filigree.

Nevertheless, despite all this attention to detail, and the exquisite pleasure of sipping the infusion, to drink tea in excess was anathema, for:

> Moderation is the very essence of tea. Tea does not lend itself to extravagance. If a tea is insipid and bland, it will lose its flavour before even half a cup has disappeared. How much more so in the case of extravagance in its use. The vibrancy will fade from the colour and the perfection of its fragrance will melt away.

It was during the Tang Dynasty that the practice of sending tribute teas to the emperor's court began. An imperial official sent a small quantity of a tea that had been lauded to the court by Lu Yu. It was so well received that he was instructed to send an annual supply. The best went to the Emperor himself, and the remainder to his household and high officials. It became so popular that each year more had to be sent. By the close of the eighth century, a workforce of 30,000 was employed to satisfy the demand.

Plucking of the imperial tea took place in early morning mists, before the leaves had been dried by the sun, and often before dawn. The plucking gangs were controlled by signals from drums and cymbals. Extraordinary precautions were taken to ensure that tea was not tainted in the plucking. The women – traditionally described as virgins – were forbidden to eat garlic, onions and strong spices. Nor were their hands allowed to touch the leaves, for they wore silk gloves, with slits in the tips, and snipped off the tea shoots with their fingernails. Jugs of water were carried so as to clean the pluckers' nails frequently. In later years, imperial plucking would become even more refined, and the tea shoots would be cut with gold scissors.

The Tang poet Lu Tung was another seminal figure in Chinese tea culture. His *Song of Tea* progresses from the first bowl, which merely moistens his lips and throat, to the seventh, which wafts him away on a breeze. In another poem he wrote the famous lines:

> I am in no way interested in immortality,
> But only in the taste of tea.

The Tang Dynasty was followed by the Sung (960–1279). It was a time of great literary achievement, and many stories and poems were written about tea and tea tasting. In 1107 the Emperor Hui Tsung wrote a treatise on tea. This went into great detail about the harvesting of tea, its preparation, and the spiritual benefits of drinking the infusion. It also documented a major change in the brewing of tea. Previously most tea had been boiled together with the water – although some early accounts are ambiguous about this – but now the water was boiled and then poured on to the powdered tea and left to brew. Before serving into bowls it was briskly whisked.

The Sung method of serving tea – powdered and whisked – became the basis of the famous Japanese tea ceremony. Although tea had been originally introduced into Japan during the ninth century, its use did not take hold until it was reintroduced from Sung China in 1171 by a Japanese Zen scholar. There was a strong association between the ability of tea to keep sleep at bay, and the Japanese desire to spend long hours in meditation. Japanese tea gardens are planted differently to others, with the bushes in long hedges. The plucking table, instead of being flat, is gently curved into uniform arches that have a Zen-like beauty. The Japanese only produce green tea, and much of this is greener than in other countries, since the plants are covered with mats for three weeks before the harvest to increase the amount of green chlorophyll in the bud.

The final great changes in the brewing of tea in China came in the Ming Dynasty. The Mings ruled from 1368 to 1644, and were the emperors when Chinese tea first came to the West. During the Ming era great developments took place in ceramic for domestic use. Previously, tea had been drunk from wooden bowls, but the Mings began to use porcelain, and this became the norm, both in China, and later in the West. Huge quantities of Chinese porcelain accompanied the tea shipped to the West. At first, as a new fashion, it was highly priced. Later, as the price fell, it became commonplace. It cost little to ship, for it was treated as ballast, which was necessary to keep the centre of gravity of the ship low in the water. (Copper, one of the few materials that the Chinese lacked, was a common ballast for the journey to China.) Wooden ships always leak, and tea is sensitive to damp. Porcelain was the ideal commodity to line the bottom of the holds, and it was almost always used as a platform for cargoes of silk and tea.

During the Ming Dynasty, tea compressed into cakes, balls, or bricks was gradually superseded by loose-leaf tea. By the time the West discovered tea, loose-leaf tea was in general use throughout China – loose-leaf tea on which boiling water was poured and then allowed to steep. The tea was poured into porcelain handle-less cups, and no longer whisked. This was the method of making tea that the West copied.

Some brick tea continued to be made, and it is still made to this day, mostly for export to the largely nomadic peoples on China's frontiers. Compressed tea has the advantages of being easy to transport and also being resistant to deterioration. There is very little air circulation inside a brick of tea, which makes it less susceptible to damp and contamination by other odours. Without doubt, however, properly looked after loose-leaf tea produces a better-flavoured liquor.

The Ming also introduced the practice of scenting some teas with flower petals. Aromatic plant oils had been used in earlier times but the Ming, with their special affinity for flowers, scented their teas with the petals of lotus, rose, gardenia, orange blossom, and especially jasmine. Half opened blossoms, full of scent, were layered between tea in a sealed pot, in a ratio of three parts of tea to one of flowers, and then boiled in water. The contents were then removed and baked.

The other major innovation of the Ming Dynasty was the production of black teas. The Chinese have always preferred green teas, regarding black teas as being only suitable for foreigners. Before the Ming there seems to be no record of black teas. Precisely how or why black teas came to be produced is something of a mystery, but they became very popular among the peoples living north of the Great Wall. Bartering for horses with tea had begun in the Tang Dynasty, but became much greater under the Ming. As many as 20,000 horses were purchased in a single year by the Horse and Tea Commission, in exchange for well over 1 million lbs of tea. Much of this tea was black, and the Commission controlled the huge tea plantations established to produce it. The first teas to find their way to the West were green, but black teas soon followed and eventually came to dominate western taste.

It was ironic that the export of China tea to the West, destined to become one of the world's most valuable crops, should have started in the time of the Ming Dynasty, for it was the Ming who had turned China into an inward-looking nation. Under the Ming the Chinese had convinced themselves that they were superior to all other cultures; that they should isolate themselves from any-thing foreign. Direct selling by the Chinese to foreign countries gradually diminished, and in 1521 was declared illegal. The selling of tea had to be handled through intermediaries – Japan-ese, Koreans, or Europeans – less the Chinese became tainted.

Tea is made from an evergreen tree. At the beginning of *The Classic of Tea*, Lu Yu wrote:

> Tea is from a grand tree in the south. The tree may grow from one or two feet to as much as twelve. In the rivers and gorges of the province of Szechwan are trees whose girth is such that it requires two men to embrace them. Those trees must be felled for plucking.

This comes as a surprise to those who have only seen conven-tional tea plantations with their 'table' of thigh-high shrubs. In fact, tea is a tree that if given space and left unpruned will grow to a height of forty feet or more. There is a wild tree growing in China, on the border of Yunnan province and Myanmar (formerly Burma), which is believed to be 1,700 years old, and which when last measured was over three feet in diameter and 108 feet tall. Even pruned trees develop a massive root system, with a taproot reaching down twenty feet or more. It is this root system, pumping up into a severely pruned bush, which results in the continual production of masses of new shoots, which when regularly plucked produce quality tea.

The tea plant is a species of camellia, *Camellia sinensis*. For many years it was believed in the West that there were two species, one for green tea and one for black. Both types of tea can, in fact, be produced from any tea plant. Nevertheless, it was not such an absurd notion, for there are many varieties of tea plant, and some are better suited to green or black tea manufacture.

Tea grows best in a deep, rich, acid soil. It likes a hot and humid atmosphere with about 100 inches of rain a year. A cooler night temperature slows growth, but produces a better-flavoured tea. This combination of requirements is found on high land within the tropics, or close to them, and this is where most tea is now commercially grown. Varieties of tea grown in China are more resistant to cold than most, and can withstand mild frost, which enables the Chinese to grow tea well north of the tropics. Yields, however, are relatively low.

Because of the northerly latitudes and high altitude in which Chinese teas are grown, the plant is plucked much less frequently than in more tropical climates. A seventeenth-century account, given to the captain of an East India Company ship by a merchant in Canton, describes the cycle:

In the month of March when the moon is half spent or three quarters the best tea is made.

In April a second or worser sort.

In May a third or worser sort, and so worse and worse.

He also adds 'that which grows on the mountains is the best,' echoing the old Chinese saying: 'Famous teas come from high mountains.'

Although some Chinese tea-manufacturing processes have recently been mechanized, in essence the methods are still the same as those developed during the Ming Dynasty. Careful plucking is essential if good teas are to be produced. The leaf used must only come from tender new shoots, and old leaves must be discarded. As the shoots develop, the leaves become coarser, so the bushes have to be picked regularly. The classic exhortation is to pluck only 'two leaves and a bud'. The very finest Chinese imperial teas were even more stringently selected, with the leaf coming from one leaf and a bud, or even solely from the new buds. Ordinary teas will contain two leaves and a bud plus a certain amount of older leaf.

The leaves are harvested into a basket slung on the plucker's back, and subsequently transported in baskets or bags to the factory. Any damage to the leaf will break some plant cells, which will release enzymes that will start the leaf fermenting (more correctly, oxidizing) and turning brown. It is important to minimize this by careful plucking and handling. The leaf must not be crushed, piled too deeply, or take too long to reach the factory. Nevertheless, once the leaf is plucked, however carefully it is handled, some bruising will occur and fermentation will start. It is important to keep this to a minimum before the manufacturing process starts. For this reason factories have to be within a few miles of the fields. Manufacturing tea needs considerable expertise and skill. All these requirements mean that is not normally possible for small-scale growers to process their own tea. Most tea factories, therefore, either serve a large plantation or a number of small farmers.

At the factory the tea leaves are spread out on bamboo trays to dry off the dew and other superfluous moisture. If green tea is being made, any fermentation is now brought to a halt by killing off the enzymes with heat. This can be done by a few minutes of steaming or roasting. The roasting is quite mild – the leaves being tossed about in a shallow iron pan and heated over a charcoal fire until they are just hot enough still to remove by hand. They are then tipped out on to the rolling table.

At the wicker rolling table the workers make balls of the

Chinese tea-rolling table

Chinese tea furnaces and drying pans

leaves, which they roll between the palms of their hands and about the table, both to expel any moisture and to put a twist on the leaves. If there is too much moisture left, the brief roasting and the rolling may be repeated a few times. Then the leaves are returned to the roasting pans for a much longer final roasting. This may take an hour or more, the leaves being continually moved around with the hands so that they do not blacken. At the end of this final roasting the tea is ready for use. All that remains is to sieve out the dust and sort the leaf into different grades.

Many of the operations needed to produce black tea are similar to those used in green-tea manufacture, though the natural fermentation of the bruised leaf is not halted, but encouraged. When the leaves are brought in from the field they are left to lie in the bamboo trays for several hours, often overnight. They are then tossed and beaten by hand until soft and flaccid, which releases the enzymes and browns the leaves, before being roasted and rolled. The final roasting is much more severe than with green tea. Instead of being put in a pan, the leaf is placed on a sieve, and hot air from the charcoal fire funnelled up through it. Finally, the sieve is covered to increase the heat, and this totally blackens the tea.

A few teas are produced by a process somewhere between those for green and black teas. These semi-fermented teas, such as *oolong*, are only allowed to half ferment before being fired. They have an appearance and flavour somewhere between black and green teas.

During the first half of the nineteenth century there was very little increase in the amount of tea British people consumed. In 1800 the consumption per head was about one and a half pounds a year; in 1850 nearly two pounds. However, it was a time of rapidly increasing population, so total consumption more than doubled. Virtually all this tea came from China.

The British were a great trading nation, skilled at exchanging the goods they manufactured or traded for the goods they wanted. The Chinese, however, desired very little from the British. They were confident that their own manufactured goods were superior to anything the British might try to sell them. They were only interested in being paid in silver. This was difficult for the British, for it seemed that the export of such huge quantities of silver might debase the British currency. The problem was slightly alleviated by the Chinese desire for cotton. So much Chinese land had been given over to the hugely profitable tea industry that it had been necessary to curtail the production of cotton. India grew cotton, so the East India Company, which of course controlled India, was able to sell cotton for silver, and then with the silver buy tea. The Chinese need for cotton, however, was nowhere near the British demand for tea. Fortuitously for the British, and for the East India Company, there was one other commodity that was in increasing demand in China – opium. And opium was produced in India.

Opium is the dried juice of the unripe seed capsules of the opium poppy, *Papaver somniferum*, which originates from southwest Asia. It was known to the Greeks and Romans, and was probably brought to India by the Arabs. When this occurred is not known, but by the sixteenth century it was being extensively cultivated and traded in Bihar, and probably exported to China.

The Arabs also seem to have taken opium to China. The Chinese have more complete written records of earlier times than the Indians, and this introduction can be traced back much further. However, it seems likely that the Indians would have received visits from the Arabs earlier than did the Chinese, and therefore would have discovered opium earlier. It is recorded that the Arabs visited Canton in the eighth century, and we also have records of the Chinese cultivation of the poppy in that century. In

973 the Emperor Sung T'ai-tsu, commissioned a medical work, in which it was written of the poppy:

> Its seeds have healing powers. When men have taken the stone that confers immortality [mercury?], feel it powerfully operating, and cannot eat with appetite, they may be benefited by mixing these seeds with bamboo juice, boiling into gruel, and taking this.

Over succeeding centuries there were many references to the use of opium for treating all manner of illnesses, ranging from coughs to dysentery. It is also clear that by the sixteenth century opium was being manufactured in China. Whether opium was being swallowed for other than medicinal use is not recorded, but given the experience of other countries, and the addictive nature of the drug, it seems likely.

The consumption of opium was transformed by the arrival of tobacco. This seems to have come to China from the Philippines, where the Spaniards had introduced it from America, in about 1620. The last Ming Emperor, Szu Tsung, who ruled from 1628 to 1644, tried to ban it, but without success, for it had become too popular. Soon people were mixing other drugs with tobacco to see what effects they had. Arsenic was used for this purpose (and still is) but the drug that became most favoured was opium.

Opium, when eaten in small quantities, is only moderately addictive, and its effects are not usually severe. Many people in the Middle East and South Asia take opium as a recreational drug and continue working, although it is debilitating. There are many accounts of westerners taking opium regularly, but continuing to function. Excess consumption, usually provoked by using it to control pain, can be devastating. Coleridge, De Quincy, and Clive of India all suffered the consequences of ingesting too much opium. To smoke opium, however, is altogether more serious. An early Chinese account puts it succinctly:

Depraved young men without any fixed occupation used to meet together by night to smoke; it grew to be a custom with them. Often various delicacies prepared with honey and sugar, with fresh fruits to the number of ten or more dishes, were provided for visitors while smoking. In order to tempt new smokers to come, no charge was made for the first time. After some time they could not stay away, and would come even if they forfeited all their property. Smokers were able to remain awake the whole night and rejoice, as an aid to sensual indulgence. Afterwards they found themselves beyond the possibility of cure. If for one day they omitted smoking, their faces suddenly became shrivelled, their lips opened, their teeth were seen, they lost all vivacity, and seemed ready to die. Another smoke, however, restored them. After three years all such persons die.

At this time the use of opium for smoking was largely confined to the coastal provinces and to the island of Formosa. Nevertheless, the Imperial government in Peking (Beijing) became alarmed, and in 1729 the sale of opium for smoking was prohibited. No action was taken against the smokers themselves, but the keepers of shops were to be imprisoned and then strangled. Opium, however, continued to be imported. Ostensibly this was for medicinal use, but in fact much was smoked. Bribes to customs officials smoothed the way. In 1727 imports had been 200 chests (a chest is approximately 140lbs of opium); by 1767 imports were 1,000 chests. Much of this came from India.

When the Mughals took control of much of India in the sixteenth century the cultivation of opium was unregulated. The Emperor Akbar (1556–1605) made purchase of the crop and its subsequent sale a state monopoly. The Mughal emperors then raised revenue by leasing out this monopoly to contractors. Cultivation was still freely allowed, but growers had to sell to a state contractor. These contractors then manufactured the opium and sold it on to dealers inside India, or to merchants for export. The export trade was controlled by various European nations, principally the Dutch, and this practice continued after the British victories in Bengal.

In 1773, the British took over control of Bengal and Bihar from the Mughals, and asserted their monopoly over opium. The monopoly was leased to contractors, who had the exclusive right to buy and manufacture all opium grown in the East India Company's territories, and also to import opium from the neighbouring states. All high-grade opium, fit for export, then had to be sold to the East India Company at a fixed price. However, the contractors oppressed the opium farmers so severely that output and revenue fell, and this led the East India Company to take over direct purchase from the cultivators. At first the opium was sold directly by the Company to China and south-east Asia, but this was found to contravene the Company's charter. Thereafter it was sold for export at auction in Calcutta, with no questions asked as to its final destination.

Outside British jurisdiction, in Indian territories ruled by independent princes, there were several important opium-producing areas. These were mostly in central India and Rajasthan, and the opium from these areas was loosely called Malwa, after one of these districts. The Dutch and the Portuguese had been exporting Malwa opium well before the British arrived in India. Traditionally it was exported through Bombay, which had come under British control, and the British put an end to this practice in 1803. Nevertheless, it was still possible to export from other places beyond British jurisdiction, and it took many years for the British either to conquer the territories concerned, or to encircle them and extract a heavy transit duty. This the British finally achieved in 1843. At its height the Indian opium industry employed nearly 1 million people.

Why the Chinese preferred Indian opium to other opiums is something of a mystery. The opium poppy grows well in China, for opium is not particularly difficult to grow and manufacture – it is nowhere near so sophisticated a process as is needed to produce a good tea. As with other consumables, it might have been just a question of habit; of continuing to enjoy what had originally been experienced. Certainly much effort was made in India to produce an opium that was acceptable to the Chinese. As a British opium official in India wrote in 1836: 'The great object of the Bengal opium agencies is to furnish an article suitable to the peculiar tastes of the population of China.'

In the last decade of the eighteenth century, two startling developments were brought to the attention of the Emperor of China. The first was that blatant smoking of opium had reached Peking itself. The second was that, although opium was supposed to be only imported for medicinal use, the amount coming into China had increased to about 4,000 chests a year. The amount of silver involved in the purchase of so much opium threatened the balance of payments. In 1796 the Emperor banned all exports of silver and imports of opium.

The ban increased the production of opium in China, but otherwise made little difference. The East India Company forbade its ships to carry opium, but was happy to license other ships to carry it. Bengal and Malwa opium were purchased by all and sundry at the Company's auctions in Calcutta and from Malwa, and smuggled into China.

The smuggling was done with the connivance of Chinese officials, who extracted large bribes. A price war between Bengal and Malwa reduced prices and increased consumption. In 1820 the Imperial Chinese government made some attempts to halt the trade, and succeeded in stopping opium cargoes being offloaded at the Cantonese port of Whampoa. A new system of smuggling began – opium was offloaded into storage ships moored at Lintin in the mouth of the Canton River. These ships were heavily armed against any attempt by the Chinese to capture them. Opium went up the river as before, paying bribes, but was now carried by Chinese smugglers. These smugglers also took silver out to make payments. Some of this silver was used to buy Chinese tea and other goods, but much of it was taken back to India to buy even more opium.

The Americans were also in the opium business. As Indian opium was monopolized by the British they had to find supplies in Turkey. Between 1818 and 1833 the Americans brought opium worth nearly $5 million into China. This was less than a twentieth of the more than $100 million of opium brought in over the same period by the British. The principal American firm was Russell & Company. Its ships flew the American flag, and one of its opium captains became head of the firm. He was succeeded by Warren Delano II, grandfather of President Franklin Delano Roosevelt.

By 1830 China was importing over 18,000 chests, 2½ million lbs, of Indian opium a year. This more than covered the entire cost of the tea being exported – about 9 million Spanish dollars. (The preferred currency in China was the Spanish dollar, although Mexican and other dollars were also in circulation. There were a little over four Spanish dollars to one pound sterling. Nine million Spanish dollars were approximately equivalent to £2.2 million.) British merchants saw opportunities to increase sales of opium further. Led by Dr William Jardine, founder of the finance house Jardine Matheson, they began to trade up the Chinese coast, creating new markets, new addicts and new profits.

William Jardine had been born on a Scottish farm in 1784. He obtained the diploma of the Royal College of Surgeons in Edinburgh when only eighteen, and then travelled out to China in the same month on an Indiaman as a surgeon's mate. Like the other officers, he had the right to 'privileged tonnage' – the right to ship goods on his own account. His allowance was two tons, which although it was only a fraction of that of the senior officers, nevertheless gave him plenty of scope for a handsome profit. Jardine did this for fifteen years, until 1817, and built up an extensive network of business contacts in the East. The next year he went from London to Bombay where he joined forces with Parsee merchants to operate a ship in the China trade. In 1822 Jardine moved to Canton and began dealing in large quantities of opium. He amassed a huge fortune. In 1828 he joined forces with a fellow Scot, James Matheson, who was also in the opium trade, to form the company Jardine Matheson. Although affable, Jardine was able and tough. It is said that, in order to expedite business, he had no chairs in his office. When presenting a document at the Petition Gate in Canton he was struck from behind hard with a bamboo pole. He did not even turn round. Thereafter he was known to the Chinese as the 'iron-headed old rat'.

Jardine and his fellow foreigners hugely expanded the opium trade. By 1838, Bengal and Malwa were exporting 4¾ million lbs of opium. It had become the world's most valuable trade commodity. China's silver was being drained into India. There it was used by the British to speed up colonization and the conquest of new territory. The surplus silver – and a huge surplus it was – was repatriated to Britain. Some £4 million a year was sent back from India in the 1830s.

The change in the balance of trade brought about by British opium is graphically illustrated by the movement of silver between Britain and China. In the decade to 1810 the British exported 983 tons of silver to the Chinese. In the decade to 1840 the Chinese exported 366 tons of silver to the British.

Meanwhile, the role of the East India Company had fundamentally changed, for Parliament had removed the monopoly the Company had enjoyed of trade between Britain and China. As from 22 April 1834 the China trade was opened to all. A year later the Company's charter came up for renewal, and its position in India was transformed. It, in effect, became an agent for the British government, administering the country and collecting taxes on its behalf. It ceased to trade on its own account. Following the Indian 'Mutiny' of 1857, the Company was stripped of this privilege too, and the British government took over the direct rule of British India. The Company was, of course, generously compensated – with money from the Indians.

China's trade with the West had orignally been opened up by the Portuguese. A fleet of their ships had first visited Canton in 1517, and they had established 'factories' (trading posts) at several places along the Chinese coast. In 1545 the Chinese attacked them. Many Portuguese were killed, and their ships destroyed. By 1549 all their factories had been closed. However, in 1557 they were allowed to re-establish themselves at Macao, a two-mile long narrow spit of land sixty-five miles south of Canton.

A British ship first visited Canton in 1637, but it was 1699 before they managed to start regular trade and establish a factory. The Chinese allocated fifteen acres for the foreigners, and the British were crowded against the other nations' factories, including those of the Dutch, the French, the Americans, the Spanish and the Danes. To avoid any suggestion that the foreigners had any rights over the land, they were only allowed to stay for six months of the year, and then had to go to Macao for the other six months. Access to the rest of China was forbidden. The foreigners welcomed the enforced sojourn in Macao, for they were forbidden to bring any women, whether wives or mistresses, to Canton. Moreover, the Chinese women were forbidden to them. In Macao the foreign men were free to keep their families, or make other liaisons, or visit the many brothels.

The Chinese, confident in their superiority, refused to have diplomatic relations with any country that refused to acknowledge inferior status. All dealings by foreign merchants were required to be conducted through a guild of Chinese merchants, the *Cohong*, who in turn were supervised by Chinese Imperial officials.

The changed status of the East India Company had serious repercussions in Canton. When the Company's monopoly expired, the British government decided that, instead of the British merchants handling their own relations with the Chinese, it would appoint a Superintendent of Trade, Lord Napier. He had instructions from the Foreign Secretary, Lord Palmerston, to present his credentials to the Governor-General of Canton.

Napier arrived in July 1834. His official letter was rejected, and the Governor-General ordered him to leave for Macao. When Napier refused, the Chinese blockaded the factories. Napier summoned two British frigates, but the Chinese blocked the river and assembled sixty-eight war junks. Napier left in ignominy on 21 September 1834, and died of fever in Macao the next month. Trade returned to normal.

As opium abuse became worse, different advice was tendered to the Emperor in Peking. Some officials, worried more about the threat to the currency than the degeneration of some of the population, wanted to legalize the drug; others wanted to take effective action to enforce the ban. The Emperor decided in favour of the latter. These advocated the death sentence for addicts (but with a year's grace to enable them to attempt a cure), and ruthless action against all opium sellers, including foreign merchants. On the last day of 1838 the leading advocate of the moral path, Lin Tse-hsu, was appointed Imperial commissioner to 'sever the trunk from the roots'.

Lin Tse-hsu was fifty-three, and had enjoyed a very varied career in the Chinese civil service. He had been a judicial commissioner, a financial commissioner, and was currently Governor-General of Hupeh and Hunan provinces. He had a reputation for being just and humane and was known as 'Lin, Clear as the Heavens'. In July 1838 Lin had sent a memorial to the Emperor, which supported strict enforcement of the laws prohibiting opium. He had recommended a policy of destroying opium-smoking equipment, a time limit on rehabilitation, and draconian measures against dealers and smugglers. He had enforced these measures within his own provinces with considerable success. Lin was summoned to Peking for consultations, where he had nineteen audiences with the Emperor, and persuaded him that he, Lin, was the man to deal with the situation in Canton.

Lin wasted no time. On 8 January 1839 he set out on a journey from Peking to Canton with a small staff. It was a tortuously slow journey, for much of it had to be done on river boats, and there were snowstorms on the higher ground. The journey took two months, but Lin sent messages ahead on fast horses and had arrests made even before he arrived. The American merchants decided to quit the opium trade, as did some of the British. This left only a handful of British merchants led by Jardine Matheson, and some Indian Parsees led by Heerjeebhoy Rustumjee.

Lin entered Canton on 10 March by boat in a formal procession. Eight days later he summoned a meeting of the *Cohong*. He berated them for treasonable activities in allowing opium to come into China and silver to go out. The *Cohong* were to arrange with the foreigners to surrender all the opium lying offshore in their ships, otherwise he would confiscate their property and execute some of them. Lin also stopped the departure of all foreign merchants.

The foreigners agreed amongst themselves to surrender 1,056 chests of opium as a gesture. This was not sufficient for Lin. He ordered the arrest of Lancelot Dent, who, he thought, was the main opium supplier, and he also blockaded the factories. Charles Elliot, the British Chief Superintendent, arrived just in time to be trapped. After a forty-seven-day siege Elliot ordered all the traders' opium to be surrendered, guaranteed that it would be paid for by the British government, and then handed it over for destruction. Most of the opium belonged to British and Parsee firms, but the Americans still had stocks and lost 1,000 chests. All together, 20,283 chests of opium, valued at $9 million, were dumped into the sea.

With so much money at stake, it was inevitable that the British would send an expeditionary force. Lord Palmerston, the British Foreign Secretary, was notoriously belligerent, and had become famous for his 'gunboat diplomacy'. He had been made Secretary at War when only twenty-four and held that office for nineteen years. Although portrayed in the Press as something of a rake, and referred to as 'Lord Cupid', Palmerston worked prodigiously hard. He toiled through to 1 a.m. most nights, standing at a special high desk to keep awake, and assiduously promoted an aggressive foreign policy across the whole world. He had been Foreign Secretary for eleven years, and used the navy against the King of Naples and the Viceroy of Egypt. He had blockaded Rotterdam and Naples, Acre and Beirut.

Palmerston consulted the opium merchant, William Jardine, who had left Canton just before the arrival of Commissioner Lin. He then gave instructions for the blockade of China's main ports. This would continue until reparations for the seized opium had been made, together with compensation for the entire cost of the expedition. He also demanded that the country be opened up to British merchants and their opium, and that a Chinese island be ceded to Britain.

Macaulay spoke for the government in Parliament. He declared that the British merchants at Canton:

> should look with confidence on the victorious flag which was hoisted over them, which reminded them that they belonged to a country unaccustomed to defeat, to submission or to shame; to a country which had exacted such reparation for the wrongs to her children as had made the ears of all who heard it tingle; to a country which had made the Bey of Algeria humble himself in the dust before her insulted consul; to a country which had avenged the victims of the Black Hole on the field of Plassey; to a country that had not degenerated since the great Protector vowed that he would make the name

of Englishmen as much respected as ever had been the name of Roman citizen.

Gladstone led the parliamentary opposition: 'A war more unjust in its origins, a war more calculated to cover this country with permanent disgrace, I do not know and I have not read of.' The Government, which insisted that any military expedition was to protect free trade, and not to impose the sale of opium, won the day. It was given authority to make war.

The Chinese totally underestimated the efficiency of the British war machine. Insulated from outside influences, the Chinese army was equipped with outdated weapons and ill-trained troops. They performed elaborate sword drills, which would be of little use against the latest muskets. Confident in their supremacy, they even had faith in martial arts devotees who would lie on riverbeds and then bore holes through the bottom of British warships.

In June 1840 the British assembled a fleet off Macao – steamers, transports with 4,000 soldiers, and sixteen warships. Palmerston did not want to engage in a provincial war in Canton, but wanted to take the war to Peking and force the Emperor to capitulate. Accordingly, leaving only a token force at Canton, the fleet sailed 800 miles north to the island of Chusan. The plan was to capture the island as a warning, then sail north to the coast near Peking, and from there present the British demands to the Emperor. The fleet borrowed pilots from the ships of the British opium merchants.

Chusan was an easy victory. At first the islanders were delighted to see the British ships, for they thought they had come to trade. The British, however, soon made clear they wanted surrender. When the Chinese refused, the British bombarded the town, reduced it to rubble and then looted it.

The fleet continued its journey north, to Taku, 100 miles from Peking. The Chinese, alarmed that the British might attack Peking itself, agreed to talks. There was, however, no agreement. Palmerston's letter and the British financial demands astonished the Chinese. The British refused to discuss Chinese demands that the British ban export of opium from their territories. The British force lacked the shallow draught vessels that would have been necessary to take the war up river to Peking, so they turned round and sailed south to pursue the war in Canton.

Lin was no longer at Canton. He had been removed from office, and exiled to the Russian border. (Lin was subsequently rehabilitated and once again became a governor-general. He ended his career as Imperial Commissioner for suppressing rebels in Kwangsi, and died in 1850 while still in office. He was canonized and several temples were erected to his memory. In 1929 the Chinese government designated 3 June, the day Lin had begun the destruction of opium in Canton, as Opium Prohibition Day. He is now very widely admired by the Chinese, both in China and overseas. A street in New York is named after him.)

Lin had been replaced as commissioner at Canton by Ch'i-shan, who had conducted the negotiations at Taku. Seeing the power of the British forces, Ch'i-shan opened negotiations with Elliot. They agreed on part of what Palmerston required, but foundered on the demand for ceded ports. The British then attacked and captured the Chinese gun batteries guarding the river to Canton. Negotiations were resumed and Ch'i-shan agreed to an indemnity and to cede Hong Kong. He was overtaken by events, however, for the Emperor was already amassing an 'Army of Extermination' to drive out the foreigners. Ch'i-shan was disgraced and taken from Canton in chains.

Elliot was also to be removed, for Palmerston thought him not firm enough:

Throughout the whole course of your proceedings you seem to have considered that my instructions were waste paper, which you might treat with entire disregard, and that you were at full liberty to deal with the interests of your country according to your own fancy.

He was replaced by Sir Henry Pottinger.

Pottinger had a reputation for decisive action. Born in 1789, near Belfast, he came from a family whose fortunes had declined. Five sons were sent out to India to make a living. Henry became a midshipman when he was twelve years old, and set out for India when only fourteen. Soon after his arrival, he transferred to the Company's army, and was commissioned in 1809. Almost immediately he was sent to accompany the Governor-General's representative on a successful mission to negotiate a treaty with the north-east-Indian state of Sind. He, and another officer, then went to Baluchistan as spies. They travelled 1,500 miles, disguised as horse-dealers or pilgrims, and brought back much useful information about a territory previously unexplored by the British.

Pottinger then became assistant to the British Resident at Poona, and was able to follow closely the machinations and wars that enabled the British to supplant the Maratha rulers in central India. Afterwards he was given his own Residency at Kutch, on the southern border of Sind, and later the responsibility of dealing with Sind and bringing it under British influence. Pottinger threatened war against Sind, and finally extracted a favourable treaty in 1839 – a treaty that allowed the British to move troops through Sind to Afghanistan. He was given a baronetcy – became Sir Henry Pottinger – and went back to Britain for leave, and to recover his health. He was still there when Palmerston sent for him. The Foreign Secretary's instructions to Pottinger were crystal clear – compensation, idemnity, ceding of Hong Kong (already occupied by the British) and at least four new ports, free trade and the legalization of opium.

On 21 May 1841 the Emperor of China's cousin sent flaming rafts into the British fleet. The British then destroyed seventy-one Chinese war junks, and seized the Chinese shore batteries. Troops were landed, who took control of the high land just outside Canton. The city was at their mercy. However, the British did not occupy the city, but demanded a ransom. The Chinese paid $6 million (£1,450,000) and the British withdrew to their ships. Exports resumed from the port downstream at Whampoa. The Americans and French returned to conduct business from Canton itself. Tea began again to leave the China coast in normal quantities.

Pottinger reached Hong Kong in August with more ships and troops. He took over command from Elliot, and sailed north. First he captured Amoy, an important port halfway up the coast; then he recaptured the island of Chusan, and the port of Ningpo on the mainland opposite. The Chinese did try to recapture Ningpo, but another of the Emperor's cousins (a distinguished calligrapher, but an incompetent general) was in command. The streets were choked with dead; 500 Chinese soldiers, and not a single British one.

The British then moved up to the heavily populated plains that bordered the Yangtze River. They occupied Shanghai, which the Chinese had abandoned. The Chinese put up some resistance at Chapu and Chinkiang, but these were captured too. This enabled the Grand Canal, which linked the Yangtze and Yellow rivers and carried much of China's trade, to be cut. Chinkiang also controlled the river to Nanking, and it now became possible to move boats and artillery to the edge of the ancient and important city of Nanking. The British began to prepare an assault. The Chinese mandarins could see that all was lost, and feared that an assault on Peking, which would almost certainly topple the regime, would follow. With some difficulty they persuaded the Emperor to sue for peace.

The Treaty of Nanking was signed on 29 August 1842. The Chinese gave almost all that Palmerston had wanted. The ports of Canton, Amoy, Foochow, Ningpo, and Shanghai were to be opened up to British trade and residence; China would pay $21 million (£5 million) for the cost of the war and compensation for the confiscated opium; Hong Kong would pass to the British in perpetuity. The only condition the Chinese refused to countenance was the legalization of opium and, rather surprisingly, Pottinger did not insist.

It was Chinese policy to treat all foreigners similarly. As a result it concluded treaties with the other major trading nations, France and America, on broadly similar lines to that with Britain.

Much as China had been humiliated in the Treaty of Nanking, implementation did not completely satisfy the British. There were disputes as to whether the British merchants had the right to settle permanently within Canton; disputes over representation in Peking. Opium had not been legalized. In consequence the British did not allow it through their treaty ports. Nevertheless, a flourishing trade in smuggled Indian opium still operated along the coast. Lord Palmerston, still Foreign Secretary in 1850, considered the whole settlement inadequate:

> The time is fast coming when we shall be obliged to strike another blow in China . . . these half-civilised governments such as those in China, Portugal and Spanish America, all require a dressing every eight or ten years to keep them in order.

Matters came to a head in 1856, when the Chinese arrested the crew of a suspected pirate ship, the *Arrow*. Lord Palmerston, after sixteen years as Foreign Secretary, and short spells as Home

Secretary, had now become Prime Minister. He was now even more belligerent than at the time of the first Opium War. The British public loved his rhetoric:

> As the Roman, in days of old, held himself free from indignity, when he could say Civis Romanus sum; so also a British subject, in whatever land he may be, shall feel confident that the watchful eye and the strong arm of England will protect him against injustice and wrong.

The British consul at Canton and the Governor of Hong Kong mounted a naval attack on Canton, and captured the Chinese Governor-General's residence. In retaliation foreign factories outside the walled city were burned, and rewards were offered for the death or capture of the British. Palmerston now saw his opportunity to finish business with the Chinese. Another expeditionary force was assembled under Lord Elgin. Following the murder of one of their missionaries, the French joined the British.

Canton was attacked in late 1857. The Governor-General was captured and exiled to India. Elgin then went north, and captured the Dagu forts that guarded the river to Tientsin and Peking. The Emperor was again forced to negotiate to save his capital. The 1858 Treaty of Tientsin imposed further heavy losses to China's sovereignty – ten more ports were opened to the foreigners; missionaries were allowed into China; foreigners could travel within China; a British diplomat would reside in Peking. This time the opium question was not avoided – the trade was to be legalized.

The terms of the Treaty of Tientsin caused great resentment in China. When the British and French returned to ratify it in Peking, they found the river blocked. There was an exchange of fire with the Dagu forts, and many British casualties. The Americans, who were supposedly neutral observers, sided with the British. Nevertheless, the British and French were forced to retreat.

In 1860 the British and French returned with a much larger expedition. The Chinese arrested a British diplomat who had gone ahead to arrange the signing of the treaty, and killed several of his party. In retribution, Peking was occupied and the Emperor's summer palace burnt. The settlement, which followed this total defeat and humiliation of the Chinese, resulted in a further unequal treaty. The Russians, who played an important role in negotiations, were given huge territories in the north of China and access to the port of Vladivostok. The Convention of Peking further increased the indemnity China would pay, opened Tientsin as a Treaty Port, and ceded the peninsular opposite Hong Kong to the British.

During all the wars and upheavals of the 1840s and 1850s, the trade in Chinese tea was remarkably unaffected. The price might fluctuate in London, depending on the news from China, but the tea kept on coming. During actual hostilities, which never lasted very long, tea shipments might be temporarily halted, but they soon resumed. If things were difficult for the British, the Americans would ship the tea out. Tea stocks in Britain never went below nine months' supply. The Chinese attempts to ban opium caused flutters in the market as merchants wondered how the silver to purchase tea would be obtained. However, whatever the Chinese authorities did at centres like Canton, there were always alternative destinations on the long coast, and some Indian opium always got through. There was such a big imbalance in value between the two crops, with opium being far more valuable than tea, that even reduced imports of opium were sufficient to pay for the tea.

The exchange of opium for tea was a disaster for China. While it was true, as the British were ever fond of pointing out, that no one forced the Chinese to smoke opium, it was also true that exports from British territory and the smuggling by British merchants undermined Chinese efforts to stem addiction. Once the Treaty of Tientsin legalized the opium trade, even more Indian opium flooded into China. Imports tripled from what they had been in 1835, before the Opium War, to peak at 93,000 chests in 1872. Britain continued to export Indian opium to China until 1911. There was also a huge rise in opium cultivation inside China, with so much land put to its cultivation that food shortages ensued. Perhaps most seriously of all, the British military expeditions sent to protect the opium-for-tea trade, destabilized the Chinese regime and fuelled xenophobia. The central government lost control of huge areas to robbers and pirates; many of the Chinese people thought the Manchu Dynasty was appeasing the hated foreigners. The repercussions would echo down into modern China.

A more pleasant feature of the China tea trade was the 'Clipper Race'. The most highly prized teas from China were those plucked first, at the beginning of the season, in the spring. Teas were believed to deteriorate with age. They certainly do if they are exposed to damp, but if properly packed in sealed containers they keep well. Nevertheless, a mystique built up around drinking recently plucked teas, especially the 'first flush' teas. It was rather similar to the present race in Britain to drink the first of the new Beaujolais.

The East India Company had used immensely strong, dumpy, heavy vessels, described as being like a cross between a medieval castle and a warehouse. Typically, these 'East Indiamen' would leave Britain in January, sail round the Cape of Good Hope, and then pick up the south-west monsoon to arrive off China in September. The entire tea harvest for that year would have been plucked by then and, with luck, it could be loaded for departure in December. Often, the ships took a roundabout route on the way back, for everything depended on the wind. They would first go east from China, between Formosa (Taiwan) and the Philippines, then south to New Guinea, before turning west. If they picked up good winds, they might be back by September. More likely it would be December or later, fully two years after they had first left Britain. Delays in China might make it necessary to spend almost a year in China waiting for the north-east monsoon, extending the round trip to nearer three years.

The East India Company disposed of many of its ships in 1814, when it lost its monopoly of the trade to India. It had continued to trade with China, but when in 1834 it lost that monopoly too, it disposed of its last ship. Many were bought by their captains or by Indian merchants, who had often been operating the ships under licence from the Company, and the ships continued to sail to China.

The Americans had developed fast sailing ships as privateers during the war against the British of 1812. These had sleek lines, a sharp bow and lots of sail. (A captured American privateer was used as a model for the British opium clippers that sailed between India and China. The first of these was the *Red Rover*, which was launched in 1829. Its captain, William Clifton, who had copied the design of the privateer *Prince de Neufchatel*, received £10,000 from the Governor-General of India for speeding up the opium run to Canton.) From these privateers the Americans developed the first tea clippers. The *Rainbow*, launched in 1845, made the journey from New York to Canton in 102 days, knocking sixteen days off the previous record. In 1849 the *Sea Witch* cut the time to seventy-four days. The repeal of the British Navigation Laws in 1849 allowed American ships to carry tea direct from China to Britain. The first American clipper to carry tea from China to London was the *Oriental*, which made the journey from Hong Kong in ninety-seven days. This was three times the speed of the lumbering East Indiaman. There was a furore in London, and a determination to rival the Americans.

The 1860s were the great days of the tea clippers. During the 1850s the British had mastered the building techniques developed by the Americans. The Americans themselves had more important uses for their ships, as they were enmeshed in a civil war. The opening up of the Treaty Ports made the races more interesting, for tea could be taken from the port of Foochow, close to the tea fields, immediately after it had been plucked and manufactured. Large sums were wagered on which would be the first boat back to Britain. The most famous race was in 1866, with forty entrants, which ended in a dead heat between the *Ariel* and the *Taeping*.

The opening of the Suez Canal in 1869 brought the races to an end, for it made the trade viable to steamships. There had been a few slow steamers on the China trade previously, but they were not efficient, for they had to provide space for large quantities of fuel. The Suez Canal route had its own coaling stations en route, which gave steamers the advantage over the clippers sailing round Africa. The last clipper race was in 1871.

One of the last clippers to be constructed was the *Cutty Sark*, launched in 1869, now on display at Greenwich, in London. It is interesting to see how tightly the chests of tea were packed in, both to make maximum use of the limited space and to prevent the cargo shifting; and extraordinary to realize that such a small ship might carry a million pounds of tea.

Despite various wars, British imports of tea from China had increased dramatically. In 1830 imports had been 30 million lbs; in 1879 imports peaked at 136 million lbs. Most of this tea was grown not on plantations, but in tiny acreages as a peasant-farmer crop. The demand was so great that the driving force was quantity not quality. The tea was plucked indiscriminately, taking off much

Chong thie Loong kee.
Most humbly beg leave to acqu
: aint the Gentlemen trading to
this kort that the above mention
: ed chop has been long established
dnd is much esteemed for its Black
and young Hyson Tea but fearing
the foreigners might be cheated by tho
: se shumeless persons who forged this
chop he therefore take the liberty to
pallish these few lines for its
remark and trust.

more than the desirable 'two leaves and a bud'. The bushes were
damaged by over-plucking. The processing was done without
care, and there was much adulteration. For several decades a
great deal of welcome revenue went to the Chinese farmers and
merchants, but they were badly placed to face any competition
from new plantations in other countries.

THREE

Victorian Enterprise – India

Tea planters in those days were a strange medley of
retired or cashiered Army and Navy officers, medical
men, engineers, veterinary surgeons, steamer captains,
chemists, shopkeepers of all kinds, stable-keepers, used
up policemen, clerks and goodness knows who besides.

EDWARD MONEY

From the very first imports the tea trade between China and
Britain was a monopoly of the East India Company until 1834,
and was hugely profitable. The East India Company's main
activities were, however, in India. It was there that the Company
had transacted most of its business, and then made the extraordinary transition from being a trading company to ruling a
nation.

The Company had established its first 'factory' at Surat on the
coast of western India in 1619. During the remainder of the
seventeenth century and into the eighteenth it established more
trading posts in India, some of them well fortified. There had
been clashes with local princes, and sometimes these had resulted
in bloodshed, but the Company remained a purely commercial
venture.

Much of India in the mid eighteenth century was under the
nominal control of the Mughal Emperor at Delhi. This regime,
severely weakened by attacks from both the Marathas of western
India and from the Afghans, was in decline. Several of the

86

Emperor's princes had declared themselves independent, and others only made nominal homage. One of the latter was the *nawab* of Bengal in east India, where the Company had a factory at Calcutta. An attack on this factory by the *nawab*, who was incensed that the Company was fortifying its factory without his permission, resulted in the temporary expulsion of the British. Retribution followed. The Company sent an army under Robert Clive, which in 1757 defeated the *nawab*. A puppet *nawab*, who had colluded with Clive, was put in his place.

The new *nawab*, Mir Kasim, became appalled by the excesses of the Company's British servants, who used private armies to enrich themselves. Clive, when he returned from a visit to England, reported that 'such a scene of anarchy, confusion, bribery, corruption, and extortion was never seen or heard of in any country but Bengal; nor such and so many fortunes acquired in so unjust and rapacious a way.' Mir Kasim broke with the Company, and put together a Mughal army to fight it. In the ensuing battle the Mughals were totally defeated.

Had they wanted to, the Company could have marched against the Emperor in Delhi. However, this might not have been a financial success, so the Company satisfied itself with assuming, in 1765, the *Diwani* of Bengal, Bihar and Orissa. The *Diwani* gave the rights, after a small annual tribute to the Emperor (soon abandoned), to all the tax revenues of those territories. The Company assumed responsibility for the administration, including the army, police and justice system. It had become a government. It also had a monopoly of trade.

Although the East India Company was the government of part of India, it was also a British company, and to some extent answerable to the British government. That relationship, under the Company's charter was, however, far from clear. Parliament became concerned, and in 1784 passed the India Act, which established a Board of Control. This could regulate 'the levying of war or making of peace, or negotiating with any native princes

Victorian Enterprise – India

or states in India,' and could also dismiss the Company's Governor-General. Subject to these limitations, however, the Company managed to retain its trading monopoly, and also retain the right to govern its territories.

The Company's armies, with help from British troops, conquered huge new tracts of India, especially in the south, so that about half of all India came under direct Company rule. There was much criticism of the Company's dual role, as government and trader. The Company lost its monopoly of trade with India in 1813. When its charter came up for renewal in 1833, some wanted to abolish its governmental responsibilities. Quite the opposite happened – the Company was prohibited from trading, except in salt and opium, and left to administer British India. Shareholders would receive an annual dividend of 10½ per cent. This dividend and the cost of servicing the 'home bond debt' would be met out of taxation in India. Since the home bond debt originated in loans the East India Company had taken out when it lent money to the British government to further its own commercial interests, there was much resentment in India over these arrangements.

In addition to these monies, the Indians also had to pay for the cost of transporting troops between Britain and India, the pensions of the Company's administrators and army, the salaries of the directors of the East India Company and many other expenses. These included the cost of war medals produced to commemorate their own conquest, and the maintenance of European lunatics from India. Together with the home bond debt, these charges became known, and reviled by Indians, as the 'home charges'. Not only Indians were outraged. Sir Charles Trevelyan, later Governor of Madras observed: '£5,000,000 sterling a year is subtracted from the wealth of India and added to the wealth of England, which is the most serious injury which India suffers from its connection with England.' There would be future resentment, too, as the cost of conquering new territories inside India and of waging war against adjacent countries was added to these debts to be paid by the Indians.

Following the revision of its charter in 1834, the East India Company's monopoly of trade between China and Britain had come to an end. Simultaneously, there were doubts in Britain as to the reliability of Chinese exports, particularly as Japan had recently severed all trade with the West. It was therefore natural that the British, through the East India Company, should consider growing tea in India.

In 1793 Lord Macartney had been sent by the British government on a mission to Peking. Macartney was determined to be treated as an emissary of an equal state, but the Chinese had other ideas. They inscribed his barges with characters reading 'envoy bearing tribute'. When he arrived he was expected to perform the 'kowtow', which involved kneeling three times before the Emperor, and each time touching the floor three times with the face. Macartney would only do this if in return the Emperor would perform the kowtow to a portrait Macartney was carrying of the British king, George III. This the Chinese Emperor refused to do, and permission was refused for Macartney to become resident ambassador in Peking. The two did exchange presents, however, and Lord Macartney was allowed to take away some tea seeds and plants:

> In crossing into Kiangsi we passed through tea plantations and were allowed by the Viceroy to take up several tea plants in a growing state with very large balls of earth adhering to them, which plants I flatter myself, I shall be able to transmit to Bengal.

The plants probably did not survive, but some seeds were successfully germinated in the Botanical Gardens of Calcutta. In 1816, Lord Amherst led another mission to Peking, just as unsuccessful as that of Macartney, and he too was able to take away some plants and seeds. Amherst's ship, the *Alceste*, hit a coral reef off Sumatra – all the people aboard were rescued, but the plant specimens were lost.

These were by no means the first tea plants to have left China. There were, of course, whole plantations in Japan, and various other plants from China were dotted around the world. It seems that some tea plants reached Holland in the seventeenth century, but were from Japan. Linnaeus, the great Swedish botanist who established the modern system of plant classification, went to tremendous trouble to obtain a living specimen of tea. He sent his assistants, employed as chaplains, on Swedish East India Company ships going to China. After an extraordinary catalogue of disasters befell his returning plants – some were lost in storms, others lost to rats, others turned out not to be tea at all – he finally acquired a plant in 1763, the first in Europe. Other plants had been established in tropical countries – including Java, St Helena and Brazil – where they seemed to flourish.

From the earliest days of the East India Company's administration it had been mooted that tea might be cultivated in India. In 1778, Sir Joseph Banks, the famous botanist who had accompanied Captain Cook, had suggested that black teas might be grown with success in parts of north India, and had even considered the possibility of recruiting Chinese growers and manufacturers. Banks had received some of the samples sent by Lord Macartney's 1793 expedition. Nevertheless, although the tea plant flourished in the Botanical Gardens at Calcutta, the Company made little effort to encourage commercial production. Some felt that this was because, secure with the China monopoly, there was no incentive for the Company to proceed. There were also doubts as to whether good tea could be grown outside China, and whether the necessary expertise could be found to manufacture a quality product. With the loss of the Company's China monopoly these doubts were examined more closely, and in 1834 a Tea Committee was established to look into the possibilities of importing plants and seed from China, to select areas of India suitable for their cultivation, and to conduct trials. This Tea Committee acted quickly. They immediately sent one of their members, C. J. Gordon, to China, to collect plants, seeds, and recruit experts in cultivation and manufacture. They also issued an official circular asking for suggestions as to where tea might be best grown in India.

Gordon managed to purchase three batches of tea seed. However, much of the seed was despatched in Gordon's absence, and turned out to be very inferior. Gordon also found it difficult to recruit suitable Chinese. Skilled tea workers were too well paid to want to emigrate. In addition it was illegal for the Chinese to pass on their skills, and Chinese workers were apprehensive lest officials should harass the families they left behind. The Dutch, who were also trying to develop tea in their eastern territories, had only managed to recruit about twelve skilled men, and all had been murdered. While Gordon was endeavouring to overcome these difficulties, a discovery was made in India that transformed the entire situation.

There had been rumours that tea might be indigenous to India for some years before the establishment of the 1834 Tea Committee. In 1815, Colonel Latter, the British Resident at Katmandu in Nepal, had observed that some of the Assamese drank tea. In 1816 he had obtained what was probably a tea plant and sent it to Calcutta for identification, but tests had proved inconclusive.

The East India Company had annexed Assam in 1826. In essence, the territory was the valley of the upper Brahmaputra, one of Asia's greatest rivers. About 400 miles long, it was bounded on all sides, except for a gap where the river ran south, by high mountains with dense forests. It is often supposed that Assam itself is mountainous, like other tea areas, but for the most part it is not. Although 300 miles upstream from the ocean, the Brahmaputra enters Assam only 150 feet above sea level, and most of the land is below 300 feet. The intense flatness of the country is what strikes visitors. A multitude of smaller rivers run down from the mountains into the Brahmaputra, often flooding the plains. Swamps abound. It is a country of excessive rainfall and extreme humidity. In consequence, for those who live there, the climate is unhealthy and enervating. For many plants, however, the climate is ideal.

The country had been ruled by the Ahoms, a Shan dynasty, who had conquered it in the thirteenth century. It was a naturally defensible valley, and the Ahoms managed to keep the Mughals and other warlike neighbours at bay. In the eighteenth century, however, the regime was weakened by a number of incompetent monarchs, and the country began to descend into anarchy. This decline coincided with a desire of the Burmese to expand their influence. They invaded Assam in 1817, quickly took control, and before departing installed a puppet ruler. This ruler was deposed and mutilated, prompting a new invasion by Burma in 1819. The Burmese put the country to the sword, and laid it waste. By 1822 Assam was totally under Burmese control. They committed terrible atrocities – 'some they flayed alive, others they burnt in oil and others again they drove in crowds into village *namghars* or prayer houses, which they then set on fire.'

> All who were suspected of being inimical to the reign of terror were seized and bound by Burmese executioners, who cut off the lobes of the poor victims' ears and choice portions of the body, such as the points of the shoulders, and actually ate the raw flesh before the living sufferers: they then inhu-

manly inflicted gashes on the body, that the mutilated might die slowly, and finally closed the tragedy by disembowelling the wretched victims.

Many fled the country, but huge numbers of men, women and children were killed or taken as slaves. It is estimated that the population of Assam was halved.

It was events to the south of Assam, however, which brought about the First Anglo-Burmese War. The Burmese had taken over the coastal Kingdom of Arakan in the late eighteenth century. Refugees from Arakan had fled north into Bengal and then made raids into Burmese-controlled areas. The Burmese had retaliated by incursions into Bengal, but been repulsed by the Company's army. A further incursion into Bengal, and the capture of an island which belonged to the Company, led the British to declare war on Burma in 1824. Rangoon was attacked from the sea, and fell to the British in 1824. The Burmese then fought back, inflicting heavy losses on the British forces, who were incompetently directed. At least 15,000 'British' troops died, nearly all Indians. The Burmese were finally defeated in 1825. The entire cost of the war was charged to the Indians. In the treaty that followed, large areas of territory were ceded to the Company, including Assam.

The people of Assam welcomed the Company as saviours. Soon, however, they hankered for self-rule, and there were various rebellions in the 1830s and 1840s, but none seriously threatened the Company's regime.

Robert Bruce, an ex-army businessman, had gone to Assam before the war looking for trading opportunities, and had become an agent for an Assamese chief whom the East India Company were backing for the control of Upper Assam. In 1823 Bruce had learnt of the existence of tea plants in Assam, and made arrangements to obtain some. Meanwhile, the war had broken out with Burma, and Robert Bruce's brother, C. A. Bruce, arrived to command some British gunboats.

C. A. Bruce, who was to become perhaps the most important figure in the development of tea in India, had led an adventurous life before he came to Assam. He had left England in 1809 as a midshipman on an East India Company ship. On the journey he had been twice captured by the French, marched across Mauritius 'at the end of the bayonet', and kept prisoner until the island was taken by the British. He then went with the British to take Java.

As it happened, Bruce's area of command in Assam covered Sadiya – the very place from which his brother was hoping to get tea plants. C. A. Bruce collected the promised tea plants, grew some in his garden at Sadiya, sent some to the British Agent in Assam to grow in his garden, and despatched leaves and seeds to Calcutta for examination. The Company's Botanical Gardens at Calcutta declined to confirm that the samples were tea rather than another variety of camellia, and the probable discovery was not pursued.

There was another discovery, by a Lieutenant Charlton who was on service in Assam in 1831, who sent plants to the Agricultural and Horticultural Society in Calcutta with the observation:

> The tea tree grows in the vicinity of Suddyah, the most remote of the British possessions toward the east, in Assam, and adjacent to British territory. Some of the natives of Suddyah are in the habit of drinking an infusion of the dried leaves, but they do not prepare them in any particular manner. Although the leaves are devoid of fragrance in their green state, they acquire the smell and taste of Chinese tea when dried.

Charlton's plants, which soon died, were also denied official recognition. Subsequently there was a huge controversy between Charlton and C. A. Bruce as to which of them was the first to 'discover' tea in India. Why Dr Wallich, the superintendent of the Botanical Gardens at Calcutta, and botanist to the East India Company, was so reluctant to concede that tea was growing in Assam remains a mystery.

The Tea Committee's circular of 1834 reached Charlton, who had by then become assistant to Captain Jenkins, Agent at Jorhat for the north-eastern frontier. A few months later he sent new samples of seeds and leaves from Sadiya to Calcutta:

> The tree I now find is indigenous to this place as well as Beesa; and grows wild everywhere, here and there, all the way from this place, about a month's journey to the Chinese province Younan, where I am told it is extensively cultivated. One or two people from that province have assured me, that the tea tree grown there exactly resembles the species that we have here, so I think there can be no longer any doubt of its being *bone fide* tea.

Wallich was finally convinced. On Christmas Eve, 1834, the Tea Committee informed the Governor-General of India:

> The tea shrub is beyond all doubt indigenous to Upper Assam ... We have no hesitation in declaring this discovery, which is due to the indefatigable researches of Captain Jenkins and Lieutenant Charlton, to be by far the most important and valuable that has ever been made on matters connected with the agricultural or commercial resources of this empire. We are perfectly confident that the tea plant which has been brought to light, will be found capable, under proper management, of being cultivated with complete success for commercial purposes, and that consequently the objects of our labours may be before long fully realized.

Gordon had already sent off enough seed from China to conduct trials. While he was away, the Tea Committee decided that the indigenous tea would probably do better in India. They were also inclined to bring Chinese experts from Yunnan, rather than eastern China. When Gordon arrived in Calcutta, however, they changed their minds, and he was returned to Canton once again to recruit experts in tea cultivation and manufacture. The 80,000 seeds he had already sent were germinated in the Calcutta Botanical Gardens. It was decided to distribute them widely to see where they grew best. Twenty thousand seedlings were sent to Kumaon in the foothills of the Himalayas, 2,000 to South India, and 20,000 to Assam.

The Tea Committee deputed a three-man scientific panel to go to Assam. They also asked Lieutenant Charlton to establish a tea nursery at Sadiya, with C. A. Bruce as his assistant. Given the controversy over which one of them had first found tea in Assam, and the Tea Committee's fulsome tribute to Charlton, but with no mention of Bruce's role, it was perhaps a relief to Bruce when Charlton was called away to subdue a rebellion. Not so fortunate for Charlton, however, who was badly wounded and invalided out of Assam. Bruce became the pivotal figure in Assam tea for many years.

It took four and a half months for the scientists to make the arduous journey up to Assam. The tea nursery was a disappointment, since it had been mostly destroyed by cattle. Of 20,000 Chinese plants put out nearby, only fifty-five survived, and they were dying. There were insurrections taking place in Assam and a frightened Dr Wallich was all for returning to Calcutta. However, M'Clelland and Griffith, the other two members of the panel, wanted to continue and a fairly full survey was made.

The scientific panel had been given instructions to find out whether tea was indigenous to Assam, whether conditions there were suitable for establishing a tea industry, which areas would be best, and whether there was any necessity to import Chinese tea seed.

The scientists failed to decide whether tea was indigenous to India. They found tea plants all over Upper Assam south of the Brahmaputra River, but mostly in clumps, as if they had been planted. Since local people harvested and processed tea for drinking, it was possible that they were old plantations, semi-abandoned during the recent years of war.

There has been much argument as to the origin of the tea plant. Both China and India have been claimed as the original source, and other countries in south-east Asia have also been suggested. It may be that in the future paleobotanists, who analyse the ancient pollen in soil samples, will be able to come to a firm conclusion. In the meantime, the most definitive study seems to have been made in 1958 by Robert Sealy of the Royal Botanic Gardens, Kew. In *A Revision of the Genus Camellia* Sealy identifies two main varieties – *Camellia sinensis* var. *sinensis* and *Camellia sinensis* var. *assamica*. The first grows up to nineteen feet high, is hardier, has relatively narrow and smaller leaves, and is perhaps indigenous to western Yunnan. The second grows up to fifty-six feet high, is less hardy, has larger leathery leaves, and is perhaps indigenous to the warmer parts of Assam, Myanmar (Burma), Thailand, Laos, Cambodia, Vietnam and southern China.

Robert Sealy also points out that groups of people in the second area used var. *assamica* as a stimulant, often leaving it to ferment in a hole in the ground before chewing the leaves or making an infusion. They did not use the plant as a beverage, until taught to do so by the Chinese or the British. He speculates that their method of fermenting var. *assamica* was adopted by the Chinese, who then tried it on var. *sinensis*, which turned out to yield a pleasant beverage.

The Tea Committee's scientific experts thought the conditions in Assam were similar to those in the tea districts of China, with regard to topography, vegetation, temperature and humidity. In fact, the Assam areas are more tropical than those in China and have a higher rainfall. These differences, however, eventually turned out to be advantageous for var. *assamica*. The scientists also emphasized correctly the need to choose areas with a well drained soil.

The scientists were split as to whether Chinese seed would be better than seed from indigenous plants. Dr Wallich argued that the indigenous plants would be better adapted to local conditions; William Griffith insisted that Chinese seeds would be best because they were the result of many centuries of selective cultivation. Griffith won the day. This resulted in Gordon being sent back to China, and large quantities of Chinese seed being sent to India by him, and others, for many years. Every effort would be made to replace the indigenous tea of Assam with that of China. Meanwhile, as there would be a delay of two or three years before any Chinese plants grew sufficiently large to harvest, Bruce was to experiment with the indigenous tea. The government was impressed with the scientific panel's positive report. In 1836 Bruce was appointed Superintendent of Tea Forests, and given authority to open up two or three plantations.

Bruce established new China tea-seed nurseries, belonging of course to the East India Company, at various places in Upper Assam – Jaipur, Chabua, Chota Tingri and Hukanpukri. At Sadiya there was both a China tea nursery and one for indigenous tea.

Bruce and his men also sought to find patches of indigenous tea in the jungle. This was not an easy job. The wars fought across Assam had caused the richly cultivated valley to revert to nature – 'six-eighths or seven-eighths of its extent covered with a jungle of gigantic reeds, traversed only by the wild elephant or the buffalo, where human footstep is unknown'.

The Assam forests received between 100 inches and 200

inches of rain a year (London, considered wet by many, receives about twenty-five inches) making for numerous streams and swamps. Trees grew tall and close, often with heavy undergrowth. On foot, it was difficult to see any distance. In addition, the jungle was full of dangerous animals, especially tigers. (In those days, in India, tigers were killing as many as 2,000 people a year.) For these conditions the ideal vehicle was an elephant – slow, but safe, and giving an excellent view over the terrain. Bruce bought four elephants at £15 apiece. In Assam conditions, an elephant needed very little extra food, if any, but Bruce indulged his animals with a yearly allowance of £5 for rice.

Once a patch of 'wild' tea had been spotted, negotiations had to be opened with the local chief. Sometimes these chiefs were cooperative, seeing possibilities for development and employment; sometimes they resented any interference from outside and had to be bribed. Bruce was a very skilful negotiator. He would sit cross-legged with the chiefs, smoke their pipes, and beguile them with sweet words. Very small sums of money often smoothed the way, but more often the chiefs were bribed with opium.

By 1839, some 120 areas with indigenous tea had been discovered, and some of these covered a considerable area. Outside Jaipur Bruce found a tract that was two or three miles long. The trees in and around these areas were felled to give the tea more light. Some of the tea shrubs had grown into tall trees, and Bruce mentions one tree that was '29 cubits high and 4 spans round' – about forty-four feet high and three feet in circumference. These trees, and all the other tea plants, were cut down to about three feet, and then the shoots that grew from these pruned trees were harvested. This type of pruning produced a much larger bush than those in China, perhaps six feet tall. Coupled with the wide spacing, the tea tracts must have looked more like orange groves than conventional tea gardens with their continuous flat green tables.

A few Chinese artisans arrived to begin the manufacture of tea. Because the patches of tea were so widely spread out, and transport was so difficult, much of the tea was already fermenting in an uncontrolled way before it arrived to be processed. This inhibited the production of quality teas. Nevertheless, with much effort, a reasonably acceptable tea was produced.

In November 1836 a small sample of tea from Sadiya arrived at Calcutta and was well received. At the end of 1837 a larger sample was sent, and considered to be of 'marketable quality'. In 1838, twelve chests of tea were sent to the East India Company in London. Some of the tea was kept for the directors, some was sent as samples to tea brokers, and some was despatched to provincial mayors to stimulate interest. On 10 January 1839, the balance of 350 lbs was auctioned. In the normal way, these teas would have made one or two shillings per lb, but in keen bidding the first lot fetched five shillings, and the last lot the huge amount of thirty-four shillings (£1.70) per lb. All were sold to a Captain Pidding, ostensibly in a burst of patriotism, more probably to obtain publicity for his range of teas.

In 1839, Bruce produced 5,000 lbs of tea, and was expecting to sell more than twice that in 1840. His work was purely experimental, but he had pointed the way for the commercial production of Assam tea. He produced an extremely detailed estimate of what it would cost to set up a plantation, which in summary showed:

	rupees
Total outlay for 10 tracts; each 400 × 200 yards (about 165 acres in total)	16,591
Less capital expenditure	4,304
Total annual outlay	12,287
Receipts	
– from 355,555 tea plants, producing 35,554 lbs	

tea @Rs 1 per lb.	35,554
Annual profit	23,267
ANNUAL PROFIT AT RS 10 = £1	£2,327

Bruce then extrapolated these figures to give an annual profit on 1,000 tracts of tea (16,500 acres) of £232,660.

With profit projections like these, and the success of the London auction, it was inevitable that British businessmen would seize what seemed like a golden opportunity to make money.

The London venture capitalists were quick off the mark. On 12 February 1839, only a month after the first auction of Assam tea, a group of merchants met in the City and decided to look into the possibilities of forming a company. Next day, some of them met the Chairman of the East India Company, who approved in principle the granting of land to the new enterprise, and the transfer to it of the Company's tea assets in Assam. The day after that, the merchants met again, and agreed to raise £500,000 to form the Assam Company. A few days later all the shares had been subscribed.

Quick as they had been, the London merchants were not the first to propose a commercial tea venture in Assam. In Calcutta, there had been a proposal to form a Bengal Tea Association, also to take over the Company's assets and exploit tea cultivation in Assam. The members were well connected, and included the chairman of the 1834 Tea Committee. They were able to force the Assam Company into an amalgamation whereby the London company put up the capital, but the men of Calcutta gained control of the enterprise. Favourable terms were given to the Indian-based merchants to acquire shares and seats on the London board, and the local management and direction would be left entirely to them.

J. W. White was put in charge of the company's operations in Assam. He set up headquarters at Nazira, where they still are. C. A. Bruce transferred his services to the company – an absolute essential for them, since he would be the only one of their senior employees to know anything about the cultivation and manufacture of tea in Assam. He ran the company's northern division, and was based in Jaipur. Presumably his old base at Sadiya had become less attractive after an 'unfortunate affair' in 1839, when an uprising had wiped out Colonel White and his garrison.

Elephants were essential for travel in the dense, tiger-infested jungle. They were also extremely useful in clearing plantation land of heavy timber. The East India Company refused to lend Bruce the elephants he had used while in their employ, and it was difficult to purchase them elsewhere. The Assam Company therefore had to build stockades to capture and train wild elephants. Later they used elephants to move made tea from outstations – six chests at a time, strapped to special *howdahs*. Finally, the company developed an elephant cart, with four great wheels, which could carry fifty-four chests, over 5,000 lbs, of tea. Elephants were also a useful sideline for some of the European staff, who bought in wild elephants, trained them surreptitiously (not difficult many miles away from headquarters), and sold them to the company as having been bought tame.

Existing cultivated tracts of tea, which had been taken over from the East India Company, were maintained and improved. The Assam Company also acquired new leases on patches of jungle where there was tea, and brought this into production. There was a ten- or twenty-year grace period before any rent would have to be paid to the government. By the end of 1840, 2,638 acres were being cultivated (an acre is about 70 yards square; half the size of a large football pitch) and 10,202 lbs of tea had been exported. Everyone was delighted, and the Annual Report predicted production would rise to 320,000 lbs by 1845.

Production the next year, however, did not meet expectations, and expenses had soared. An agent of the company, J. M. Mackie, was sent to Assam to investigate. Meanwhile, White and Bruce entered into acrimonious correspondence with the company in Calcutta, and then resigned. Mackie reached Nazira in October 1843. What qualifications he had for the task in hand, other than being a 'gentleman of high standing and character' was unclear, and when the company had received no report from him by June 1844 he was dismissed. To add to all these problems, the account books were ten months in arrears.

The company had been operating without proper incorporation, and with unlimited liability. This meant that if the company became insolvent, the shareholders would be liable for its debts. These problems, and the discouraging news from India, were enough to frighten some shareholders, and these forfeited their shares rather than pay what was due on them. The company was finally incorporated in 1845 under a special Act of Parliament, six years after it was founded. Its seal depicted a tea bush and an elephant, surmounting the motto '*Ingenio et Labore*' – 'by ingenuity and hard work'. In 1845 the company declared a dividend. Presumably this was to placate shareholders, for there was no profit to justify this largesse and the money had to be borrowed from its bank. Such was the state of the company's finances that some of the directors wanted it liquidated. However, no buyer could be found.

Drastic cost-cutting ensued. The company's steamer and saw-mill were sold; the estates in the north and east were abandoned. The Calcutta board kept their nerve while London panicked, and they changed the management in Assam. The concentrated group of tea tracts left in production became better managed, the quality of tea improved, and in 1847 the tide began to turn. In 1848 the company made its first profit. By 1850 the company had cleared its debts. Some abandoned estates were brought back into production, and in 1852 the company paid a genuine dividend.

Within a decade the Assam Company had raised tea production from 10,000 lbs to 250,000 lbs. Five years later, in 1855, it was 583,000 lbs. At that date they were still the sole exporters of tea from Assam, but the situation was about to change. In the early 1850s a number of small estates were opened up to follow the example of the Assam Company. Many of them, indeed, were started by British employees of the Assam Company. They found it convenient to buy a plot adjacent to the land they were managing for the company, where they could keep a close eye on things, and perhaps 'borrow' the company's seed or labour. In 1859, a large new public company came into operation – the Jorehaut Tea Company. It absorbed several of the existing small tea gardens as a nucleus, and then expanded to become a major force. By the end of 1859, in addition to the Assam Company and the Jorehaut Tea Company, there were fifty other tea estates in Assam.

Darjeeling was another area of India where tea was planted in the early years. The amount of land suitable for tea was limited, so that Darjeeling would never produce large quantities of tea. The quality, however, turned out to be excellent, and Darjeeling teas would eventually become the benchmark against which all other fine black teas would be measured.

Darjeeling had been in the domain of the rajahs of Sikkim until the Gurkhas, who had taken control of Nepal in 1768, annexed much of it. This gave the Gurkhas a long border with British territory, into which they started to make raids. When the Gurkhas captured some small British forts in 1814, the British declared war. The Gurkhas were totally defeated, and in the settlement which followed ceded 4,000 square miles of annexed Sikkim territory to the British. The British, who wanted to establish a buffer state between themselves and the Gurkhas, handed the territory back to the Rajah of Sikkim.

In 1828, Captain Lloyd visited Darjeeling while investigating a border dispute between Sikkim and Nepal. The town, which had been a Gurkha garrison, was completely abandoned. Nevertheless, since it was 7,000 feet above sea level and had a healthy climate, Lloyd saw potential for a British sanatorium. He submitted a report, and was authorized by the East India Company to enter into negotiations with the Rajah of Sikkim. In 1835, in return for a small annual allowance, the Rajah ceded a strip of land in the Darjeeling Hills to the Company, including the small deserted town.

In 1839, Dr Campbell of the Indian Medical Service was appointed Superintendent of the District. He soon set up a flourishing sanatorium for the Company's troops and servants, established revenue and justice systems, and built roads, houses and a bazaar. Thousand of immigrants flocked in from Nepal, Sikkim and Bhutan. Dr Campbell was interested in horticulture, and experimented with various plants in his own garden. In 1841 he obtained some China tea seeds from Gordon's plants at Kumaon. These did well, as did others planted lower down the hills, and Dr Joseph Hooker, the eminent botanist, reported that they 'might be cultivated at great profit'. In 1847 the Company set up a nursery to propagate tea plants for the British planters who had begun to take plots of land.

Meanwhile, however, the Sikkim government had become more aggressive. A number of raids culminated in 1849 with the seizure of Dr Campbell and Joseph Hooker. Both were imprisoned and Campbell was beaten. Retribution inevitably followed. The British mounted a military expedition, and Sikkim surrendered without a shot being fired. The captive Britons were released, the Rajah's allowance was terminated, and a further 640 square miles of territory adjacent to Darjeeling was annexed.

A decade later Sikkim raiders made further incursions into British territory. This time the British sent a larger force, and captured the Sikkim capital, Tumlong. The British also had trouble with raids and kidnappings organized from Bhutan, which prompted another expedition. In the settlements the British imposed after victory in 1865, further territory was added to British Darjeeling. What had started as a small sanatorium ended up as a district of 1,164 square miles.

Tea development in Darjeeling was rapid. The British found the climate made it an attractive place to settle. There was also the view: 'quite unparalleled for the scenery it embraces', Joseph Hooker reported from one house, 'commanding confessedly the grandest known landscape of snowy mountains in the Himalaya, and hence in the world'. Finding labour was never the problem that it was in other areas of India, for there was a large supply of willing workers from nearby Nepal. By 1866 there were 39 estates in Darjeeling with 10,000 acres of tea. By 1874 there were 113 estates with over 18,000 acres of tea planted. Production was 4 million lbs and rising fast. Moreover Darjeeling was beginning to establish a reputation for good teas.

Rainfall in Darjeeling varies between 70 and 150 inches a year. At the foot of the valley the temperatures are tropical, whereas 7,000 feet up they can fall at night almost to freezing. This affects the rate of growth, and the teas planted at the upper altitudes yield less than those below. These lower yielding and slower growing teas, however, have more flavour and are more prized.

The plucking season begins at the end of March, and continues to the end of November. Plucking is strictly supervised so that only the new buds and the two young leaves on the stalk below are harvested. Tea produced in the rainy season is from the fast growing shoots, and not of the very highest quality. The finest, most delicately flavoured, most expensive teas are taken early in the season, just before the monsoon breaks. The 'first flush Darjeeling' is eagerly awaited by the connoisseur. However, it is the second plucking – the famous 'second flush Darjeeling' – which is considered to give the very finest tea. Another favourite tea, the 'autumnal Darjeeling', is harvested late in the season when growth is slow and the flavour again prominent.

Altitude is not the only arbiter of quality. There is considerable variation in quality and the price obtained between teas grown on estates at the same height. Some of this can be put down to supervision of the plucking, or to growing and manufacturing techniques. However, different soils probably also play a part, as does the degree of hybridization of the original Chinese tea with the Assam plants that were brought in later. Quality has to be the mantra of the Darjeeling planter, for yields are only a fraction of those in lush areas like Assam.

The year 1857 was cataclysmic in India, for it was the year of the 'Mutiny'. For a decade, the Company had been adopting an aggressive policy of acquisition. It had been Indian custom for the rulers of princely states, who did not have natural heirs, to adopt a son to inherit the title. The Company refused to recognize these titles, and acquired vast new territories, including Satara, Udaipur, Jhansi and Nagpur. Resentment over this was added to in 1856 when the Company deposed the 'effete' King of Oudh, and took over his kingdom. There was also unrest among landlords and farmers over changes to land tenure. Meanwhile, there was trouble in the Company's army. A law had been enacted that made Indian soldiers liable to serve overseas. There were religious objections to this by some Hindus. The final straw came in 1857 when, in order to load a new type of rifle, soldiers were ordered to bite off the tip of the cartridges. These were coated with animal fat. The Hindus were forbidden by their religion to eat cow, and the Muslims forbidden to eat pig, so both refused. Regiment after regiment was lined up under British artillery and, after refusing to load the new cartridges, disbanded.

The revolt began in May 1857 at Meerut, forty miles from

EXECUTION OF "JOHN COMPANY;"

Or, The Blowing up (there ought to be) in Leadenhall Street.

Delhi. A number of soldiers who had refused to load the new cartridges had been manacled and imprisoned. While their British officers were at church, three regiments mutinied. They freed the prisoners, killed several officers, and set off for Delhi. The Indian soldiers at Delhi welcomed their comrades, and took over the city. The revolt spread all over the highly populated Ganges plain, but only occasionally beyond. The British, using British and Indian soldiers, eventually regained control. There was great cruelty perpetrated by both sides. British civilians – men, women and children – were massacred. When the British regained control they exacted terrible revenge, burning whole villages. Many innocent men were hanged. Indians suspected of complicity were tortured, and tied to the mouths of cannon for execution. Peace was eventually declared in July 1858.

Although the rebellion had lasted over a year, it did not spread to much of India. Nevertheless, it had profound effects. What trust there was between the British and the Indians had largely gone. The British became even more arrogant; even more confident of their racial superiority. To tighten their control, they boosted their military forces in India, especially those manned with British soldiers. The British had spent a great deal of money on suppressing the rebellion. Eventually, the total cost would be charged to India, as would future expenses incurred in expanding British garrisons. In the meantime, however, a bridging loan had to be made from Britain. The ambiguous role of the East India Company had been tolerated as long as money flowed into the British treasury. Now it was time for the British Parliament to assert itself. In August 1858 all the Company's powers in India were assumed directly by the British government, and the Governor-General, Lord Canning, became the first Viceroy.

Assam was too far from the main areas of rebellion to be greatly affected. A mutiny among troops at Chittagong did cause some anxiety. A few hundred men from the Naval Brigade were sent to deal with possible trouble. A plot to murder some Christians was discovered, and this led to some planters temporarily abandoning their estates. The biggest inconvenience was the interruption in river transport. In other tea areas of India there was also some disruption, but in general the effect on development was very temporary.

The spread of tea cultivation to areas beyond Assam had been slow. Darjeeling had a number of planters from the 1850s. Small government nurseries and plantations, planted with Chinese seed, were established in Kumaon and Garwhal on the foothills of the Himalayas. Privatization of the government gardens was slower than in Assam, but other private plantations began to be established from 1856. By 1863, seventy-eight plantations were dotted about Kumaon, Dehra Dun, Garwhal and Simla. Unlike in Assam, a number of wealthy Indians, including the Maharajah of Kashmir, developed estates.

The Assam variety of tea plant turned out to be much better suited to Assam conditions than the Chinese plants brought in by Gordon in the 1830s. In Assam these native plants gradually replaced the Chinese plants, but not, however, before some harmful cross-pollination occurred. The result was known as 'hybrid' tea, and the consequent poor performance of these plants was particularly pronounced since many of Gordon's plants and seeds (actually despatched when he was not in China) were of inferior stock. Outside Assam most tea was grown at higher altitudes, between 2,000 feet and 6,000 feet above sea level, where the nights could be cold. In these conditions the Chinese plants did well, and efforts were made to bring in new Chinese plants of a good variety.

The East India Company despatched Robert Fortune to China in 1848 to search for good tea stock. Fortune was one of the great plant hunters of the nineteenth century. Born in 1812, he had been apprenticed as a gardener near Edinburgh, and then moved to the city's Royal Botanical Garden. In 1842 he become superintendent of the Horticultural Society's hothouses at Chiswick near London. The following year the society sent him to collect plants in north China. This was difficult territory for westerners to travel in, especially in the aftermath of the Opium War, and Fortune managed to persuade the society to provide him with a shotgun and two pistols. He had to use these when the junk he was travelling in from Shanghai to Chusan was attacked by pirates. Very coolly, although ill with fever, he waited until the pirate boat was within twenty yards and then jumped up and fired both barrels of his shotgun into the pirates. He then incapacitated a second pirate boat by shooting the helmsman. The pirates fled, and Fortune reached Chusan safely, to continue his plant hunting. He found many plants previously unknown in the West, from rhododendrons to palm trees, several of which were named after him. It was on this first visit to China that Fortune became the first westerner to realize that both green and black tea were made from the same variety of tea plant, but by using different methods of manufacture.

Robert Fortune was favourably impressed by rural life in China: 'I fully believe that in no country of the world is there less real misery than in China . . . I doubt if there is a happier race anywhere than the Chinese farmer and peasantry.' Fortune travelled extensively in China from 1848 to 1851 to find the most promising varieties of tea plant. He journeyed into the high quality tea areas inland from Shanghai, places that were closed to foreigners, by disguising himself as a Chinese merchant. He had already grown a pigtail, and he shaved the rest of his head, and adopted Chinese dress, as soon as he left Shanghai. Travelling by boat, or carried by chair, he made copious notes on climate, soils, planting, plucking and manufacture. He sent 20,000 tea plants back to India, by four different ships to ensure that some arrived safely.

The plants were packed in Wardian cases. Nathaniel Ward, a London doctor, had accidentally germinated some seeds in a closed bottle in which he was keeping a chrysalis. In the sealed atmosphere, the plants survived for four years without water. Ward then developed a glass case, well protected with wooden slats, for the transport of plants. With the cases on deck, or slung over the ship's sides, it was found possible to move plants long distances safely by sea through extremes of hot or cold weather. If not fresh, tea seed can be difficult to germinate, since a gap opens up between the seed and its sheath, and this space can become waterlogged. Fortune solved the problem by planting the seeds inside these Wardian cases, and leaving them to germinate en route to Calcutta. He also managed to recruit eight highly qualified tea men, and purchased quantities of implements. On his return to India, Fortune was able to see his plants successfully transplanted in Garhwal and Kumaon, and good quality tea manufactured by the Chinese he had engaged.

In Cachar, just south of the tea areas of Upper Assam, 'wild' tea was identified in 1855, and this led to a number of small estates being opened up by the end of the decade. In south India, tea was very much a subsidiary crop to coffee. Experimental planting had started as early as 1832, but by 1881 there were still less than 5,000 acres in cultivation, mostly in the Nilgiri Hills.

The government, keen to expand the tea industry, made land available on very generous terms. Plots had to be surveyed at the cost of the lessee. One quarter would be rent-free for ever; three quarters rent-free for fifteen years. Thereafter the rentable three quarters would pay a minimal rent. There was, however, an obligation to clear the land – one eighth in the first five years; one quarter within ten years; one half within twenty years; and three quarters within thirty years. The possibility this opened up of acquiring land, without having to find any money for it for several years, fuelled a speculators' paradise.

By 1860, it was clear that there was money to be made in

growing tea in India. A classic scramble to buy tea shares or tea land developed. No one worried about the profit that could be made by growing, producing and selling tea – 'gardens were made to sell, not to pay.' Companies and individuals rushed to buy land for tea. In one district of Cachar alone applications for tea land in 1862–3 totalled over half a million acres. As a government report later pointed out:

According to the clearance conditions of the rules, the applications for these lands would have been bound to bring into cultivation nearly 140,000 acres in ten years. To do this they would have required about 140,000 laborers, while it was well known that the total population of the district at that date scarcely exceeded that number.

The applicants for tea lands had to advance the money for a compass survey. These surveys, through dense jungle, often turned out to be wildly inaccurate when proper surveys were eventually made. In some cases errors were so large that the tracts of land did not in reality exist at all; in others, the land was in areas under the control of belligerent indigenous people and totally uncultivatable. Acreages were exaggerated. Many of these lands were sold on, often to companies fronted by the landowner himself, with fraudulent intent.

Nevertheless, despite all the chicanery, the quantity of tea produced increased dramatically – in 1862 it was 2 million lbs; by 1866 it was 6 million lbs. However, much of this tea was produced at great expense and was of inferior quality. The average price of tea fell by a third. Most of the newer plantations were producing at a loss. The end came when there was a financial crisis in the London money market. In India, the Agra bank collapsed and the Calcutta markets became nervous. The banks demanded repayment of the monies they had advanced on speculative tea estates. This prompted forced sales of these estates, the value of tea companies plummeted, and the bubble burst.

Tea mania and the subsequent collapse checked the growth of the Indian tea industry for a year or two. Fortunes were lost, and unproductive land abandoned. However, with more caution and with a greater attention to cost, production soon began to expand again. By 1873, 75,000 acres of tea were producing a crop of 15 million lbs. By 1880, 208,000 acres, three quarters of which were in Assam, were producing 43 million lbs. The great bulk of tea from India went to Britain. It had a great advantage over Chinese tea, on which an import duty of 35 per cent had to be paid, for it came in duty-free. In general, also, it was of a higher quality than the Chinese teas. In 1888 Indian production rose to 86 million lbs, and a major landmark was reached – for British tea imports from India had become greater than those from China. It was an imperial dream come true.

For the early planters transport was by elephant, palanquin or boat. The marshy conditions over much of the land did not suit horses or bullocks, and the general use of these had to await better roads.

Palanquins, known locally as a *palkee*, were commonly used both in Calcutta and beyond. In essence it was a long stout box, with sliding shutters on the side, in which the passenger lay. A long pole ran the length of the roof and projected at both ends, on to the shoulders of four bearers. The *palkee-wallahs* were famous for their stamina and would carry passengers over amazing distances in well-organized relays. Dr Joseph Hooker was carried by *palkee* from Calcutta to Darjeeling in 1848:

> the dust when the slides are open, and the stifling heat when
> shut during a shower, are conclusive against the vehicle, and

A Palkee, from *A Tea Planter's Life in Assam*, 1884

on getting out with aching bones and giddy head at the journey's end, I shook the dust from my person, and wished never to see a *palkee* again.

Palkees had their limitations, and could take little baggage. Nevertheless, it was an important method of transport on certain routes, and there were no alternatives. The bearers would cross ravines, ford streams, and negotiate dense leech-infested jungle. A road was eventually constructed along a six-mile stretch Hooker had travelled, and it needed 300 bridges. The *palkee-wallahs* moved amazingly fast, normally covering thirty miles in a day. However, by using relays and travelling day and night, they could achieve much more. The journey from Calcutta to the foothills of Darjeeling, which involved a trek of 400 miles, could be done in only ninety-eight hours.

The planters relied on the mail service to communicate with the outside world. Postal deliveries to the main centres were also extraordinarily well organized, and surprisingly fast. The British had introduced a fortnightly mail service from Bombay to Calcutta in 1790. Relays of *dak* (mail) runners, carried the post from Bombay across India to Masulipatam, and from there south to Madras and north to Calcutta. The runners, changed every eleven or twelve miles, were accompanied at night by bearers carrying flaming torches, and in some localities by a drummer to scare away wild animals. In Rudyard Kipling's poem *The Overland Mail* there is a verse paying tribute to the intrepid runners:

> Is the torrent in spate? He must ford it or swim.
> Has the rain wrecked the road? He must climb by the cliff.
> Does the tempest cry 'Halt'? What are tempests to him?
> The Service admits not a 'but' or an 'if'.
> While the breath's in his mouth, he must bear without fail,
> In the Name of the Empress, the Overland Mail.

A letter from Bombay to Calcutta took about twenty-six days. In 1820 a direct *dak* runner service from Bombay to Calcutta via Nagpur was introduced. During the 1840s some stages of this route were converted to carriage by horses, and in the 1860s to rail. The telegraph service from Bombay to Calcutta was inaugurated in 1860. *Dak* runners, however, were the main service on many routes, and were not finally phased out until the second half of the twentieth century. In the early days of the Assam tea estates, relays of postal runners would take the mail up to the Assam border at Dhubri. From there the post went up the Brahmaputra River by two-man canoe, the crew changing every fifteen miles or so, to Upper Assam. As early as 1840, a letter from the Assam Company at Nazira reached Calcutta in only eleven days.

From Calcutta, mail would normally take five months to get to Britain. However, if money were no object, it could be carried in relays by the postal men who ran the 1,356-mile cross-country journey to Bombay. It was then taken by ship to Suez, overland to Cairo, by steamer to Alexandria, by ship to Marseilles, and by horse to the English Channel and Britain. This journey could be done in about two months.

In the very early days of the Assam plantations the journey from Calcutta to Assam was by 'country boat'. These small boats, perhaps forty feet long, could if the wind was right, occasionally sail up the rivers. Normally, however, five or more men would drag the boats upstream.

The boats went north from Calcutta up the Bhagirathi River to the River Ganges at Pabna. They then went east, downstream on the Ganges until they reached the Brahmaputra River, and went north again upstream to Gauhati in Assam. Progress would depend on the amount of water in the rivers and the strength of the currents. The 500-mile journey often took over three months. The upper stretches of the Brahmaputra River within Assam were difficult to navigate, and the onward journey from Gauhati to Saikowa might take another two months.

The East India Company was quick to introduce steamers into India. A government steamer service was inaugurated on the Ganges in 1834, from Calcutta to Allahabad. Soon afterwards an irregular service was operating from Calcutta to Gauhati in Assam. These steamers were too large to go up the Bhagirathi River, so they would go downstream from Calcutta to the Bay of Bengal, and then negotiate a way through the *Sundarbans*, the mouths of the Ganges. As these waterways were constantly shifting, this required great expertise. The steamers cut the journey time to Assam to a mere three of four weeks.

The steamer service was, however, infrequent and unreliable. Much traffic continued to use country boats. The Assam Company put its own steamer into service in 1842, but it was not designed for the difficult conditions on the Brahmaputra and was withdrawn. Twenty years later, in 1862, the India General Steam Navigation Company finally introduced a regular Calcutta to Assam service, sailing right up to Dibrugarh in Upper Assam. Shallow draught paddle steamers were used, which also had sails.

They towed wide barges, known as 'flats', which were dropped off as the steamers went up the Brahmaputra, and later collected, loaded with tea, for the return journey to Calcutta.

When the first tea planters arrived in Assam there were virtually no usable roads. The Ahom kings had built an extensive network, but these had almost all been neglected in the anarchy before the British conquest. Many of these roads had been raised above flood level on large embankments, and the tea estates were able to rehabilitate short sections for their own use. A trunk road was built through Assam by the government in 1866, but otherwise little progress was made before 1880. In many tea-growing areas the estates had to build roads themselves, and hope for a government grant towards the construction. During the rains, a planter might be marooned on his estate for several months.

The railway took many years to extend as far as Assam. In 1862 the line from Calcutta was taken through to Kushtia on the Ganges, close to where the country boats had entered the river. This made the first leg of the journey to the Brahmaputra much faster and easier. In 1879 the railway was continued north to the Tista River, almost to Assam. Two years later it crossed the Assam border, and during the 1880s was extended into the tea districts.

In the early days, the lack of good roads, and the dispersed nature of the plantations, meant that there was very little socializing among the European planters. The Assam Company might have half a dozen planters bunched together in one area – and some of these set up the first club in Assam, the Hatti Putti Billiard Club, in 1881 – but many of its planters lived on isolated estates many miles from each other. On the smaller estates a planter might have just one colleague (who hopefully was congenial), or else be on his own, many miles from the next plantation. There was almost no social interaction with the Assamese. There were other Europeans in Assam – mostly government administrative officers and missionaries – but not many. In general, neither of these groups was too keen on mixing with the planters.

European planters, as a whole, had had a bad reputation in mid nineteenth-century India. This was largely due to the excesses of the indigo planters. India has a long history of cultivation and manufacture of the blue dye, but it was European planters who turned it into a major export, with large-scale planting and production. Huge tracts of land were acquired by indigo planters, particularly in Bihar, where one estate alone covered 300 square miles. Planters with experience of the slave plantations in the West Indies came to Bihar. Tenants were forced to grow indigo for very little return. This was achieved by private armies and coercion. The planters' men beat the peasants, put them in stocks, or inflicted what a government circular to magistrates in 1810 delicately called 'acts of violence, which although they amount not in the legal sense to murder, have occasioned the death of natives'.

One of the most notorious offenders was William Orby Hunter, who was the proprietor of a number of indigo plantations in the Tirhut District of north Bihar. Three lower caste girls upset Hunter and his Indian mistress. It was charged that he:

> Had their noses, ears and hair cut off, and one of them her tongue cut out. That they had fetters put on their feet, that they were wounded in their private parts, and were affected with the venereal disease (of which disease Mussammant Kinojee, who was brought to the magistrate in a litter, after-wards died in Tirhoot), and that they had otherwise been treated with great cruelty. It was alleged by all the females that they had been forcibly violated by Mr Hunter, and one of

them stated that she had, under a sense of dishonour, attempted to drown herself in a well.

The case came to trial at Calcutta in 1797. Hunter was found guilty of all charges. Pleading 'the ruinous expense of the prosecution' he was allowed to escape with paying damages and a fine of 100 rupees.

The government was reluctant to do much to curtail the abuses on the indigo estates, since the crop brought in much revenue. There were some attempts at self-regulation through an indigo planters' association, but excesses continued until the end of the century, and were only ended by the collapse of the industry that followed the invention and manufacture of synthetic indigo.

The indigo planters were despised by both Indian peasants and by government officials alike. John Beames, District Collector and Magistrate of Champaran in 1866, described the planters there as 'rough, uneducated men, hard drinkers, loose livers and destitute of sympathy for the natives'. The enmity of the peasants towards the indigo planters made it difficult to recruit labour for the new tea estates. The low regard of British officials put planters at the bottom of the European social scale, and ensured only the fairly desperate applied for jobs on the tea plantations in the early years. The indigo planters' culture – of profit before humanity – also influenced the attitudes and behaviour of the tea planters.

In 1860 there were only about a hundred Europeans working on the tea estates. By 1880 this had risen to about 800. One of the reasons for the collapse of the tea-bubble was the quality of plantation management. In 1860 the most experienced planters worked for the Assam Company, the Jorehaut Tea Company, and on a handful of new small estates, often owner-managed. Tea mania attracted a rush of men who had failed elsewhere. As an official report put it:

Tea planters in those days were a strange medley of retired or cashiered Army and Navy officers, medical men, engineers, veterinary surgeons, steamer captains, chemists, shopkeepers of all kinds, stable-keepers, used up policemen, clerks and goodness knows who besides.

On the larger estates an 'assistant' was placed in charge of each estate, answerable to the superintendent at headquarters. These assistants were invariably European. In the early days of the Assam Company the superintendent had suggested that they might be better off with Assamese or Bengali assistants since a 'European entirely ignorant of the language and equally to every part of his duty can be worse than useless.' His suggestion was ignored and European assistants were to manage the vast majority of tea estates in India for a hundred years. At first, most were already resident in India, or had even been born there, but later they tended to be recruited directly from Britain.

The Europeans were typically appointed on a first contract of five years. If they signed on for another tour of three years, they would get their fares paid to take leave in Britain. The journey to and from Calcutta, going round the tip of Africa, might take five months each way. In the early days the journey from Upper Assam to Calcutta might take another four or five months. All together, allowing for contingencies, the journey from an estate to Britain could take a year each way. With six month's leave in Britain, a planter might be away from his estate for two and a half years.

Assam planters' bungalows were originally built of wood and mud, with a very heavy thatched roof. The floor was usually just of mud. Later, to keep away damp, wooden floors were raised several feet above the ground. The thatch extended well away from the walls, over a raised verandah where the planter would spend much of his time. A thatched porch would often be placed over the front steps. Windows and doors would be of bamboo

Assam Bungalow, from *A Tea Planter's Life in Assam,* 1884

frames covered with woven grass. The building itself would be about sixty feet by forty feet, and normally had three rooms – a central sitting and dining room, with bedrooms off each side. The bathroom, to minimize problems with stagnant water, would be some distance away. The kitchen, too, would be well away from the house.

This small residence would have many staff. Some would be Hindus, recruited from the plantation labour force, but there would also have to be Muslims, recruited from Calcutta, to deal with the non-vegetarian diet. George Barker, an Assam planter, drew up a list of servants in the 1880s:

> Each person has a kitmutgar, or waiter, to attend to his wants at dinner, a species of butler in fact; next there is a bearer to look after the bedroom and act as a valet, then the khansama (cook) and his assistant, two or three pani-wallahs (water-

carriers), the mater (sweeper), two chowkeydars (watchmen), one for night, the other for day duty, punkah-wallahs (two or three for pulling the punkah during the hot weather), syces (one for each horse), malee (gardeners, according to the size of garden), mooorgie-wallah (to look after the chickens), gorukhiya (cow-herd), and a few others.

The *punkah* was a feature of all European and wealthier Indian residences and offices. In essence, a large plank, or wooden frame covered with cloth, was suspended vertically to somewhere above head height. Ropes would lead out through holes in the wall to the back or side of the house, from where the *punkah-wallah* would pull the *punkah* back and forth to create a cooling draught. In the hot weather this work continued day and night.

The planter's routine would be to wake at five a.m., have a small breakfast, work until eleven a.m., take lunch and rest until two p.m. He would then work through until six p.m., bathe and dine, relax, and go to bed at nine-thirty p.m. These timings were observed across the tea districts, so that if a planter dropped in to visit another, he could be entertained without disrupting the schedule. The planters were very hospitable, even to those they did not know – 'although an utter stranger, is he not a white man?'

Chicken was the main meat dish: 'chicken in every form, chicken cutlets, steaks minced, spatchcocked, rissoled, roasted, boiled, curried, in soup, on toast, fried, devilled, and in many other ways'. Tinned provisions were purchasable in Calcutta, but too expensive for most planters. The one luxury most planters found the money for was alcohol. The very early planters preferred brandy, which was also easy to transport. Brandy, however, largely disappeared in the 1870s as a result of a disease in the French vineyards. It was supplanted by whisky. Beer also became popular as transport improved. Planters had a reputation for heavy drinking, and it was said that when the last planters had left India their only monument would be a cache of empty bottles behind their bungalows.

Many of the British in India thought that alcoholic drinks, particularly red wines, had medicinal value. Those at risk of influenza were advised to 'drink deep' of port. Cholera, on the other hand, was thought better warded off with brandy. There were stories of miraculous cures. It was said that Sir John Lloyd had been despaired of by his doctor, who announced that the patient 'cannot survive two hours more'. The coffin bearers were summoned, but Sir John escaped death. He was 'indebted to claret for his unexpected recovery,' said the doctor, 'during the last week of the disease we poured down his throat from three to four bottles of that generous beverage every twenty-four hours; and with extraordinary effect.'

The biggest problem for the early planters was their health. Assam was notorious for malaria, or its more severe form known as 'jungle fever', and for cholera. In its first year of operations, in 1840, the Assam Company had a European staff of about twenty. During that year, three of these died and three left because of ill health. Next year the Assam Company appointed its first medical officer – he died of fever a year later. Whereas the Assam Company and other big companies employed medical officers, the smaller plantations relied on the few government doctors. Getting to a doctor or hospital was often extremely difficult, and might involve an arduous journey by boat or palanquin. Quinine was used to control malaria, but some found it ineffective, or that it led to black water fever – so called because the urine was black – and they then had to leave Assam. Chlorodyne – a painkiller then containing chloroform and morphine – became popular for cholera and stomach upsets. Many of the planters, however, had strong constitutions, and kept relatively healthy with 'quinine every morning, castor oil twice a week, and calomel [the purgative, mercurous chloride] at the change of the moon'.

The premiums of the life assurance companies illustrate how

A Planter, from *A Tea Planter's Life in Assam*, 1884

unhealthy India was. Even for the British civil servants the premiums were double what they were in Britain. The early graves of the British in India tell only half a story, for many more left the country in broken health before they died. The graveyards of Cairo and Aden are full of those who never finished the journey home.

From the earliest days some planters were accompanied by their wives and families. Among the men of the Assam Company buried in the cemetery at Nazira there are several women and children. Life for the men was isolating enough, but for the widely dispersed wives, who might not see another planter's wife for months, it must have been very hard. If they had young children, this might have been a solace. However, it was not considered healthy for the children to remain in India when they were older, and many were sent 'home' to relatives in Britain when they became seven or eight.

Most of the planters, however, were single. Some took Indian mistresses, usually surreptitiously, for there was no prospect of such women being accepted in European society. Such a liaison would be invaluable for a new planter wanting to understand a totally new culture, and learn the language. These 'sleeping dictionaries' were a feature of planting life, and were tolerated if discreet. After the Mutiny attitudes hardened – it was as if the British perception of attractiveness had shifted. Even so, George Barker's views in *A Tea Planter's Life in Assam* might have been extreme – or perhaps not, as the book was issued by the leading publisher in Calcutta:

> Many years ago, the Burmese made an incursion and overran Assam, carrying off a large proportion of the female population. To judge by the intense ugliness of the present race, it is probable that the Burmese are men of taste, and selected only the beauties of the valley, leaving their plainer sisters to raise up a generation that is unsurpassed for hideousness.

This contempt for the Assamese was matched by the contempt shown by many planters towards their imported labour.

FOUR

Victorian Enterprise – the '1st class jungley'

*The mortality among immigrants to the tea districts
in the early days of the industry is generally understood
to have been very great; but few people, I believe,
realize how appalling it actually was.*

J. W. EDGAR, Junior Secretary to the
Government of Bengal, 1873

It was clear from very early on that labour would have to be
brought into the Assam estates from outside. To grow tea required
a great deal of labour – cheap labour. An acre of tea needed the
services of one, or even one and a half, labourers for most of the
year. This was in addition to the managers and foremen, and the
skilled labour needed for manufacture. A factory needed a good
acreage to be efficient – ideally 500 acres or more – making for a
labour force of at least 500. Any new tea plantations needed
relatively cheap labour, since the tea had to compete with another
cheap labour country, China.

In general, the Assamese were not interested in plantation
work, especially not for the wages on offer. Following the Burmese invasions, the population had been decimated, and there
was little surplus labour. Most of the inhabitants had crops
of their own, which needed their attention for much of the
year. They would sometimes do a little work in their off season,

but this could not be relied on. A few Assamese did become regular workers, especially in the factories, but they were the exception. The tribal people who lived in parts of Assam had assisted Bruce in his experimental harvesting of wild tea, but being much addicted to opium they were not good or reliable workers.

The first outsiders to be recruited to the tea estates were Chinese. Three tea-men recruited by Gordon on his first trip to China joined Bruce on his Assam experimental plots in 1836. Within a year two of them became ill and died. Another five Chinese recruited by Gordon went to Assam in 1838. There was a considerable Chinese community in Calcutta, and the government, which seemed to believe that every Chinaman was a tea expert, engaged the services of a Dr Lumqua to recruit some of them for Assam. Lumqua arrived in Assam in 1840 with eighteen men, and another twenty-four followed behind. En route the government transferred their services to the new Assam Company.

Dr Lumqua proposed an extraordinary scheme for recruiting Chinese labourers. He suggested that they might be brought from the Chinese province of Yunnan by foot. As this was a journey of 800 miles, over high mountains and inhospitable country, it was not a realistic scheme. Nevertheless, a Chinese agent was recruited and sent off to Yunnan with official letters, and expensive presents. He was never seen again. Dr Lumqua died of fever later in 1840, and the scheme was terminated.

Meanwhile, the Assam Company had begun recruiting Chinese from Malaya. There was trouble when the first batch of 105, on the way up the Brahmaputra River, were involved in a fight with some villagers. The Assam Company's assistant managed to extricate them, and deliver them to Assam, but it took all the company's efforts to quash charges of assaulting the police.

In February 1840, another 247 Chinese from Malaya landed at

Calcutta. There, a fight amongst them left five men seriously wounded. On the way up to Assam, at Pabna, there was a battle with the inhabitants. Two of the townspeople were killed and two critically injured. The District Magistrate arrested fifteen of the Chinese. The remainder then refused to travel further without their compatriots. Three months later, as none of the assailants could be positively identified, all the Chinese were acquitted. The Chinese were reluctant to proceed to Assam, and after several warnings, all except four were dismissed. On their way back to Calcutta further fights broke out. In Calcutta itself, the Chinese coolies went on the rampage, were arrested, and then exiled to Mauritius.

There were no more attempts to recruit Chinese coolies. (The word *coolie*, or *cooly*, used to describe cheaply hired Oriental unskilled labourers, then lacked the derogatory connotations it later acquired, especially in South Africa.) Over the years a few more Chinese experts were engaged, but only after properly ascertaining they were indeed skilled in tea making. Future efforts to recruit coolies for manual labour were confined to the Indian subcontinent.

There were few educated Assamese, and clerical work on the estates was mostly done by Bengalis. They also became the first medical staff. The planters could not do without the literate and numerate Bengali *babus* but they were held in general contempt. This was not only in the tea districts but also in government circles. Lord Macaulay, the famous historian, was a member of the Supreme Council of India at Calcutta from 1834 to 1838. He composed the Criminal Code for India, and instituted the education of Indians in English. In his essay on Warren Hastings he wrote:

> What the horns are to the buffalo, what the paw is to the tiger, what the sting is to the bee, what beauty, according to the old Greek song, is to woman, deceit is to the Bengalee.

Large promises, smooth excuses, elaborate tissues of circum-
stantial falsehood, chicanery, perjury, forgery, are the weapons, offensive and defensive of the people of the Lower
Ganges.

This antipathy towards the Bengalis remained with many of the
British. In 1933, Oscar Lingren, who went out as a planter to
Assam in 1877, wrote about an Indian visitor from the company
employing him: 'the Partner who came up was a typical swine of
an overbearing Bengali.'

Slavery had been common in British India in the eighteenth
century. Most Europeans kept household slaves. The East India
Company traded in slaves until 1764, and it was not until 1789
that their export was prohibited. The Calcutta newspapers of the
late eighteenth century have many advertisements concerning
slaves, such as this one in 1784 from a lieutenant, J. H. Valentin
Dubois:

> *Slave Boys run away.* – On the fifteenth of October last two
> slave boys (with the letters V.D. marked on each of their right
> arms, above the elbow, named Sam and Tom, about eleven
> years of age, and exactly of a size,) ran away, with a great
> quantity of plate, &., &. This is to request, if they offer their
> service to any gentlemen, they will be so kind as to examine
> their arms, keep them confined, and inform the owner. A
> reward of one hundred sicca rupees will be given to any
> black man, to apprehend and deliver them up.

Slavery was finally abolished in British India in 1843. This was
a decade later than in most other British possessions but, by
declaring that such a status had never legally existed, India

avoided the problems of compensation that arose elsewhere. It was not long, however, before a new type of slavery was invented for the Indians.

The practice of recruiting Indian labourers for work on distant plantations grew out of the abolition of slavery. The Emancipation Bill went through the British parliament in 1833. Although this legislation gave rights to the slaves, and compensation to their owners, its immediate effects were limited since the ex-slaves were forced to become 'apprentices' for a number of years before they were free of their masters. Nevertheless, eventually the workforce in the British plantations in the Caribbean, Mauritius and South Africa began to decline, and the planters began to look for new sources of cheap labour. India, with its millions of poor, was an obvious choice.

The French had exported labourers from India to their plantations on the island of Bourbon (now Réunion) from as early as 1826. At first these Indians came from the French enclaves of Pondicherry and Karikal, but later the French began to recruit in Calcutta. The British insisted that the labourers went before a British official to confirm that they were going voluntarily. Usually they went on a five-year contract, with a guaranteed wage and free food. At this time there was an attempt to send some Indians to the British island of Mauritius, but the recruits proved unsuitable. In 1834, there was a more 'successful' shipment of thirty-nine Indians to the sugar plantations of Mauritius. By 1838, about 25,000 Indians had arrived there.

The majority of these early emigrants came from the hills of Chota Nagpur in south-west Bengal. These hills were heavily populated with Adivasis, aboriginal peoples who had been isolated by the invasions of the Aryans and the Mughals. As their population increased, and the land could no longer support their shifting cultivation, they began to descend to the plains for agricultural work. With no formal education, and with no experience of more settled societies, they were easily exploited. This

131

seemed to make them ideal for work on the plantations. John Gladstone (the father of William Gladstone, the future Prime Minister), who took Chota Nagpur coolies for his sugar estates in Demerara, was informed by his agent in India that they 'are always spoken of as more akin to the monkey than the man. They have no religion, no education, and in their present state no wants beyond eating, drinking and sleeping: and to procure which they are willing to labour.'

The Government of India passed legislation in 1837 to control this emigration. These regulations were also applied to Assam, which was so remote from the recruiting areas as to be almost a foreign country.

The Assam Company began recruiting Indians from outside Assam for manual work in 1839, its first year of operations. A number of Europeans were sent to likely areas to recruit labour. Potential recruits were offered advances against a contract. The first successes were close to the western border of Assam at Rangpur, where 400 labourers were recruited and then marched the 160 miles to Gauhati. Others were engaged in areas of Bengal west of Calcutta. At the end of 1839, W. S. Stewart went to Hazaribad and Ranchi, areas of Bihar that had been successful hunting grounds for the indigo planters. Three months later, Stewart started out with 637 coolies to march the 400 miles to Assam. Halfway there cholera broke out, and in the night all the coolies fled. The Assam Company lost 10,727 rupees. Stewart was sacked – not for this débâcle, but for drunken abuse towards his colleagues.

During the 1840s and 1850s the majority of coolies recruited by the Assam Company – by far the largest employer – came from nearby areas of Bengal. A few came by steamer from further down the Brahmaputra River, but the government-run service was irregular, and it was totally withdrawn to move troops in the Second Burmese war of 1852–3, and also during the Indian Mutiny of 1857–8. By 1860 there were only about 12,000 workers in total on all the tea estates of Assam and the rest of the Brahmaputra valley.

The 1860s brought about a huge expansion in the tea acreage and in the recruitment of labour. This was aided by the inauguration of a regular steamer service up the Brahmaputra River in 1862. Labour contractors and their agents were paid for each coolie delivered alive. What physical condition the coolies were in was no concern of theirs, as long as the coolies survived the journey. Indeed, as a government Special Commission of 1862 noted that 'persons had been despatched who were at the time on the point of death'. The poor health of those recruited, combined with the appalling conditions of the journeys on foot or by boat, resulted in terrible mortality. Often half of a consignment died before reaching the estates. This was regarded as an acceptable risk, for as the Special Commission observed:

> The supply of labourers was regarded as an ordinary commercial transaction between a native contractor and the planter, 'all parties considered their duties and responsibility discharged when the living are landed, and the cost of death adjusted.'

The government decided to intervene, and in 1863 the first legislation to govern the recruitment and transport of coolies into Assam was introduced. This provided for the licensing of recruiters, the medical examination of all coolies before departure, and for adequate sanitation during transportation. This checked some of the grossest abuses, and reduced mortality in transit. Judged by normal criteria, however, conditions were still appalling.

In just under five years from 1863, to the north-east alone – Assam, Cachar, and Sylhet – 108,980 coolies were despatched. In spite of the new Act not all of these reached the estates. There were 4,250 deaths, mostly from cholera. Another 759 managed to escape.

Even though the majority of coolies survived the journey, the condition of those who arrived could hardly be described as good. The Civil Surgeon of Dibrugarh in Upper Assam wrote:

> In 1864 and 1865 as many as 1000 a month used to land . . . I saw all these coolies. The majority were in tolerable health on the whole, but fully 25 per cent were debilitated; in particular batches as many as 75 per cent were debilitated.
>
> As a general rule, coolies on arrival were unable to march out six miles without dozens falling out. In one instance, a batch of 800 were going to a garden about 12 miles out on the Seebsagor Road; Dr Green, who happened to be coming up, fell in with them, and found them in numbers lying about dead and dying on the side of the road. This was in July 1865. I had already weeded out the worse men. I had no further room, having sixty or seventy men sick in a small building.
>
> A system of inspection that did allow a large percentage of cripples, idiots, lepers, and people in far advanced stages of chronic diseases, to come up here as laborers, was nothing more or less than a farce.

Most of this labour came from Chota Nagpur and other districts of Bengal, with others coming from Orissa, and the North-west Provinces and Oudh. About 30 per cent were women, and many of these brought their children with them. It was very difficult to engage coolies for Assam and other remote areas in the north-east. The estates were so far away from the main labour recruiting areas that contact between the coolies and their families was impossible during the contract, and many also feared that even at the end of their contract they might never return to their homes. This was a very sensible fear, for very few ever did return. However, for many people there was little choice, for the recruiting areas were gripped by famine. In 1865–6 the rains had failed in Bihar and Orissa. Official figures, now generally considered to be underestimates, put the number of deaths at 1,435,000, with 4,500,000 severely malnourished.

Appalling though the conditions were in transit to the north-east, conditions on the estates were often even worse. Incredible as it might seem, little thought had been given to how the labourers might be fed. There was simply not enough food in Assam for all the immigrants. In consequence most coolies were malnourished, and not strong enough to withstand the rigours of plantation life. In addition, accommodation was badly constructed and over-crowded; malaria was rampant; water was polluted. This led to deaths from fever, diarrhoea, dysentery and above all from cholera. Statistics were collected for six-month periods, when mortality was typically 20 or 30 per cent, or even higher. In the second half of 1865, for example, out of 282 labourers on Gilladharee Estate in Upper Assam, 111 died. Conditions in Sylhet were no better – in the same half-year on Cherragong Estate, out of 203 labourers, 113 died.

Statistics from the early years are sparse. However, it is recorded that in the three years between 1 May 1863 and 1 May 1866, some 84,915 labourers were landed in Assam and the adjoining districts. At the end of June 1866 only 49,750 were left. The others had either run away and not been recaptured (in which case they probably died in the jungles) or they had died on the estates. Since some coolies were probably landed in May and June 1866, we can assume that in the three years there were more than 35,165 deaths.

Many coolies deserted. The planters were angry that labourers, for whom they had paid the contractors good money, often fled before finishing their contracts. In 1865, the Bengal government introduced a bill to regulate employment on the estates. This provided for a minimum wage for a nine-hour day, three-year contracts, medical officers on the larger estates, and for the appointment of labour inspectors who would be able to cancel contracts in cases of ill treatment. On the insistence of the planters, however, it was amended so that absconding became a breach of contract. The planters were given powers of arrest to enforce this. In addition the planters were allowed to demand longer contracts, of up to five years. These became the norm.

Refusal to work became an offence, and many coolies were sent to prison. The Bengal Tea Cultivation Committee of 1868 reported that in several cases 'we have been informed that a short period of imprisonment had a good effect, and that the cooly has returned to the garden, and become a steady labourer.' Contracts that were enforceable with power of arrest and imprisonment led to the continuation of low wages, bad conditions, and ill treatment on many estates, because they stopped any free market in labour. It became impossible for dissatisfied labour to move to the better-run estates.

If the coolies had been able to see in advance the conditions on the worst estates, they might have thought twice about putting their mark on contracts. With this in mind, a government Act of 1882 was supposedly framed to make it possible for coolies to travel to the tea areas, and then sign contracts if they were happy with conditions. These pious sentiments were totally nullified by designating Goalpara District a tea area. Goalpara was just inside the Assam border. Its main town, Dhubri, had no tea and was far from the tea districts. Labourers were no more likely to discover the true state of affairs there than from their home districts. The labour recruiters in areas far from Assam then avoided any of the regulations framed to safeguard coolie recruitment and transportation. They sent the coolies to Dhubri and officially recruited them from there. This abuse was not rectified for thirty-three years.

In 1881, just before the new Act came in, the planters had formed their own organization, the Indian Tea Association. Originally based in Calcutta, it soon acquired branches in many of the tea districts, including Assam. It was this organization that so successfully petitioned the government when the 1882 Act was being framed. Over the years it became very powerful and, working closely with the Indian Tea Districts Association in London, managed to block many attempts to reform labour legislation.

Some tea estates sent their own men to recruit coolies, for which they received a substantial commission. In general, this was a better system than using contractors, since there was at least an incentive to enlist healthy labourers. These *sardars*, or headmen, usually went back to the areas from which they had originally come. Then, as George Barker relates, they were supposed to induce recruitment by

> pointing out the exhilarating effects of cultivating the tea plant, the enormous fortunes to be acquired by industrious coolies, and to what an improved position they can hope to aspire; but forgetting to mention the deadly climate, the miseries of being in a strange country, and other drawbacks.

After the 1882 Act, however, the *sardars* often worked in league with the unlicensed labour contractors who were sending coolies to be engaged in Dhubri.

Most of the coolie contractors were based in the Bihar District of northern Bengal, but many of the labourers came from Chota Nagpur District in south-west Bengal. Chota Nagpur was home to the Adivasis, the most popular workers with the planters – the '1st class jungley'. As one of the planters, David Crole, observed:

'planters, in a rough and ready way, judge the worth of a coolie by the darkness of the skin.' In the last two decades of the nineteenth century 350,000 coolies went from Chota Nagpur to Assam. Another 350,000 coolies also went to Assam from other areas – mostly from the plains of Bihar and the United Provinces. Large quantities of coolies also went up to Dooars and the other tea districts. About 10,000 coolies a year were exported to Burma, the Straights Settlements, Mauritius and other places overseas. The main depots were in Raniganj in the north-east of Bengal, on the way to the tea areas. The conditions were appalling. A doctor's inspection in 1888 reported overcrowding, bad water and food, and 'dead bodies which at present are thrown into the river or half buried'.

Coolies were ordered from the contractors, either directly by the estates, or through coolie-broking firms in Calcutta. Most of these firms were controlled by the British managing agencies that ran many of the tea estates. The coolie contractors employed *arkattis*, recruiting agents, to scour the villages for potential coolies. Some contractors employed over 1,000 *arkattis*. In the Ranchi District of Bihar alone there were estimated to be over 5,000 *arkattis*. They might be paid twenty rupees a head by intermediaries, the *sudder arkattis*, who then sold them on to the contractors for perhaps fifty rupees. The coolies would eventually be sold to the planters for twice that.

In 1888 Superintendent F. Harrington Tucker of the Indian Police Service was sent to Bihar to investigate the many complaints against the contractors and their men. The *arkattis* were, he reported

> as a rule, the scum of the country, and unscrupulous to a degree. Amongst them have been found ex-convicts, burglars,

thieves, dacoits [bandits], and notorious badmashas [bad characters], all of the deepest dye, and who resort to every vile practice to obtain their ends, i.e. a poor unfortunate coolie.

He then gave a list of the malpractices adopted by the recruiters and *arkattis*:

a. Enticing men away under promise of getting them service where they will be well paid, not mentioning Assam and Cachar.
b. Enticing away girls under the promise that they would be provided with well-to-do husbands, jewellery, etc.
c. Enticing away girls and women under promise of marriage and deserting them after putting them on board the steamer at Dhubri.
d. Assuming various disguises by which they induce men and women to join them in pretended enterprises, and somehow getting them under pecuniary obligations and taking them to recruiting depots, and there making their victims over to contractors who ship them off to Assam etc.

Superintendent Tucker initiated a series of successful prosecutions against some of the worst *arkattis*, but the abuses were too widespread for him to be able to make much of an impact. As an official report, inspired by Tucker's findings, pointed out: 'the radical defect of the existing law is that it authorizes the execution of labour contracts by emigrants under circumstances of place and time which put them at a disadvantage, and practically render it impossible for them to refuse the required consent.'

The government of Bengal was in favour of some reform. This, however, was blocked by the government of India, which took the planters' side, for it was keen to see the plantations expand.

The structure of British governance of India was complicated and frequently changed. Throughout the nineteenth century there was a government of India, under the control of the Viceroy (before 1858 a Governor-General) based in the Indian capital, Calcutta. In the late nineteenth century, beneath the Viceroy and the government of India, British India was divided into twelve local governments. One of these was Assam, which had been excised from Bengal in 1874. Another was Bengal (officially Lower Bengal, although that name was rarely used) under its own Lieutenant-Governor. Bengal was divided into four provinces: Bihar, Orissa, Chota Nagpur and, very confusingly, Bengal, which to avoid misunderstanding was sometimes called Bengal Proper.

Although Assam had its own government, answerable directly to the government of India, most of its labour was recruited from Bengal, so recruits for Assam started out under the jurisdiction of the Bengal government. This led to some tension between the government of Assam, the government of India and the Bengal government, for Bengal had considerable autonomy. In general the Bengal government pursued a more liberal policy than the Chief Commissioner of Assam and the government of India, both of which tended to favour the Assam planters.

The government of India refused to abolish a system where contracts were usually executed hundreds of miles from the labourers' homes, and from where they had no money to return. 'The recruiters are well aware that, once safely landed in Assam,' the Bengal government observed, 'the labourer will have no choice but to enter into a five years' engagement, and are therefore ready to hold forth any promises, and sometimes even to use force, to get him to start on the journey.'

There had been another reason for sending Superintendent Tucker to Bihar, for there had been a number of 'coolie raids'.

Coolies in transit to the tea districts had been captured by armed gangs, and then sold illicitly. This not only deprived some tea estates of labourers whom they were expecting, but also meant that the British coolie-broking firms in Calcutta were out of pocket. The cash invested to put the coolies on their journeys was lost; the expected commission on their 'sale' evaporated. This was a situation none of the governments could tolerate.

A number of coolie raiders were arrested and prosecuted. A typical case was the one against Kristo Nath Mitter and his *arkattis*. Two *sardars* of tea estates in the Dooars were travelling near Gaya with potential coolies – fifty-two men, women and children. They were intercepted by a force of *arkattis*, and imprisoned in a makeshift jail for two days. The coolies were sent to Calcutta where they were made over to the son of a Mr Mackertish, a licensed contractor. He then sold them to the British firm of Begg, Dunlop and Company. They sent the unfortunates to Dhubri, where they were forced to sign contracts, and sent to work on an estate in Upper Assam. Fortunately for the coolies (or perhaps not), they were 'rescued', for the *sardars* managed to escape from a train in Bihar. They reported the theft to their estate manager, who informed the authorities, and the coolies were eventually retrieved.

The most notorious of the coolie raiders was John Henry Lawton, a cashiered British soldier. Superintendent Tucker secured several convictions against him and his *arkattis*, for which they were sent to prison. In one case, a *sardar* was escorting thiry men, women and children to a Dooars tea estate, when Lawton and his men arrived. Lawton pretended that he was a police officer, and took everyone to a nearby depot, ostensibly to check their papers. They were then forced to give up their money and food, and imprisoned for eleven days. During that time, the potential coolies were forced to touch Lawton's pen as he put a mark of assent on contracts. The coolies were then put in bullock carts to start the journey to the tea districts. Meanwhile, the enterprising *sardar* escaped, together with a blanket, which he sold to finance a journey to Calcutta. There he borrowed the fare to his estate, where he told his story to the manager and the authorities. The coolies were eventually found on a Cachar tea plantation, Kaspore Estate, where Lawton had sold them to the manager.

It can be seen that there was an element of luck in these convictions, for they followed on the escape and determination of estate *sardars*. Many other cases must have remained unsolved and, of course, the entirely legal despatch of coolies to Dhubri continued. Despite pleas to keep Tucker in the recruiting areas, where he could have continued to keep watch on the abuses, the government withdrew him to save money.

Before he left Bihar, Superintendent Tucker did one last favour for the coolies whom he had tried so hard to benefit. He met John Beames (the same John Beames who had been so scathing about the indigo planters some twenty years before), Commissioner of Bhagalpur, and arranged a single supervised route for coolies going up from Chota Nagpur to the Dooars. Clean water was made available at regular intervals, and there were police to stop the coolie raiders. In the first three months of operation, Tucker supervised the movement of over 10,000 labourers and their families to the Dooars, and none were stolen or caught cholera. Nevertheless, the coolies continued to be fought over, for now that it was difficult to steal from the estate *sardars*, the contractors and their agents took to fighting among themselves, and to stealing coolies from each other.

The attitude of the planters to these abuses was probably, judging from what reminiscences we have, similar to that of Samuel Baildon, an Assam planter, who wrote in 1882:

The present position in obtaining coolies, and the red-tapism connected with their journey to the tea localities, is extremely far-fetched, and almost devoid of real good. Anxious as planters always are to do their utmost for labourers, it would be strange if they did not feel that as cherished *protégés* of Government, a great deal of unnecessary fuss is made with coolies, especially in the districts in which they are recruited.

Whether they were travelling by land or by steamer, the potential coolies were heavily guarded lest they escape. Prior to the 1882 Act, this restraint would have been legal, for the labourers would have already signed away their freedom. After the 1882 Act came into force, the coolies would in theory have been at liberty to change their minds on the journey up to the tea districts or, if destined for Assam, before they arrived at Dhubri. Every effort, however, was made to prevent their escape, and illegal force was often used. Most coolies, however, were totally destitute, so desertion was not an option.

Once they had signed contracts and begun work on the estates the coolies were still guarded. Planters regarded the coolies as a commodity they had bought, and took precautions to prevent them from going to another estate or fleeing altogether before their contracts had expired. One planter was put on trial in 1867 for confining his 'unruly' coolies in stocks. Houses were ringed with high fences, and coolies were not allowed out at night. The compounds were guarded by numerous watchmen. Nevertheless, many coolies managed to escape.

There was some resentment among the native Assamese towards the imported labour, and this was utilized by the planters to encourage them to hunt for absconding coolies. The standard reward for recapture was five rupees – a month's wages – and this was then deducted from the coolie's future earnings. Some estates used tracker dogs. Despite all these obstacles, about 5 per cent of coolies escaped each year and were never recaptured.

Whether many of them escaped to freedom is doubtful – most probably died through disease or starvation, or were killed by hostile tribes. Captured coolies were taken back to the estates, then usually tied up and flogged. Many died from these floggings. A few planters were put on trial, but in the early days there were few checks and most planters operated outside the law.

As late as 1873 planters were still writing letters to officials extolling the virtues of corporal punishment to prevent desertion. They urged that the flogging be done by the government and preferably ordered by planters who should be made honorary magistrates. The manager of Dilkhosh Tea Estate in Cachar wrote to the Deputy Commissioner: 'coolies as a rule do not care for imprisonment in the least, and if flogging was introduced, it would stop a great deal of absconding and other faults.' The manager of Napook Tea estate was equally enthusiastic: 'the stick has a great terror for these innate thieves and scamps, – especially, without hurting the man too much, the quiet, firm, systematic way the Government floggings are conducted.'

Flogging was almost ubiquitous on the early tea plantations, both of men and of women. Not only were escaped coolies flogged, but flogging was also widely used on labourers who failed to work sufficiently hard. The Junior Secretary to the Bengal government, J. W. Edgar, writing in 1873 described the 'practice of tying up and flogging coolies who were really physically unfit for work of any kind when the amount of daily task did not come up to what the manager considered they ought to do'. He added: 'I have reason to believe that this practice was almost universal in Cachar when I first went there in 1863, and I had it on excellent authority that it was at least equally common in Assam.'

Although the planters had powers of arrest, extra-judicial floggings were of course illegal. There were very few pros-ecutions, however, for the estates were a closed world – almost private kingdoms. In 1883 the government tried to rescind the legislation that barred Indians in the judicial service from trying cases against Europeans, even for very minor offences. The 'Ilbert Bill' (named after the official who introduced it) brought tremendous protests by the British community in India. 'What a stiletto is to the Italian a false charge is to the Bengalee,' one of their lawyers, echoing Macaulay, told a huge meeting in Calcutta Town Hall. 'Do not forget that there are wily natives, snakelike, who creep where you cannot walk, because you cannot walk unless you walk upright.' He then urged them to fight the bill lest 'the greasy Baboo is to sit upon you in judgement'. There was wild applause from the 3,000 or so Europeans present.

The Indian Tea Association was at the forefront of opposition to the Ilbert Bill. There were many meetings in Assam and other tea districts, and messages of support were telegraphed to Calcutta. Eventually the government was forced to back down, and only allow trials of Europeans before a native judge if at least half the jury were European. European juries rarely convicted a fellow European, particularly if the offence was murder. As Lord Curzon observed in 1900, just after he became Viceroy, 'There is no justice in this country in cases where Europeans and Natives are concerned.'

The tea planters, upset at the reputation they had acquired, always maintained that it was in their own interest to behave well towards their labourers, for they needed the healthy and the willing. As one put it: 'an employer likes to get as much out of his labourers as they are capable of giving him, and not to kill the goose that lays the golden eggs.' They resented any interference by government. In fact, however, many of them, trying to turn jungle into tea gardens as quickly as possible, had put the interests of their labourers conveniently aside. Planters were under financial pressure from shareholders, and also from leases that the government could cancel if land was not developed on schedule. This blinded them to their longer-term interests, and fostered inhumanity on a terrible scale. As the Assistant Commissioner of Burpettah put it:

> It was against the interests of the planters to have the blind, the maimed, the insane, and others physically unfit for labour sent up to them as coolies; yet contractors' agents and others in their employ had sent up such people. It was against their interests to make no provision for epidemics on the passage to Assam, yet such omission had taken place. The dying had been allowed to struggle with their agony along with the living, destitute of medical aid, and scenes the most revolting to humanity had resulted. It was against the interests of planters to leave their coolies houseless on arrival, to give them insufficient food, and to make no provision for medical aid; yet all these acts of neglect had occurred.

The truth is that tea production in Assam should never have been allowed to develop so quickly. The government should have controlled immigration until it was confident that labourers would be humanely treated and that a proper system of monitoring had been established. Many British administrators saw the need for these controls, but they were ignored by a central government that was more interested in commercial development than in humanity.

Indentured labour was, of course, also supplied to the Dooars and other tea areas in north India. In general, however, the abuses in those places was less than in Assam, for they were less isolated. In areas outside Assam the planters had no private right of arrest. Nevertheless, there were many terrible incidents on these estates too. Many coolies trying to escape *were* forcibly detained, and often whipped or beaten. And, of course, many died of abuses on the way up to these estates.

In south India indentured labour was also better treated than in Assam. This was primarily because of competition from over-seas. Huge quantities of labour went from south India to Natal, Mauritius, Réunion, Martinique, Guadaloupe and Fiji. In addition, there was mass emigration to the new tea estates in Ceylon. In 1888, for example, 78,302 coolies went from Madras Presidency to Ceylon, and perhaps another 60,000 to other destinations.

In order to secure enough labour, the south India planters developed another mechanism – that of debt bondage. The planters gave their *kanganies* interest-free loans to recruit labour by means of cash advances. These *kanganies* were a combination of north Indian estate *sardar* and contractor. Not only did the *kanganies* recruit the coolies, but they also supervised the work on the estates and received a percentage of the coolies' earnings. In some cases the potential coolie was already in debt, and the debt was merely transferred; in others cases a new debt was created. Either way, it was almost impossible for the coolie to repay the *kangany* out of the subsistence wage, and the coolie was bonded to the plantation, often for life. If indebted coolies tried to escape, the police arrested them.

In general, as the century progressed, the lot of the coolies on the tea estates slightly improved. Government administration in the tea districts was progressively strengthened, and given more resources for the inspection of labour conditions. The planters, running well-established estates, were not under the same press-ure to open up land as their predecessors, and tended to be a little more humane. Flogging for failing to achieve work targets became less universal, but was still common. There was a general improvement in housing – although, of course, the housing compounds were still heavily guarded to prevent escape. The provision of clean water and the introduction of basic medical facilities on some plantations reduced mortality. Labourers were allowed to have small plots of land to grow fruit and vegetables, and grain was made available for purchase from the estates at a price fixed by government.

It could be cold in the early morning among the dew-covered tea bushes. The planters took to buying quantities of ex-army greatcoats – the legendary uniform of the British 'redcoats' – which they sold to the labourers. The brilliant red of the coats against the brilliant green of the tea gardens was a famous sight.

In spite of these improvements, life for the tea estate labourers was still hard. Throughout the nineteenth century, wages on the estates were kept low. For the period 1865 to 1900 they were supposedly five rupees a month for men, and four rupees for women – from 1882 this was the legal minimum. The Chief Commissioner of Assam, Sir Henry Cotton, discovered that in 1900 many estates were not paying even this statutory minimum wage. The price of grain had doubled over this thirty-five-year period, and by 1900 this minimum wage was only half of what an agricultural labourer outside the tea estates in Assam received for work. Cotton also discovered that

in some instances only a few annas (or pence) found their way into the hands of a coolie as wages in the course of a whole year, the managers having deemed that they were justified in making deductions right and left so long as they kept their labourers in good condition like their horses and their cattle.

Sir Henry Cotton was Chief Commissioner of Assam from 1896 to 1902. At first he had been an ardent supporter of the planters, and it was only when he started to investigate conditions on the estates closely that he realized how exploited the coolies were. Even on the most respectable estates he found evidence of whippings and beatings. He also discovered other iniquities:

148

It is needless to say that it was only a small percentage of abuses which could come to my knowledge. But I had cases brought to my notice where contracts of sickly and unfit labourers were cancelled for the purpose of keeping down the rate of mortality among contract labourers, and of others where deaths had been treated as desertions for the same reason. I knew of cases where it was the practice to expel sickly coolies who became unfit for labour. I have seen with my own eyes a Government hospital full of sickly and dying coolies whose contracts had been cancelled and who had just been expelled from his garden by one of the oldest and most respected planters in the province. I have seen dead and dying coolies lying in the ditch by the roadside and in the bazaar.

The coolies saw Sir Henry Cotton as their saviour. When he visited Cachar in 1901 the roads were lined for fifteen miles by coolies holding lanterns and shouting 'Cotton Sahib ki jay!' (Long live Cotton!). On his tour of East Bengal later that year, the roads were lined with banners – 'Mr Cotton, the Protector of the Dumb Coolie.'

Initially, the Viceroy, Lord Curzon, backed Sir Henry Cotton in his attempts to control abuses on the tea estates. However, when Cotton was subjected to a campaign of vilification by the planters and the Press – especially by *The Times* in Britain – Curzon withdrew his support. Cotton, who had been born in India and whose father and grandfather had also been administrators in India, resigned. He returned to Britain, became a Liberal Member of Parliament, and from there continued to fight for the coolies.

Official reports, in general, underestimated the abuses on the tea estates. They tended to suggest a wholesale improvement since the early days. When inspections were made of water supplies and housing conditions, these were probably accurate. The planters had to keep statistics concerning mortality, and where it was especially high it was investigated. These figures, however, were often manipulated. Moreover, it would have been difficult to get information about general working conditions from vulnerable labourers who were in fear of reprisal and who were often coached to give favourable answers.

In 1894, to encourage recruitment, a group of Adivasi headmen were taken on a tour of twenty-seven Assam tea gardens. The government official who accompanied them reported positively on the working conditions. This was flatly contradicted in the group's damning report, which was suppressed. They found that conditions on twenty-three of the plantations were unacceptable: floggings were common, both of men and women; there was no paid sick leave; women had to return to work within six days of giving birth. The headmen also found that wages were too low, especially given the high price of grain, and considerably less than on other enterprises that recruited labourers. They heard testimonies from many coolies who, despite having been on the estates for fifteen or twenty years, were too poor to return home. Workers described the estates as a *phatak*, a prison, from which they could never escape.

There was an opportunity for some labourers to improve their lot. At the end of their five-year contract they could opt for renewal on a local contract for just a year at a time. Many coolies, however, were bullied or bribed into signing another five-year contract under the 1882 Act. This was easily imposed if the labourer was in debt to the estate, as many were, especially if they had been ill.

As a bribe to sign a fresh contract the men might be offered a woman to marry, for government officials allowed tea estate managers 'the disposal in marriage of all imported female coolies'. One of the more liberal planters, David Crole, who worked for the Jokai Tea Company in the 1890s, condemned this system in his book, *Tea* (1897). In it he described an even more iniquitous system, whereby the marriage was arranged in such a way that the husband's and wife's contracts expired at different times. The planter could then threaten the one whose contract expired first with expulsion from the estate, and separation from their spouse, unless they signed another contract. This contract would be dated to finish after the other's contract expired, and the process would continue, binding the couple to the planter for ever.

Children, of course, were expected to work with their parents. Indeed it was often the only way families could earn enough to survive. Normally they started to work when aged five or six and, if they were on one of the better plantations, might get one and a half rupees a month.

If they did not owe money, time-expired labourers were in a relatively strong bargaining position. They could demand a bonus for resigning, and a slightly enhanced wage. They might also opt for a local contract, sometimes for only a year, which gave them freedom from arrest by the planters. They could also choose to live outside the labour lines. Even more importantly, they could move to an estate where conditions were better. As the century came to an end many time-expired labourers took advantage of these rights.

Many workers never exercised these options, however, for they died before they completed their contracts. Although mortality was much reduced as the century progressed, it was still shockingly high. This was particularly true of the workers recruited under the infamous 1882 Act. Their statutory wage, if indeed they received it in full, was probably not sufficient to keep them from being malnourished. Consequently the mortality among 1882 Act labourers was higher than for other workers, whose own mortality was higher than those employed outside the estates. The average coolie recruited under the 1882 Act stood a one-in-four chance of dying before the end of the five-year contact. On many estates, of course, the mortality was greater than the average. Planters and government tried to explain this away by suggesting that the coolies had imported the diseases themselves. Sir Henry Cotton showed that it was correlated to low wages and high workloads. Doctors linked the high death rate to the absence of sick leave, and to the coolies being forced to work hard when debilitated by disease.

Towards the end of the nineteenth century, conditions on the better estates markedly improved. David Crole described better houses 'constructed to hold only one family to four families, instead of an indefinite number ranging perhaps up to eight'. He also spoke in a much more humane way of the labourers: 'A batch of new coolies are generally given a day or two in which to settle down and find out their friends and relations, if any, among the coolies in the garden.' He added, 'I am sure that a policy of reasonable kindness and conciliation is never thrown away on any sentient being, much less on one of our own species, even though he be of another race.'

On many estates, however, the old ways continued. The twentieth century began with a number of high-profile conflicts between the planters and their labour. In 1901 an Assam planter, Horace Lyall, had some of his coolies beaten for threatening to appeal to the authorities after he had refused sick leave for one of them. Two coolies were seriously injured. A European-dominated jury acquitted him, but on review the High Court imposed a fine and imprisoned him for a month. The Indian Tea Association protested, but Lord Curzon, the Viceroy, confirmed the sentence.

In 1903 another Assam planter, Peter Bain, caught an absconding coolie and beat him to death. The man's wife and niece were also whipped for accompanying him. A local European jury found him guilty of 'simple hurt' and he only received a six-month sentence. Again, the planting community vigorously supported one of their own.

Indenture finally came to an end because it was no longer politically acceptable. Members of Parliament, missionaries and liberal opinion in Britain and India kept up pressure on the governments of both Britain and India to abolish it. The practice became an embarrassment for the authorities. In 1901 registration and supervision in the recruiting districts were reintroduced; in 1908 the Assam planters lost their power of arrest; in 1915 coolie contractors had their licences terminated, and recruitment could thereafter only be done by estate *sardars*. Closer government supervision of recruitment had lessened the number of coolies the contractors could find and, in consequence, the contractors had put up their prices. Cheap labour had become expensive, and planters had begun to see it was in their interests to improve conditions and pay higher wages to attract willing labour. The number of coolies indentured under the infamous 1882 Act rapidly declined after 1901, and the whole system was finally abolished in 1926.

By 1900 over 200,000 acres of tea had been planted in the jungles of Assam. This cost the lives of a few British planters and of several hundred thousand Indian coolies.

It has been argued that some of these coolies would have lost their lives anyway, had they stayed in their villages, and especially so in the years of famine. This may be true, but does this excuse the excesses of the British coolie contractors and planters? This tragedy was encouraged by government legislation, but it was enacted by tea planters who had a contempt for the Indian coolies, and their lives – a contempt they had acquired from the indigo planters, who had themselves brought in attitudes acquired in the Caribbean slave plantations. It was the planters' own Indian Tea Association that fought against almost every safeguard. By no means all the planters behaved badly, and a

Victorian Enterprise – the '1st class jungley'

few behaved admirably, but the well-documented cruelties and death toll taint the majority. However, for the planters, it had some compensations, for as one of them, George Barker, wrote of Assam in 1883:

> This is the last remaining district where any sort of respect is shown for the Europeans; in all other parts of India the black man is as good as the white, a fact that is speedily brought home to a new comer. It is here, in Assam, that nearly all the old rights of servility that were exacted by Europeans in the days of the East India Company, are still in existence, and flourish to the general better feeling amongst the whole community. Here no heavy babu swaggers past with his umbrella up, jostling you on the way; but with courtly mien, on seeing your pony coming along, furls up the umbrella, steps on one side, and salutes with a proud salaam. A mounted native will dismount until the white man has passed by, and drivers of a conveyance will turn off on one side; but this gives rise to a difficulty in the case of the road being narrow and the sahib's buggy wide, a difficulty that is surmounted by the simple expedient of turning the cart off the road. If the block occurs, as it frequently does, on a raised road, with a steep embankment on either side and a paddy field at the bottom, the result is disastrous. It is pretty certain that the ghari will break away and career into the most sticky spot, have to be unloaded and dragged to the top, by persuasively twisting the tails of the bullocks, and then reloading; but the dignity of the sahib must be maintained, no matter what inconvenience to the native.

At the end of the nineteenth century India was producing nearly 200 million lbs of tea. Of this 85 per cent was exported to Britain. There were over 500,000 acres (780 square miles) of tea across the country – 200,000 of these were in Assam, 130,000 in Cachar and Sylhet, 130,000 in Bengal, and there were smaller

Victorian Enterprise – the '1st class jungley'

acreages in the Punjab, the North-western Provinces and in the southern India states of Madras, Travencore and Cochin. Virtually all this tea had been planted in only forty years – but at a terrible cost.

FIVE

Victorian Enterprise – Ceylon

Sir Jellaby Jingle and Admiral Sneeze
Have each got a son in Ceylon.
If I stand you five thousand, you can, if you please,
Make a fortune. Come say, are you on?

HAMILTON and FASSON, 'Scenes in Ceylon', 1881

In the late nineteenth century the great rival to Indian tea was not tea from China, but from Ceylon. To understand the development of tea in Ceylon it is necessary to first look at the development of coffee, for Ceylon tea was built on the ruins of Ceylon coffee.

Ceylon, renamed Sri Lanka in 1972, is a large tropical island lying twenty miles off the south-eastern coast of India. Shaped famously like a teardrop, it is 270 miles from north to south, and 140 miles from east to west. Much of it is low lying, but the central mountains rise to over 8,000 feet. Most of the population are the descendants of peoples who originally came from India – the Sinhalese from north India, and the Tamils from south India – migrations that probably began in the first millennium BC.

The principal rain-bearing monsoon comes from the south-west. This waters the south-west coastal plain and then the central mountains. At which point, the monsoon is exhausted: there is nothing much left for the other parts of the island – north and east – and these are known as the Dry Zone. (This zone does receive some rain from a north-east monsoon, but this is much less generous.) The Wet Zone is where the plantation crops

156

flourish. These parts of the island are very fertile, and receive up to 100 inches of rain a year, with pockets receiving over 200 inches.

Ceylon was famous for the spices it produced, particularly cinnamon. In the first millennium AD, Arab and Chinese merchants sailed to the island to buy spices, gems, pearls and elephants. Inevitably, Ceylon came to the notice of the Portuguese, as they opened up routes between the East and the West. They first arrived on the island in 1505. Soon afterwards they set up fortified trading posts on the western coast, and in 1619 they annexed the Tamil-dominated northern stronghold of Jaffna. Further south they were less successful in subjugating the Sinhalese, and the kings of Kandy defied them.

The Dutch had their equivalent of the East India Company – the United East India Company, founded in 1602. Like its British counterpart, it had the right to raise armies, build forts, appoint governors and judges and to make treaties. The Dutch Company was at first only really interested in cinnamon. At the invitation of the King of Kandy in central Ceylon, it arrived in 1636 to exploit this trade, and in return undertook to help fight the Portuguese. Although in this treaty the Dutch recognized the sovereignty of the King of Kandy over most of Ceylon, they secured for themselves the sole rights to overseas trade, which would give them economic control over the country.

In 1644, the Dutch betrayed the King of Kandy. They concluded a truce with the Portuguese, and formed an alliance against the kingdom. However, the Sinhalese were so powerful that in 1649 the Dutch had to re-enter into an alliance with them against the Portuguese. The Dutch defeated the Portuguese at Colombo in 1656, and became the economic rulers of Ceylon.

The Dutch, through the United East India Company, controlled Ceylon for 140 years. As Ceylon was the world's only supplier of high quality cinnamon, the Dutch monopoly over the cinnamon trade was immensely profitable. Any interference with this monopoly – smuggling out the spice or its oil, or merely damaging a plant – carried the death penalty. The export of cinnamon and a few other luxuries was the main objective of the Dutch Company. If necessary they used military force to enforce these privileges, but otherwise they kept to their small enclaves.

During the eighteenth century the British consolidated their power in India. They also expanded their navy. Ceylon was so close to India that it was only a matter of time before the British would covet it. In 1782 the British captured the important eastern port of Trincomanlee. They soon lost it to the French, however, and in the Treaty of Paris of 1784 the port reverted to the Dutch.

Events in Europe gave Britain the opportunity it wanted. The French, who were at war with the British, invaded the Dutch Low Countries. The British in India then offered their 'protection' to the Dutch in Ceylon. Without waiting for an answer, they seized control of Trincomalee. The British then persuaded some free-lance Dutch troops to switch sides. They also entered into a treaty with the King of Kandy by which they would replace the Dutch as the kingdom's protector in return for trading privileges. In 1796 the Dutch surrendered their principal city, Colombo, and the British took over their role in Ceylon. All this was done in the name of the East India Company at Madras, and it was the Company, rather than the British government itself, which became the new ruler.

The East India Company traded from Ceylon but, fearful that events in Europe might transfer Ceylon back to the Dutch, did little to consolidate their position. In 1802 the British government decided to take direct control of the Company's possessions in Ceylon, and these became a Crown Colony. On various pretexts Britain then waged war against the Kandyan kingdom, and in 1815 took complete control of the entire island. The British then showed that they intended to stay – they established a large army, and built roads to transport it quickly.

In the Dutch era, Ceylon had been largely a subsistence economy, with the Dutch merely exporting the island's natural resources. They had managed to plant a little cinnamon to supplement the wild cinnamon harvested in the interior, and a little coffee to supplement the small patches of existing coffee. However, both these enterprises were on a very small scale. In contrast, the British soon transformed Ceylon from a subsistence into a plantation economy. They did it remarkably fast, with coffee.

Coffee is a tropical evergreen shrub. The main cultivated species, *Coffea arabica*, originated in Ethiopia. Another variety, *Coffea robusta*, which also originated in Africa, is grown on a smaller scale. At the start of the eighteenth century the colonial powers – Portugal, Spain, Holland, France and Britain – began to grow *Coffea arabica* in their tropical possessions. Brazil became the biggest producer of coffee, and it still is. The plant flourishes best at about 85°F (29°C) in a moderate rainfall of 40 to 60 inches a year (which is on the lower end of the requirement for tea) at an altitude of about 4,000 feet. Three or four years after planting it produces very pretty clusters of sweet-smelling white blossom. These develop into red berries, inside which are two seeds, or 'coffee beans'.

In a fairly simple process, the outer skin is removed in a pulper, the mucous beneath is washed away, and the beans are dried in the sun or by artificial heat. This is normally done on the plantation. Later on, the husk that encloses the beans is removed at a trader's warehouse. The coffee beans are then ready to be roasted and ground, which is best done just before the coffee is drunk.

In Ceylon, the Dutch had grown coffee on the coastal plains, where the climate was totally unsuitable. The first British planters made the same mistake, planting on the southern coast. In contrast, the hills around Kandy, in the centre of Ceylon, have an ideal climate for coffee. In 1823–5, the first successful plantings were started there, by the governor himself and by the military commandant. A number of other high civil servants and officers, including even the chief justice and the auditor-general, purchased land for coffee. (It was only in 1845 that alarm about conflict of interest caused such ownership of land to be prohibited.) Coffee did not immediately become a profitable crop, for it was in competition with coffee from the West Indies, that enjoyed a special tariff advantage for export to Britain. This obstacle was removed in 1835 when coffee from Ceylon was given equal preference, and this opened the way for the establishment of the Ceylon coffee industry.

By 1835, 4,000 acres of heavy forest around Kandy had been cleared and planted. Rumours reached Britain that fortunes were to be made. Land was bought purely for re-sale, and a speculative 'bubble' developed. All uncultivated land was regarded as Crown land, and available for acquisition by potential planters. Any title the natives of Ceylon might have had was ignored, and much common land was sequestered. In addition, although this was illegal, the inhabitants of entire villages, inconveniently located in the midst of land required by the British, were expelled. With so many high government officials involved in land speculation themselves, there were few checks.

Nearly all the new owners were small entrepreneurs, typically employees or ex-employees of the East India Company, or ex-officers, or men pretending to be: 'they were all Captains from Kondegalla down to well into Pussellawa, and even there also the Captain flourished.' A fellow planter put it more bluntly: 'In the course of time all the riff-raff of the round world came here

. . . and we came to'have a floating scum of coffee planters.' The amount of land sold by government – initially at £1 for every four acres, then at £1 an acre – rose from 337 acres in 1834 to a total of 78,685 acres in 1841. By 1845 there were 37,000 acres planted with coffee.

In 1847, a financial crisis in Britain, coupled with some import concessions given to coffee from Java and Brazil, caused the price of coffee to fall. The profit projections of the Ceylon planters began to look wildly optimistic. Those who had bought land as a speculation tried to sell it quickly. The banks called in their loans. Estates were hurriedly sold at a fraction of their cost, and much land that had been acquired for coffee was abandoned.

The slump lasted three years. By 1850, those who had held their nerve were planting out new acreages. By 1869 there were 176,000 acres of coffee. It was in that year that disaster struck.

Early in 1869 the superintendent of Galloola Estate noticed that the undersides of some coffee plant leaves were covered with yellow powdery blotches. These were quickly identified as a dangerous fungus. He was advised to strip off and burn all the affected leaves. He soon found, however, that his labourers could not keep pace with the outbreak, and it soon enveloped the estate. Within five years coffee rust fungus had spread to every estate in Ceylon.

The fungus did not kill the coffee bush. The affected leaves usually dropped off the evergreen plant, and sometimes it was completely defoliated, but the plant normally survived. The disease, however, enfeebled the bush and dramatically reduced the yield of coffee berries. Within ten years of the disease reaching Ceylon (possibly on the monsoon wind from Africa), the average yield of the Ceylon plantations dropped from 500 lbs to a little over 200 lbs an acre.

At first the planters thought the disease might go away. They changed their methods of pruning, gave the plants extra fertilizer, and tried countless other stratagems. These had no effect. Meanwhile, encouraged by higher world coffee prices, they continued to expand. More coffee was planted out, mostly in new areas that hopefully were free of disease. By 1880 there were 275,000 acres of coffee all told.

Many of these acres were, however, no longer being cultivated. The fungus had made the crop too small to be economic. In 1870 Ceylon's exports of coffee were over 110 million lbs – by 1880 it was half this, and by 1890 it was less than a tenth.

The decline of Ceylon coffee was almost exactly mirrored by the rise of Ceylon tea. William Ukers, the great historian of tea and coffee, observed: 'dead coffee trees, stripped, with branches cut level, were being exported to England to serve as legs for tea tables.' This was a fact, but it is also a neat allegory.

Tea was slow to take hold in Ceylon. The Calcutta Botanical Gardens had sent some Assam seed to its counterpart in Ceylon, the Royal Botanical Gardens at Peradeniya near Kandy, in 1839, and sent some plants the following year.

Botanical gardens were a great feature of the British Empire, and were established in most British colonies. They had been encouraged by the great gardens at Kew and Edinburgh, which relied on them for specimens and research. Gardens like Peradeniya, established in 1821, also had beautiful grounds for the British to promenade in. Set in a bend in the river it was considered the most beautiful tropical garden in the world. Giant bamboos from Malacca lined the riverbank, there was a great avenue of royal palms, and flowering trees were everywhere. Other gardens, such as that in Calcutta – which in the early days was difficult to reach from the city – were purely functional. The main purpose of all these gardens, however, was to find plants that could be grown commercially.

Some of the tea plants from Calcutta were put out at the Peradeniya botanical gardens, and some in a plot on the Chief Justice's estate. In a parallel development, a coffee planter, Maurice Worms, visited China in 1841 and brought back some tea seedlings. These were planted out on his Rothschild Estate – so named because he was related to Baron de Rothschild. It is said that a Chinese worker was also brought in, and a small sample of tea made at great expense. Some of these plants may have been spread to other estates, but nothing substantial was done with tea until the 1860s.

Even when coffee was still an enormous success, some of the Ceylon planters had been keen to investigate the possibilities of diversifying into other plantation crops. One of these crops was cinchona, from which quinine, used to prevent malaria, is extracted. (Cinchona had its own 'boom and bust' story – it was first planted out in Ceylon in 1861; by 1883 there were 64,000 acres of trees under cultivation; in the mid 1880s the world price of quinine collapsed; in the 1890s most of the Ceylon estates were abandoned.) Planters also tried growing nutmeg, cloves, vanilla, cardamom, cotton and cocoa. There was also some interest in tea.

The Planters' Association sent one of their members, Arthur Morice, on a tour of the Indian tea districts in 1867. He produced a detailed report concluding that 'there is every possibility of Tea being successfully grown in Ceylon.' In general his report made little impact on the coffee planters, who were too obsessed with their highly profitable coffee to take a long-term gamble on tea, which could not be expected to produce a profit for at least six years. The Planters' Association General Committee was dismissive:

> Among the subjects of *less* importance the Committee have to notice the publication, in the course of the year, of the report of the Tea Districts of India by the Commissioner of the Association, Mr Arthur Morice.

The director of the Royal Botanical Gardens, however, was more impressed, as were a few planters. With extraordinary speed, tea seed was ordered from Calcutta, received, and planted out in that same year of 1867.

The first planting was by James Taylor, the superintendent of Loolecondera Estate. It was a commercial planting of nineteen acres. Taylor had been born in the small Scottish town of Laurencekirk in Kincardineshire, from where a number of young men had gone to Ceylon. He was engaged through an agent to be assistant superintendent of a Kandy coffee estate for three years, on a salary of £100 a year, out of which he would pay for his passage and kit. Taylor arrived in 1852, when only sixteen years old. He was transferred to the adjacent Loolecondera Estate a few weeks later, and would, in 1892, die there (just after being sacked for refusing to go on sick-leave). Fortunately for him, the estate was taken over in the 1860s by owners who were keen to diversify. First they encouraged Taylor to plant cinchona, then to try tea.

James Taylor had a mechanical bent, and soon mastered the technique of processing tea – a technique he picked up from local coffee planters who had been employed in tea when in India. He equipped the verandah of his bungalow with rolling tables and charcoal fires, and managed to produce a good tea for the local market. He soon moved into a proper factory, for which he built a rolling machine driven by a water wheel. By 1875 there were 100 acres of tea on Loolecondera.

Other estates were quick to follow. By 1875 there were a couple of dozen other plantations growing tea, with 1,000 acres of tea between them. After 1875 the pace began to accelerate. Nevertheless, although everyone wanted to expand as fast as possible because of the depredations of the coffee fungus, this was not easy, and by 1880 less than 10,000 acres of tea had been planted up. Some tea was planted between rows of coffee, for many half-hoped that some remedy might be found against the

James Taylor (right) with his cousin, Ceylon 1864

coffee fungus. On some estates there were even fields with three crops intermingled – coffee, cinchona and tea.

A number of small coffee estates had Sinhalese owners, and some of these moved into tea. A group of wealthy Indian Parsees also planted some tea. The great majority of tea estates were, however, British owned.

The slow expansion of tea was largely because of the financial problems that had followed the collapse of coffee, but there was also a lack of expertise, and a shortage of tea seed.

Tea seed soon became more readily available as unpruned tea plants grew into mature seed-bearing trees. In the clamour for seed, however, much was distributed from poor stock, and this led to the establishment of many poor quality gardens. It was many years before finances improved. After the failure of the Bank of Ceylon in 1847, the Oriental Bank Corporation had become the country's leading bank. In 1884 it, too, failed. This led to many coffee estates being abandoned. About a quarter of estate managers left Ceylon to try their luck elsewhere.

In spite of these problems, tea continued to be planted out – both on the old coffee estates and also on new land. There was the 'low-grown' tea on the relatively few estates near the south-west coast; the 'mid-grown,' mostly on the old coffee plantations that lay between 2,000 feet and 4,000 feet above sea level, around Kandy; and the 'high-grown' on the central peaks above 4,000 feet. As had happened in India, the Assam varieties tended to do better at the lower altitudes and the China ones at the higher, but there was much hybridization between the two. By 1885 there were over 100,000 acres of tea in Ceylon, and by 1900 there were 384,000 acres.

To plant up 374,000 acres of tea in twenty years was an extra-ordinary achievement, which required a great deal of capital and labour.

In the early years, tea in Ceylon had been opened up quite differently to tea in India. In India the driving force had been the Assam Company, which originally had a total monopoly, and that company had retained its pre-eminence right up to the end of the nineteenth century and beyond. It was a limited liability company with many investors and a share capital of £500,000. Big companies also developed much of the other tea in India, with individual planters only having a minor role. In contrast, in Ceylon most of the early tea was opened up by small-scale planters who had originally been in coffee.

Some of the estates belonged to a number of partners, based in Ceylon or in Britain, who employed superintendents and assistants to manage the properties for them. There were only a few larger companies. When one of the estates became insolvent it might be taken over by a bank, but that was the extent of involvement by big financial institutions. In the last fifteen years of the nineteenth century, this structure changed considerably.

The most conspicuous newcomer was Sir Thomas Lipton, a dynamic salesman. Lipton had started as a small grocer in Glasgow in 1871. By selling cheap, then massively advertising this to the public, he had managed to establish a chain of 400 shops. In 1889 he started to buy tea at auction in London, and through his shops and agents managed to sell 4 million lbs that year. In 1890 he sold 6 million lbs of tea. In that year, on the way to Australia, Lipton stopped off at Ceylon.

Following the financial crisis, there were several Ceylon tea estates for sale. Lipton, whose motto was 'cut out the middleman', seized the opportunity and bought several. Although his name became synonymous with Ceylon tea in Europe and America (where many thought he owned the whole Ceylon tea industry) his purchase of 3,000 acres was only about 15 per cent of the total tea acreage. These estates could only supply a fraction of Lipton's needs, and he bought much tea from India. Nevertheless, the tremendous advertising of Ceylon tea by Lipton put it firmly on the world map and hugely stimulated demand.

In the 1890s a number of tea estates amalgamated to form new tea companies. Some were incorporated in Ceylon and some in Britain. New money for development was either raised privately, by tapping friends and relatives or business acquaintances, or by a public prospectus. In general, the money came from individuals willing to take a gamble rather than from institutions, for these were wary of the past record of the Ceylon planting industry.

As had happened in India, a number of agency businesses

developed. Based in Colombo, they arranged the warehousing, shipping and selling of tea for a group of estates. They often supplied management services for absent landlords. The 'Visiting Agent' became a power in the industry, and his visits to the estates were awaited with trepidation. There was another set of agencies in London, which arranged the sale and disposal of tea shipped from Ceylon. It became usual for many of these agencies, both in Colombo and London, to invest in the companies they were servicing.

The planters of the late nineteenth century were different too. The early planters had come in via coffee, and were mostly working class. They might have been trained as gardeners, or perhaps served in the ranks of the army. Their manners were rough, especially if they were single. James Taylor of Loolecondera, for example, had an aversion to the first beer from a bottle. This he would splash on to the floor, so that at the end of a drinking session the house would be awash. Towards the end of his career he felt isolated among the new breed of planters. As one of the older planters commented:

> I am not sure whether the new social ways came in with the ladies or with the leaf disease. I only know our simple ways suddenly changed in many places; such as dressing for dinner and that sort of thing, never heard of in the jungle before the sixties.

And planters really did dress for dinner. Professor Ernest Haeckel related what happened to him in the early 1880s:

> I arrived after sundown, at a very remote plantation, and the hospitable master gave me very clearly to understand that he expected to see me at dinner in a black tailcoat and white tie. My sincere regrets and explanation that my light tourist's kit for this excursion in the mountains could not possibly include black evening dress, did not prevent my host donning it in

my honour, nor his wife, the only other person at table, from appearing in full dinner toilet.

It became the fashion for young men 'of good family' to come out to Ceylon as tea planters. Some would have relatives who owned shares; others merely knew someone who knew someone. They are nicely satirized in Hamilton and Fasson's *The Shuck Estate*, where Sir John Folingsby gives advice to his second son:

> Planting coffee or tea, or we'll say sugar cane,
> From your self-respect could not detract, Sir;
> But Lombard Street, or that d. .d Mincing Lane,
> I cannot abide, that's a fact, Sir!

> Sir Jellaby Jingle and Admiral Sneeze
> Have each got a son in Ceylon.
> If I stand you five thousand, you can, if you please,
> Make a fortune. Come say, are you on?

By the end of the century, aided by better roads, this new breed of planters had established a very social way of life. They built croquet lawns and tennis courts on their estates; they built clubs to drink and to dance; they played cricket, golf and polo. White women were scarce, but not so scarce as previously. As they spread across the tea districts they brought more formal standards.

Elephants were very much a feature of plantation life. At first they were shot for sport and ivory; later they were domesticated for work.

Hunting was a skill the planter needed to open out the jungle. Wild pigs were dangerous, and they could also soon uproot a new planting. Weighing as much as 400 lbs, they were shot or caught in camouflaged pits. Smaller animals, particularly rats and porcupines, could also cause great damage to young plants. Leopards would kill the planter's fowls or dogs. Many of the planters kept packs of sporting hounds for hunting pigs and sambur deer. These deer were known as 'elks', and could weigh up to 600 lbs. The planter had to be nimble for, although the dogs might grab the animal, it was up to the hunter to kill it with a long knife. Several planters were killed in these encounters.

But the animal the early planters most loved to hunt was the elephant. The British found an island teeming with elephants, and set about culling them with vigour. They shot the males and the females, even though, unlike the African elephant, the female Ceylon elephant has no tusks. Only 60 per cent of the Ceylon male elephants carried tusks, and the majority of these were very small, but this did not deter the British military, administrators and planters. The most famous of the elephant-hunting planters was Major Thomas Rogers, who:

> When, six years ago, he had reached his thirteen hundred, he ceased reckoning any longer. His whole house was filled with ivory, for among the hosts of the slain were sixty tusked elephants. At each door of his veranda stood huge tusks, while in his dining room every corner was adorned with similar trophies.

Fortunately, perhaps, Major Rogers' career was brought to an abrupt end. He was killed at the age of forty-one, by lightning.

The coffee planters had felled the jungle, burnt most of the wood, and left the tree stumps to rot. When the tea planters cleared land they generally liked to remove the stumps as well, for these obstructed the closer planting, and also encouraged root fungus. For this work the elephant was invaluable. In addition elephants were extremely useful for moving heavy loads, such as tea machinery, over difficult terrain, and for the building of roads and bridges. In order to maintain and expand the population of tame elephants, regular wild elephant hunts were organized.

The planters loved to join these elephant hunts, but the work was really done by the expert Ceylonese. A thousand men might be required. To capture the elephants a large stockade, a *korahl*, was constructed of heavy poles and beams. It had a winged opening, to allow the elephants in. This could be barred with massive horizontal poles. Ceylonese beaters would locate a herd of maybe fifty elephants in the forest, and drive them toward the stockade. This needed great skill and might take weeks. Once the elephants had entered the wings of the *korahl*, they would be urged inside by the beating of drums and the discharge of guns. Then the entrance would be closed off.

The wild elephants were tamed with the assistance of tame ones. Each wild elephant would be sandwiched between two tame ones, and then secured with ropes. They could then be tethered, watered and fed. The tame elephants would help the *mahouts* calm the newcomers until, after perhaps two months, they might be ridden. It would take another four months of training before the new elephants could be safely put to work.

Ceylon was relatively small, and because the military had quickly built a network of strategic roads, transport was never the problem that it was in India. Nevertheless, in the early days it was a slow business, for almost all transport was by bullock cart. First the coffee would be taken to Kandy, on country roads that were extremely primitive and sometimes out of action altogether in the rains. Until these roads were improved, this first part of the journey could often only be undertaken by pack bullocks, rather than bullock carts, and might take a couple of weeks. On the road from Kandy to Colombo, which opened in 1832, bullock carts could do the ninety-mile journey in four days – if the weather was good. In the early days, it could cost more to get the crop to the coast, than to ship it 11,000 miles round the Cape from Colombo to England.

A railway to link Kandy and Colombo was opened in 1867. Subsequently, this line was extended into the plantation districts. This railway was in place for the opening up of the first tea estates, and proved invaluable for moving tea and tea machinery to and from the coast. The labour force that produced this tea was not so fortunate.

It was clear from the early days of coffee planting that local labour would not suffice. The Sinhalese showed little desire to work on the plantations, although they had assisted in clearing land. They had their own plots to cultivate, and as a contemporary observed: 'working for hire is repulsive to their national feelings, and is looked upon as almost slavery. Then being obliged to obey orders, and to do just what they are commanded is galling to them.' A few Singhalese did work on the estates, but they were only ever a small proportion of the total workforce.

Coffee was very labour-intensive in the harvesting season, but this was only for four or five months of the year. The work for much of the labour force, therefore, was seasonal. Conveniently, this season alternated with that of the rice crop in nearby India, and the practice began for labourers to come to the Ceylon coffee estates after they had harvested the rice of south India.

In the early days the planters sent their own men to do their recruiting. Later on, knowing the route, the labourers formed themselves into groups and came on their own. They selected one of themselves as headman, or *kangany*, to negotiate terms and be their supervisor on the estate. For this he received a small payment from each. Later, there was a different type of *kangany*, who was an agent of the planter.

Ceylon pluckers, from *Golden Tips*, 1900

The route to the estates was extremely arduous. The Tamil labourers took small boats across the twenty-mile-wide Palk Strait to north-west Ceylon, and then walked. The North Road – actually little more than a path – went through some of the most inhospitable jungle of Ceylon, where malaria was rampant, and good drinking water was scarce. The road then climbed up through rugged mountainous country to the estates.

Many of the *kanganies* were anxious not to spend more than necessary of the allowance they had been given by the planters for the labourers' food. They drove their charges relentlessly, for seven or eight days. It was to their financial advantage to take a few expendable men to cope with any loss. The journey was 150 miles or more, with no shelter or medical facilities: 'the roads choked up with the sick, the dying and the dead'. Some effort was made to bury the Christians, but the ground was too hard to dig deep graves: 'the consequences were that the jackals dug into them and fed on the corpses, sometimes even drawing them out of the graves, so that there might be seen, scattered about, bleached skulls and bones.'

Even more of the Tamils, weakened by the journey, and unable to take the colder altitude, succumbed on the estates. Those too ill to work were often forced off the estates by ruthless planters and left to die by the roadside. Those who survived were housed in appallingly overcrowded and insanitary conditions, where many of them died of cholera and other diseases.

There was considerable unease in some sections of British society in Ceylon about the treatment of the Tamil immigrants. Government and planters tried to blame each other for the lack of facilities. They argued about who should pay for improvements. Exactly how many of the coolies had died since 1841 was acrimoniously debated in the local newspapers of 1849, and the figures have been debated many times since then. Exact statistics were not available as to how many travelled to and from unregistered ports, although this was probably not a great number. The statistics did show a total of 272,000 arrivals but only 133,000 departures, and it was estimated that at the most only 50,000 had stayed on. The general consensus is that at least 70,000 died.

In the second half of the nineteenth century there were a number of famines in south India. This drove many of the inhabitants to risk the journey to the Ceylon estates. The famine of 1854 caused relatively few deaths, but there was much malnourishment. There was also a great loss of cattle, an essential of life in rural India – one third of the cattle died in some districts, and as many as four fifths in others. The Madras famine of 1865–6 was much more severe, and at least 450,000 Indians died. These famines greatly encouraged emigration to Ceylon, to the benefit of the coffee planters.

The tea planters found a ready source of labour from even greater calamities in India. From the first, there were a number of what government reports euphemistically called 'scarcities' – these were partial failures of the crops, which led to great hunger but not many deaths. In 1876–8 a major famine struck Madras. This had devastating consequences, and it took many years for the people to recover. The country was dependent for rain on the south-west monsoon in the middle of the year, and the northeast one later in the year. In 1876 both monsoons failed, and some districts received only a tenth of their normal rainfall. Eighteen seventy-seven was an abnormally hot year, which 'completely burnt the already parched country'. The south-west monsoon failed again. The late monsoon broke the drought, but by then over a million people had left their land for the food they received on government relief projects. They were the fortunate ones, for at least 3½ million Indians died.

It was these harsh conditions in south India that drove labourers to the Ceylon tea estates. In the 1877 famine, 167,000 south

Indian Tamils – men, women and children – went to the Ceylon plantations. Although 88,000 Tamils returned to India that year, there was nevertheless a net gain to the plantation workforce of 87,000. There are no reliable statistics until 1889 about those who took boats to Colombo. However, it is clear that until nearly the end of the century the great majority of coolies came across the Palk Strait in small boats and then walked the notorious North Road to the estates. Later, many of them walked back the same way. In some years more Tamils returned to India than arrived. Decade on decade, however, more arrived than departed, and the plantation workforce rapidly increased. By 1900 it had reached 337,000. The vast majority were Indian Tamils.

After 1855, some effort had been made to improve conditions on the North Road, and as coffee was replaced by tea the lot of the immigrant Tamils improved. By 1880 the government had built hospitals, dispensaries, shelters and wells along the route. Those too ill to continue walking were rescued by regular patrols and taken to hospitals. These improvements much reduced the deaths on the road, although there were still periodic fatal outbreaks of cholera, bubonic plague and smallpox. Effective control of these diseases would have required quarantine arrangements on arrival in Ceylon, and these were not introduced until the end of the century. The authorities cynically relied on the journey itself to weed out the sick. In consequence, many of the Ceylonese in the villages adjoining the road were infected, and these districts were depopulated.

In 1890 new steamer routes were introduced between the ports in south India and Colombo. In theory these made the North Road redundant. However, from habit, or because they could not afford the steamer fare, some labourers continued to use the old route. The planters were also keen to keep the North Road open, especially those on estates in the northern highlands. However, in 1897 there was a serious outbreak of plague in south India. To prevent it spreading, the Governor of Ceylon introduced

Ceylon pluckers sorting the leaf outside the tea factory, from *Golden Tips*, 1900

stringent controls on the Colombo route, and he closed the North Road. It never reopened.

The conditions of engagement for Tamils of south India on the Ceylon plantations were entirely different to those on estates in India or in other countries that took Indian labour. The labourers who went to Ceylon were 'free' – that is, they were not indentured on long-term contracts. They were taken on a weekly or monthly basis. Although they were only paid if they worked out that period, they could leave whenever they wished. The proximity of Ceylon to south India led the authorities in India to leave the migration unregulated. It refused, however, to allow recruitment from more distant parts of India.

The tea planters inherited the system developed by the coffee planters of using *kanganies* to recruit labour. These men, often from the same villages as the men they recruited, were given advances to cover the journey to the estates. The *kangany* and his gang would then be in debt to the estate until they had worked this amount off. Although they were 'free', the Ceylon coolies, unlike other Indian plantation labourers, had to pay the cost of their transport and recruitment. This started them in debt – a debt that they found hard to repay, and which effectively tied them to their *kanganies*. Some Tamils avoided debt and returned to India from time to time, but this became more and more unusual. This suited the tea planters, for tea was not a seasonal crop, and required permanent labour. To enhance their hold on the labourers further the tea planters were generous with any cash advances the labourers might need to supplement their inadequate wages. The planters also usually paid wages well in arrears – often two months late – to entrap the coolies.

The *kanganies* were notorious for pocketing most of the advances themselves. The potential coolie was completely at their mercy, for the *kangany* had total control over who did or did not get taken on by the estates. Often there was a tiered system, where the estate dealt with a head *kangany*, who himself had several sub-*kanganies* based in the villages of his area. These *kanganies* continued to supervise the labourers once they reached the estates, and all dealing by the planter with his labour would be through the *kanganies*. This managerial function gave the *kanganies* further leverage over their men. It can be seen that there was much scope for abuse in this system – and the *kanganies* did consistently abuse it, to the loss of both the planter and the coolie. In 1904 the planters set up their own labour commission to supervise the system, and ensure the labourers actually got the cash advances they had to repay. Nevertheless, the unreformed *kangany* system continued to operate on numerous estates for many more years.

Though wages on the tea estates were low, they were higher than in India. In the 1870s they were relatively generous. In the 1880s they were cut when the price of tea fell, and were never restored. They became even lower, relative to the cost of living, as the century progressed.

The estates provided the coolies with rice at a fixed price. This removed pressure on the planters to increase wages at times of scarcity and high prices – increases that they feared might become permanent. Although the planters were fond of explaining how generous they were in years of high rice prices, in fact they made a profit in other years – a profit that more than compensated for any temporary loss. The planters also, rather bizarrely, organized the coolies' laundry and the cutting of their hair, which they debited against their wages. The price of foodstuffs other than rice increased by 50 per cent over the last two decades of the nineteenth century, while wages remained static. Many labourers found they could only make ends meet by taking out bigger loans, which tied them further to their *kanganies*.

Accommodation on the estates was extremely basic. William

Sabonadière who planted coffee in Ceylon from the early days, wrote in *The Coffee Planter in Ceylon* in 1866: 'The best way to punish coolies is to stop their wages, by striking one or more days' work out of the check-roll. They feel the loss of money far more than corporal punishment, which I consider injudicious.' By the standard of the time, he was probably rather liberal. He also provided some medical facilities for his labour. We can assume, therefore, that he was more generous than most in providing accommodation: 'Rooms twelve feet by twelve are very fair size, and will hold ten coolies, as they have no objection to being packed tolerably close.' Things had slightly improved in 1900, when Henry Cave wrote *Golden Tips*:

> A coolie line is usually a long building of one story only, divided into a large number of compartments. Each apartment accommodates about four coolies, and it is obvious that they do not enjoy the luxury of much space; but their ideas of comfort are not ours, and they are better pleased to lie huddled together on the mud floors of these tiny hovels than to occupy superior apartments.

The lines often lacked sanitation. Worried by the high mortality, the government appointed medical inspectors. These doctors, however, were in a tricky position, for on remote estates they usually stayed with the estate manager, and then found it difficult to write a critical report. Nevertheless, one or two did. This led to a great outcry in the settler press and the government terminated the experiment.

Physical punishment was never so barbarous as in Assam. Nevertheless, beatings were common, even though some planters like Sabonadière disapproved. In 1852, James Taylor of Loolecondera Estate wrote of the owner George Pride thumping a coolie for nearly half an hour. In 1900, Henry Cave, who visited a number of Ceylon tea estates, recorded that laziness 'brings a fine of half pay and in many cases a taste of the cangany's stick'.

Work in the fields was hard. It was made particularly tiring by the absence of any break, even for a midday meal. The planters feared that if they allowed the labourers to stop in the middle of the day they might not return. Perhaps, as a result of the general ill health this had happened. Whatever the reason, it was extremely onerous for those doing hard manual work. The coolies ordinarily had to work from six a.m. to four p.m., without break or food. As a doctor who examined tea estate labourers over many years observed:

> Nine coolies out of ten go nine hours without anything to eat ... I think that the long hours without food prevents a great many arrivals from India from developing into strong labourers. I do not think long hours – perhaps 10 or 11 hours without food is likely to be anything but prejudicial to a coolie who arrives physically not in a strong state.

To fortify themselves against hunger the labourers ate a large meal before arriving in the fields. Because of the early start, this was usually of cold rice, cooked the night before – not a good start on cold mornings. And it was often cold, particularly on the higher estates, with the day starting at 50° F (10°C) and the bushes covered with dew. It might also be raining, and windy too. The Tamils of the hot south India plains, often none too healthy, were not well suited to these conditions. It would have helped if they had been well clothed, but they often only had the *cumbly*, a coarse cotton cloth, to cover themselves. These *cumblies* would soon get soaked, and most coolies could only afford the one. There were many deaths from bronchitis and pneumonia.

Ceylon child pluckers, from *Golden Tips*, 1900

Children began to work in the fields when they reached the age of five. They earned a few cents a day – perhaps a third of the adult wage. Photographs of these worker children, clad in almost nothing even in the cold, are heartbreaking.

As on the Indian tea estates, those coolies who could afford it bought army-surplus coats. William Skeen put it to verse in 1868:

> Some clad in cumblies, and some deck'd
> In scarlet tunics, some in blue,
> ˙Old regimentals, odd to view
> On such a swarthy, bare-legged crew.

The government was outraged by this unauthorized use of military uniforms and in 1896 made this attire illegal, but the law was flouted for many decades afterwards.

By 1900 there were 384,000 acres, 600 square miles, of tea in Ceylon, producing 150 million lbs of tea for export, mainly to Britain. This made the tea industry of relatively tiny Ceylon nearly as big as that of India. Nearly all this planting had been done in only twenty years – an extraordinary achievement. That it had been largely financed, not by big companies, but by individuals and small partnerships made it all the more remarkable.

The manual work, however, had been done by south Indian Tamils, and had been accompanied by death and hardship. It is fair to say that, exploited as they were, the Tamils were probably better off in Ceylon than they would have been in famine-racked India – which is why they came. It is also true that the planters in Ceylon behaved infinitely better towards their labour than did the planters in Assam. Nevertheless, it was a tragedy that so many of the British planters showed so little compassion, and made so little effort to improve life for their labourers beyond what was strictly in their own interest. They, and many of the other British in Ceylon, saw the Indian coolies as cheap labour and nothing more, lucky to escape from a worse life. Henry Cave summed up the British view:

> The Tamil coolie in Ceylon may be a shocking barbarian in point of intellect and civilisation as compared with his British master, but having regard to his own race and opportunity he is by no means an unfortunate or despicable creature.

The arrival of so many labourers from outside Ceylon was resented by the native Sinhalese. In 1900 there were about

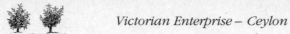

300,000 Indian Tamils working on the estates. The total population of Ceylon was under 4 million. Moreover, although the first Tamils to come to the coffee estates had been itinerant labour, returning to their homes in India once the crop was harvested, many of the tea estate workers had become permanent settlers. This would become a major problem in the twentieth century, with serious repercussions for both Ceylon and the Tamils.

SIX

New Empires

Pile it high, sell it cheap.

SIR JOHN COHEN, founder of Tesco supermarkets

For the British the twentieth century divided sharply into two halves. The first half saw their empire consolidated into a massive commercial enterprise that covered the globe and sent back tribute. In the middle of the century a huge war drained their finances. They lost most of their empire, and the manufacturing industry that had fed it, and the Americans took their imperial mantle. In the second half of the twentieth century the British reverted to being traders, but on a global scale.

At the beginning of the twentieth century Indian tea production was just under 200 million lbs. At Independence in 1947 production was over 560 million lbs. Over the same period in Ceylon production also doubled. These huge increases had been partly achieved by planting out greater acreages, but more so by improved agricultural techniques.

Fertilizer had been used from the early days of the British-owned tea estates. Indeed, the Chinese had been using human manure for many centuries. However, although there is no doubt that human manure is good for tea plants, and significantly raises yields, it is also most unhygienic, and rapidly spreads disease throughout the workforce. A much better alternative is animal dung. Cattle manure was used on many estates in the nineteenth century, and is still used. Chemical fertilizers have also been used for many years. *The Tea Planter's Vade Mecum* advocated the use of sulphate of ammonia and nitrate of ammonia in 1885, and suggested that they be blended with stable manure, wood ash and bone fertilizer.

The Indian Tea Association appointed its first scientific officer in 1900, and in 1912 established the famous research station at Tocklai in Assam. The Tea Research Institute of Ceylon was set up in 1925. Both these centres did much to make tea growing more scientific. The increased use of fertilizers, especially of those containing nitrogen, became the norm. Closer planting of tea bushes (four feet by four feet became common), better selection of seed-bearing trees, improved pruning techniques and control of disease and pests all helped to increase yields. Many early fields that had only produced 100 or 200 lbs of tea an acre began to yield 500 or 600 lbs. In Ceylon the magic figure of 1,000 lbs an acre was first reached in 1884. This, however, was exceptional and yields of this magnitude were not common until well into the twentieth century. When India and Ceylon achieved independence in the 1940s, yields were typically 1,500 lbs of made tea an acre.

Conditions for the labourers on the plantations markedly improved towards the end of British rule. More liberal attitudes seeped into British society and these were reflected by tea estate managers. In addition the coolies began to be more assertive. This was particularly true in Assam, where at the beginning of the century, the labourers were still treated appallingly.

At the close of the nineteenth century, the Assam coolies had received inspiration from Sir Henry Cotton and a vocal section of the Indian middle class. Assam was no longer a country to itself, existing in isolation. Improved transport within Assam helped spread news between workers on the scattered estates, and with a newfound confidence the coolies started to take action. A number of riots erupted against conditions on the worse estates. A manager's bungalow would be burnt down, or he might be assaulted. It needed, however, serious mismanagement to bring this about, for as one Indian planter observed:

> A tea garden is like a small town by itself, with the barracks for labourers and the stately bungalows for the managers and their assistants. Nobody, not even the policemen can enter this kingdom without the manager's permission. A manager may assault a labourer, insult him, and take girl after girl from the lines as his mistress, yet there will be none to dispute his action or authority. It is only when the manager's cruelty surpasses all bounds that the labourers set upon him and assault him.

On the estates there were weekly markets, to which nearby villagers would bring produce to sell to the coolies. The planters exercised strict control over what was sold, and who could come from outside to sell or even merely to visit. In 1920 Mahatma Gandhi launched the Indian National Congress's noncooperation programme. This involved a boycott of British cotton and other manufactured goods – much promoted in the estate markets. Naturally, the planters were vehemently opposed to the boycott, and refused to allow Congress workers on to their land. The Congress responded by setting up alternative markets outside the estate perimeters. These were usually quickly closed down by the government. Nevertheless, the interaction of the coolies with the Congress volunteers gave the coolies support.

The 1914–18 World War inflated the price of tea, enabling the tea companies to make large profits, and declare large dividends. It also inflated the price of essentials for the tea estate labourers.

Their wages, however, remained pegged. Throughout the early 1920s there were sporadic strikes for better pay and conditions.

Relations between managers and coolies were poisoned by another blatantly unfair criminal trial. A planter on Khoreal Tea Estate had wanted to take a coolie girl as his mistress. When she refused, he shot her father. The planter was acquitted in a lower court, but the High Court ordered a retrial. A British-dominated jury then acquitted him again. This led to strikes on Khoreal and other tea estates.

The most spectacular withdrawal of labour, however, was in Sylhet. Strikes had failed to improve wages, so over 8,000 labourers, inspired by Gandhi's pleas to people to return to their villages and lead simple lives, walked out. They sold most of their belongings and tried to take trains back to their original homes. They could not afford the fares, and the government refused to help, for it feared an even bigger exodus. The coolies were harassed by the police, and weakened by epidemics. Eventually, Congress and others managed to raise money for transport, and most did reach their villages.

Although the Assam indentured labour system had come to a complete end in 1926, the harsh treatment of labourers who tried to leave continued on some estates. The 1931 report of the Royal Commission on Labour in India recorded many instances, even though witnesses had to give testimony in front of their managers. Many other labourers submitted to illegal force, for as one put it: 'a lot of people do run away, but I have not run away because I am frightened in case I am beaten with a whip. The skin all comes off your back.'

In the late 1920s the Assam tea workers started to unionize. The British Trade Union Congress sent a delegation to investigate and advise. The All-India Trade Union Congress despatched an organizer, but he was arrested and imprisoned. Nevertheless, a number of lightning strikes were arranged, and these forced the estates to increase wages.

The tension was somewhat eased by a decade of good tea prices. By 1930 wages were nearly twice what they had been in 1920. Other strikes against mistreatment forced the planters to moderate their behaviour. From 1930 onwards the Assam coolies were well enough organized to fight for a living wage and to keep serious abuses in check. Conditions in Assam became no worse than on tea estates in the rest of India. Judged against the poverty of much of India, by the end of British rule the tea estate workers were living a better life than many other workers.

Since independence relations between Indian tea estate managers and their labour has often been poor. This has been driven by resentment against low wages, which have tracked low world tea prices. The huge gulf between workers and management, still symbolized by the difference between the labourers' basic housing, and the managers' palatial bungalows (often those of the old British managers), has helped to perpetuate this antagonism. There have been sporadic strikes and riots throughout Ceylon and India, right up to the present day.

Assam, where the legacy is so bitter, has continued to be the most troubled area. For example, in the year 2000, security guards opened fire on a group of protesting workers at Naharkatiya Estate, owned by the Indian Tata Group, and killed a labourer. In 2001, workers on Towkok Estate, owned by the Indian Birla Group, confronted the general manager to protest against one of them being beaten by security personnel. When the meeting got out of control, the manager took out his revolver and shot four labourers including a woman. He was then beaten to death.

Within the limits possible, given current tea prices, many employers in India now try to treat their workers fairly. In December 2001 I visited a large Indian-owned tea estate in the Nilgiri Hills of south India, Chamraj Estate. Sir Robert Stanes, who had cotton mills, coffee plantations and engineering businesses in south India, bought the land in 1923 and it developed into a flourishing estate. In 1960 the Stanes family sold their interests to the Amalgamations Group, chaired by a leading south Indian industrialist, Mr S. Anatharamakrishnan. Chamraj has 2,000 acres of tea.

Wages on Chamraj are low, as they are on almost every tea estate in the world. Wage disputes in 1971 caused several managers to be beaten up by militant workers. In 2001 the basic wage for the women pluckers was only just over £1 a day, although with scope to earn more in the main plucking months. These wages were under threat from the falling tea prices of ordinary teas, down from over 50p. a lb. in 1989 to only 30p. a lb. in 2001. The estate was starting to grow green, organic and decaffeinated teas for niche premium markets. It was also using its higher land – above 6,500 feet – to produce a carefully plucked and processed 'Darjeeling-type' tea.

On my visit I saw the usual small and basic workers' huts. I then had lunch in the extensive and beautifully furnished manager's bungalow, with its perfect lawns of brilliant green surrounded by electric-blue-flowered jacaranda trees. All this I had expected, and it was not much different to when I had been a tea planter thirty years before.

The welfare facilities, however, were a surprise. The group of estates supported four primary schools, and two higher schools, with two hostels for pupils from outlying plantations. The schools were well equipped, and had good computer facilities. There were over 1,300 students in all. Even more impressive was the estate hospital. This employed a qualified doctor and nurses, had x-ray and ultra-sound scanning facilities, and also had a fully equipped operating theatre for visiting surgeons. Workers were

treated free, and non-estate patients from the surrounding area –
some 25,000 a year – were treated for a nominal one rupee
(1½ p.). There was also a company pension scheme. These
philanthropic activities had benefited the business, enabling it to
obtain a premium price for its 'fairtrade' tea, but they had also
made life much better for the workforce.

At the beginning of the twentieth century the British empire was
the world's biggest producer of tea, and British companies controlled the international tea trade. Wealth from these Victorian
enterprises flowed back to their tiny island.

The consumption of tea in Britain had reached new heights.
In 1851, when almost all tea had come from China, consumption
was less than 2 lbs a head; in 1901, fuelled by cheap imperial
imports, it was over 6 lbs and still rising. The growth in the British
population in those fifty years increased demand further, so that
total consumption rose to 259 million lbs. This demand was easily
met by the production of India and Ceylon, and there were 100
million lbs of extra tea available for others to buy.

Tea had become part of the British way of life, both inside and
outside the home. The temperance movement of the mid nineteenth century gave a big impetus to tea drinking. At thousands
of temperance meetings across the nation tea was served as a
statement against alcohol. The reports of these meetings in the
temperance journals hardly ever fail to mention the serving of tea.
On 21 January 1850 the Islington United Teetotal Society 'com-
menced operations for the promotion of our glorious cause with
a tea festival and public meeting'. A week later in Soho the St
Ann's Young Men's Society 'held its first Tea Festival and Public
Meeting'. This obviously had an invigorating effect, for 'when tea
was concluded a few members sung the *Marseillaise*.' (There was
even a Tea Club in Calcutta, although it is doubtful whether it was

part of the temperance movement. It opened in 1819 with a rule: 'the member who slops the table, or spilleth the hot beverage in his neighbour's lap, shall forfeit two annas.')

The great pleasure gardens, which had done so much to popularize tea drinking in the eighteenth century, had mostly closed down in the early nineteenth century, with Vauxhall Gardens finally closing in 1859. Tea, however, was available in many of the coffee houses that catered for those who wanted to avoid the pubs and taverns. Then, in the 1880s coffee gave way to tea, with the advent of the tearoom.

Legend has it that the first tearoom was at the ABC (Aerated Bread Company) bakery shop at London Bridge station. The manageress started to invite a few favoured customers to drink tea in a back room. The success of this experiment, and the potential to sell accompanying food, led ABC to establish over fifty teashops by the end of the decade. Others soon followed suit – Lockharts, Express Dairy, Kardomah – and in 1894 the most famous name of all, Lyons.

Lyons had originally been tobacconists. They had moved into catering by providing refreshments, including tea, at big exhibitions. At an exhibition in Glasgow in 1888 they had built the temporary 'Bishop's Palace Tea Rooms' and clothed their waitresses in Mary Stuart costumes. In 1894 they opened the first Lyons Tea Shop in fashionable Piccadilly. Next year they opened fourteen more branches; by 1900 there were 250 Lyons Tea Shops. The phenomenal success of Lyons for over half a century was well explained in one of their reports:

Hitherto, there had been nowhere for Mama and the children to have a cup of tea or a midday meal. Prices too had been extortionate. In short, Lyons introduced to Londoners, and later to the provinces, good cheap food with exceptional smartness and cleanliness: it also gave fresh dignity to the occupation of catering. The new white and gold tea shops with their uniformed and attractive waitresses, shone forth in a London drab with drinking dens, dingy coffee houses and 'Slap Bangs' which were staffed by slipshod waiters and unkempt girls serving beer, coffee or tea.

Lyons set the standard, but there were cheaper imitations and grander ones. Perhaps the most elegant of all, and still functioning now, was the Willow Tea Rooms in Glasgow, designed by Charles Rennie Mackintosh in 1903. This had his famously high-backed silver chairs, a pink chandelier, and wall panels of beaded silk. The very grandest tearooms were in the expensive hotels, with gilded ceilings, palm courts, and elegant tea dances. All these establishments, simple and grand, sold much besides tea, but the main attraction was the tea.

It was an obvious step to move from selling cups of tea to selling leaf tea for use in the home. Lyons had begun selling tea to the public when catering to exhibitions. In 1904 they started to wholesale their own label packet-tea to grocers. By 1907 they had a network of 15,000 outlets.

Packets of tea were first sold in about 1826, by John Horniman. He offered tea in a hygienic foil-lined packet, safe from adulteration, and of a guaranteed weight. The name on the packet also promised a standard good-quality product. Grocers were at first reluctant to stock the packets, since it gave them less scope for making a profit than by making up their own blends. However, by massive advertising and selling through chemists and confectioners, Horniman created public demand, and packeted tea gradually invaded the market. The company prospered throughout the nineteenth century, and was eventually bought out by Lyons in 1918. John Horniman also invented a crude machine for filling the packets, but hand-filled packets of tea dominated the trade until well into the twentieth century. Thousands of women, earning low wages, filled the packets more cheaply than by machine.

Lyons was one of the 'big four' tea brands that dominated the British wholesale and retail trade for much of the twentieth century. The others were Brooke Bond, the Co-op, and Ty-phoo. Lipton continued to be a significant business, but gradually lost momentum as Sir Thomas Lipton grew old. Lipton's major mistake was to concentrate on his own retail shops. He opened over 600, but other shopkeepers saw this as competition and opted to stock other brands. Sales withered away, Lipton's own shops began to close because of bad management, and the Lipton name slowly disappeared in Britain. In other countries it remained a successful wholesaler, so that now Lipton's name is famous for tea almost everywhere except in the land of his birth.

A similar, but worse, fate overtook Mazawattee. Founded in about 1870, as Densham and Sons, it went straight into packet-tea wholesaling. With the striking brand name, Mazawattee, combined with aggressive advertising it soon became a market leader. It vied with Lipton in trumpeting that it had just paid the biggest weekly tea-duty cheque – both companies manipulated the figures to suggest they had over half the total British market. Disaster struck in 1905. Densham went abroad on sick leave, and in his absence the other directors decided to open a chain of lavishly equipped shops. They acquired 164 premises. As they began to open, Mazawattee retailers started a boycott. Densham returned hastily and re-assumed control. He closed all the shops – which had only been open for two months – but the company had lost so much goodwill that it never recovered.

Brooke Bond was founded by Arthur Brooke in 1869. There was never a Bond – the name Brooke, Bond & Company was invented to give the enterprise prestige. Brooke began as a retailer with a few shops in Lancashire and Yorkshire. He never really expanded the retail business, using it merely to test public reaction

Lipton advertisement, c. 1894

to his blends, and he concentrated on wholesaling. Like the other 'big four', Brooke Bond relied heavily on advertising. To suggest that its tea might aid digestion it launched the brand Pre-Gest-T. This was later shortened to P.G. Tips, and famously advertised with chimpanzees' tea parties. Another sales-aid was the 'dividend'. Stamps on each packet could be stuck on to a special card, which when full could be redeemed for cash or gifts.

Brooke Bond's promotions were entirely legitimate, but other companies were not so straight. At the turn of the century there was a rash of schemes to attract the gullible. Nelson and Company was the most notorious. They offered pensions to women who became widowed, in return for the purchase of regular small quantities of tea. These 'pension teas' became so popular that the company managed to attract 250,000 customers. At first, the company could pay the annual £25 pensions out of its increased profits. Within five years, however, there were 19,000 widows. In the court cases that followed insolvency, it was estimated that to fund these pensions the company would have needed £30 million, but it had assets of only £20,000.

Brooke Bond's dividend stamps sought to emulate the main attraction of the Co-op. The Co-operative Wholesale Society was founded in Manchester in 1863 as a manufacturer and wholesaler to the 500 co-operative societies that had been established across Britain. These societies were owned by the members who were their customers, and these received a profit dividend every year. The more you spent at the co-op, the bigger your dividend. This was a powerful incentive to buy Co-op tea. By 1912 the Co-op was selling 25 million lbs of tea. It continued to be a major player for the first half of the twentieth century, but then began to lose market share to the aggressive marketing of its three main rivals.

The other 'big four' tea seller was Ty-phoo. The Sumner family had run an apothecary and grocery business in Birmingham since 1820. John Sumner became quite a specialist in tea and published *A Popular Treatise on Tea* in 1863. Throughout the nineteenth century the fashion was for whole leaf teas, and the smaller grades of broken leaf produced in the manufacturing process were available very cheaply. John Sumner junior, reputedly encouraged by his sister who had found small-leaf tea good for her digestion, decided to buy some chests of small 'fannings' from Ceylon and packet them.

With the alliterative, oriental-sounding brand name Ty.phoo Tipps (the full stop later became a hyphen; the double p was a misprint, later imitated by other companies), the tea sold well. There was no blending – the tea was shipped direct from Ceylon and merely packaged. In contrast to the other tea companies, Typhoo offered just the one blend, at the one price. Exploiting the supposed digestive advantages of the smaller leaf, they advertised that their tea was 'free from injurious gallo-tannic acid', and initially marketed it largely through chemists. Such was the belief in its medicinal qualities that 4,000 doctors supported a successful campaign to exempt it from the pooled tea scheme in the First World War.

These four great tea companies grew to dominate the British tea market. With the advantages of bulk buying, combined with massive spending on advertising, they gradually squeezed out most of the smaller companies. Only the very small or very specialist tea businesses, such as Twinings, managed to avoid annihilation. The 'big four' were themselves not immune from market forces, and became involved in mergers and acquisitions that incorporated them into multinational corporations. Their brands, however, were what counted, and these names continued, largely unaffected by changes of corporate ownership. The government investigated the tea monopoly in 1970 and found that the four brands – Brooke Bond, Typhoo, Lyons and the Co-op – had captured 85 per cent of the total market.

Although three of the four giant tea packers had bought tea estates, as had Lipton, the vast majority of their tea was bought at auction. Following the end of the East India Company's monopoly on imports from China in 1834, the auctions of tea at East India House (which stood where the new Lloyds insurance building is today) came to an end. The Company was allowed to sell its stock in hand, and the last sale was in July 1835.

No arrangements had been made to sell the tea being shipped from China by the new merchants. The first auction, on 8 October 1835, was hurriedly organized and held at Caraway's coffee house. So many merchants, brokers and dealers turned up that the auction was moved to a nearby dancing academy in Change Alley. The first lot that was offered for sale provoked a farce. There was some doubt as to whether it was genuine tea that had been passed by the government inspector. Amid cries of 'Unfit for sale except as poison', and 'Withdraw! Withdraw!' it was removed from sale.

The dancing academy was obviously not a suitable venue for such a heavily traded commodity. It was agreed to move the auctions to the London Commercial Salerooms. These salerooms had been built in 1811 to provide accommodation for the produce dealers in the area, mostly traders in wine and sugar. The building was on a grand scale, supposedly having been modelled on a Roman temple. It was in Mincing Lane, between Fenchurch Street and the Thames. The first auction was on 20 November 1834. Mincing Lane then became famous as the hub of the tea industry of Britain and of much of the rest of the world for the next 136 years.

Many of the tea brokers and dealers had offices near the old East India House, and it took some time before they migrated to Mincing Lane. Gradually, however, Mincing Lane became paramount. Most tea that entered Britain came to the Pool of London, and most of the tea companies were based in the City of London. The Co-op relocated its tea operations from Manchester to London. Ty-phoo remained in Birmingham, but nearly all its tea was bought through Mincing Lane. Most of the other companies, large and small, had warehouses within a mile or two of Mincing Lane.

The World War of 1914–18 caused massive disruption for the tea industry. For two years business continued much as usual, then German submarines started to sink British shipping. Queues became a feature of British life, tea prices rose, and people began to complain of profiteering. The government fixed the price of the cheaper 40 per cent of all tea imports. Meanwhile, however, these imports had sharply declined, for the government had classified tea with 'luxury foodstuffs and drinks'. It was soon realized that tea was essential to maintain the nation's morale. The government took over its importation, and imposed price control on 90 per cent of sales. This 'pooled' tea was crudely divided into four grades. In 1918 all tea became 'government tea' in just three price categories. Rationing was also introduced, with a weekly allowance of two ounces.

Two ounces of tea a week was a very meagre ration. In peacetime, Lyons shops had used a pound of tea to make 85 cups. This generous measure would have only provided a cup and a half a day from a two-ounce ration. A more frugal user might have squeezed two or three cups a day or even more from the ration, but the liquor would have been thin.

Auctions resumed at the end of the war in 1919. Consumption of tea, thought to have reached saturation point, rose to a peak of 9½ lbs a head annually by 1931. The London Commercial Salesrooms became too cramped, so the tea men decided to construct a building of their own. A huge complex of offices, with an imposing auction auditorium, was built on the corner of Mincing Lane and named Plantation House. At the opening in 1937, chests of Assam tea were unloaded at St Katharine's Dock, and delivered to Plantation House by elephant.

All this concentration of tea in the City of London was asking for trouble when the Second World War broke out in 1939.

Amazingly enough, though, very little tea was damaged in enemy raids. Mincing Lane itself was less lucky. On the night of 10 May 1941, over half the tea brokers' offices were destroyed.

The tea industry had planned for war and, remembering the previous conflict, expected rationing and the government pooling of tea. Two days after war broke out, the government took over all tea stocks, and put the brokers in charge of distribution. From the very beginning, the government regarded tea as essential to morale, and made every effort to maintain imports. Nevertheless, in the enemy blockade tea stocks dropped to a quarter of their pre-war level.

Following the closure of the Mediterranean to British shipping in 1940, tea was rationed. In exchange for coupons adults were given two ounces of tea a week – the same allowance as in the previous war. At the work place extra was given to those deemed to be on essential work – fire fighters and railwaymen, harvesters and steelworkers. The over seventies received an extra ounce from 1944. When the war ended in 1946, rationing continued – the allowance occasionally going up to two and a half ounces – and was not finally removed until 1952. Tea was never pooled for sale by the government. The Minister of Food, Lord Woolton, a great advocate of tea drinking, was strongly against uniformity: 'If we had given up during the war the blending of tea, the use of brands, we should have lost something of our national life.'

The Second World War was quickly followed by loss of empire. India and Ceylon, where the British had built up massive tea plantations, and which had supplied them and the world with most of their tea, gained independence. These countries could no longer be expected to export tea profits back to Britain.

Auctions at Plantation House resumed in 1952. The auction auditorium was now too big, since the quantity of tea being auctioned within the tea-producing countries had vastly increased. Auctions had been established on a regular basis in Calcutta from 1861. Initially, very little tea had been sold there, and even that had often been re-auctioned in Mincing Lane. With India's independence in 1947, there was a strong feeling that India should control its own tea sales, and most Indian teas were subsequently sent for auction in Calcutta or Cochin.

The Assam companies began to resent the Bengalis taking their percentage, and they set up an auction floor of their own in Gauhati. Other tea-growing areas then established their own auction floors, so that now almost every tea district in India has its own auctions. Ceylon almost ceased to send tea to the London auctions, and sold it in Colombo. All these changes were accelerated by improved communications. It had become possible to airfreight tea samples before an auction to anywhere in the world, and for bids to be made by phone or fax. The major British tea packers also deserted the London auctions, because the cost of handling and warehousing tea in London had risen, and it had become attractive for the packers to buy directly from the overseas producers.

In 1971 the London auctions moved from Plantation House to the much smaller Sir John Lyon House. It was a mundane 1960s block on the Thames, downstream from Blackfriars Bridge, with none of the architectural splendour of earlier venues. Soon, even this building proved too large for the rapidly diminishing business. In 1990 the auctions moved to the London Chamber of Commerce. It was there that, on 29 June 1998, the London tea brokers held their final auction. It was the end of a ritual that had lasted for 311 years.

Tea drinking and marketing in the twentieth century was fundamentally changed by an American invention – the tea bag. It is said that about 1908 a New York tea dealer, Thomas Sullivan, started to send out samples of tea to his clients in small silk bags. Some thought they were meant to be infused (a not dissimilar process to using the already invented metal infusers) by immersing the bag in hot water. They told Sullivan that the silk was not very satisfactory, as the mesh was too fine, and he subsequently issued the first proper tea bags in gauze sachets.

Tea bags soon became popular in America, but they took a much longer time to cross the Atlantic. British travellers described the horror of American tea bags in tepid water. Tetleys introduced the tea bag on to the British market in 1935, but it was not until the mid 1950s that sales began to take off. By 1970 tea bags still had only 10 per cent of the British market. Sales then rose at a phenomenal rate. By 1985 they had 68 per cent of the market, and by 2000 about 90 per cent.

Tea bags were easy to use, and they left no mess. They turned tea from being a drink of ceremony into a drink of convenience. They enabled the multinational tea packers to standardize the product. This standardization, massively promoted by advertising, greatly reduced interest in fine teas. Purchasing a box of tea bags was far removed from a visit to an Edwardian grocer where the customer could linger over a choice from a multitude of teas.

Tea bags could be filled with very broken leaf or even dust. This could be sold at a price which loose tea could not match. Weight for weight the liquor was stronger, and made more cups. The dust infused fast, so that the tea was 'quick brew', which suited a convenience society. Tea factories across the world changed their manufacturing process to supply more of the broken leaf and dust that filled the tea bags. The days of finely grading teas came to an end on all but a few prized estates. 'Orthodox' teas were largely superseded by the new 'CTC' teas – initials which stood for Cut, Tear and Curl. Tea manufacture became a continuous conveyor-belt process. The withered green leaf was first pushed through the appropriately named McTear Rotorvane – a giant mincing machine that squeezed and then chopped the leaf. From there it was usually fed into a CTC machine. A popular alternative to the CTC machine was the

Lawrie Tea Processor, which pulverized the rotorvaned tea with hammers.

Tetleys grew fast by championing the tea bag. The other big tea packers soon followed. Such has been the power of the tea bag, that even among those who do prefer fine teas, most now buy them in bags. Twinings and Lipton now sell most of their Earl Grey and Darjeeling teas in bags. Tetleys was taken over by an American corporation in 1961, but became British-owned again in 1972 when it was acquired by Lyons.

In 1978 Lyons Tetley was itself taken over by Allied Breweries. Of the other big packers only the declining Co-op managed to stay independent. Typhoo was absorbed by Cadbury-Schweppes; Twinings by Associated British Foods; Brooke Bond and Lipton by Unilever. Tea had become just another beverage in the armoury of the food multinationals.

The food companies tried to imitate their success with instant coffee by marketing instant tea. This found uses in the iced and dispensed tea markets, but did not achieve big sales. Decaffeinated tea captured a small market. Organic tea, promoted to meet concerns about the harmful chemicals in many foods, was more promising. A number of estates switched some of their existing gardens to organic production by leaving them free from chemical applications for the stipulated three years.

The extensive and expensive promotions of the big four tea packers seemed to make their capture of almost the whole market inevitable. Only one force managed to challenge their supremacy – the supermarkets.

Although some of the big supermarket companies were founded in the nineteenth century, they did not really begin to capture a large share of the grocery market until well into the twentieth century. The Sainsbury family opened their first shop in

Drury Lane, Covent Garden, in 1869. At the outbreak of war in 1914 they had a chain of 115 shops. Tea was an important line, and in 1920 Sainbury's introduced their own label tea. This was sold as an extra item, but only complemented and never supplanted sales of tea bearing the popular labels of the big packers.

Tesco started much later. Its founder, Jack Cohen, began as a London street-market trader in 1919. He had a shaky start, lost money on soap, and the bank closed his account in 1924. The markets were tough areas to do business. Cohen's nephews, who helped him, were told: 'Hold your hands over the money, and, if necessary, be prepared to run.' Cohen persevered, and he bought up bargains wherever he could find them – jam, metal polish, fish paste. He repackaged goods where labels were damaged, or packets torn. He became known as a 'grocery doctor' who would take over unwanted lines of stock. He discovered some cheap tea in Mincing Lane, and bought four chests, at a price of 9*d* per lb. This he put into ½ lb. packets, which were priced at 6*d* and sold well. He needed a brand name, and took the initials of the tea dealer, T. E. Stockwell, together with the first two letters of his own surname, to make Tesco.

Soon, Jack Cohen was selling fifty chests of Tesco tea a week. He then moved into other lines. In the 1930s Tesco started to open conventional shops, and by the end of the decade had over 100. In the 1940s Tesco began to experiment with self-service stores, an idea Cohen had seen in America. The lower overheads, and the lower prices that followed, revolutionized the British grocery trade. In the 1950s Tesco began to take over smaller chains of grocers. Cohen's shops, and those of imitators who had also introduced self-service, grew in size and became known as 'supermarkets'.

Jack Cohen also led the attack against retail price maintenance. RPM, whereby manufacturers fixed the retail price of their goods, had been a feature of the British retail market since the late nineteenth century. Any attempt by shops to discount goods

was discouraged, and could lead to legal action. Many retailers, particularly smaller ones, supported RPM. They felt that it gave them a 'fair' profit margin. Cohen thought it kept margins artificially high, and that it discouraged competition. Tesco advertised heavily against RPM. It persuaded its customers, and eventually the government, that removing RPM would be in the public interest. RPM was largely abolished by legislation in 1964–5. The supermarkets then cut their margins, thus making many smaller grocers, who could not buy in bulk, unviable, and so they had to close.

Tea was a grocery line that was particularly exposed to cost cutting. In the battle to capture market share the big supermarkets would often use 'loss leaders' – popular lines that were offered so cheaply that no profit was made on their sale. A favourite loss leader was tea. As a result, many small tea retailers were driven out of business. The supermarkets tried to push their own label teas, by cost cutting and other methods. Nevertheless, they found that they still had to stock and sell the big packers' brands, for these had a very loyal clientele built up by massive advertising and by blending a standard but distinctive tea.

As the twentieth century progressed, the number of supermarket chains diminished, and their share of the grocery market increased. By the year 2000 the big supermarket groups had over 80 per cent of all food business, including tea. The business was dominated by four big names – Tesco, Sainsbury's, Asda (which had been acquired by the American retailer, Wal-Mart), and Safeways. The biggest was Tesco, whose profits exceeded £1 billion.

The Second World War was not a good time for the tea estates in India. Many managers went off to fight in the war; construction work on military roads, bridges and airfields drained away large numbers of tea estate workers. Wages for those still employed rose sharply, in line with wartime inflation. The profits of the tea companies became minimal.

Just before independence in 1947 India was partitioned. A few tea estates were situated in the east of the new country of Pakistan. This part of Pakistan broke away in 1971 to become Bangladesh. These estates in Sylhet and Chittagong were important to the impoverished Bangladesh economy, but only represented 7 per cent of total Indian production. The British owned about half of these estates when they abandoned the subcontinent, and they still owned them at the end of the century.

Tea companies with estates in India fell into two categories – the sterling companies, which were incorporated in Britain; and the rupee companies, which were incorporated in India. Almost all were ultimately controlled by British companies, but rupee companies had access to Indian capital. When India was British, the distinction was not particularly important, for the two currencies were easily exchangeable. After independence, convertibility ceased, and the exchange control authorities regarded the rupee companies as 'Indian', and their profits as something to be kept in India.

Following on independence, the Indian government began to plan extensive nationalization of key industries. Tea featured in some of the recommendations, and many British companies took fright and began to run their estates down. They spent as little as they could on maintenance and renewal, and sent the inflated 'profit' back to Britain. They also sold some estates to Indians. Various other legislation over the next two decades restricted profits, and prompted further sales. By the 1970s about two thirds of the total tea acreage belonged to Indian companies.

The sterling companies amalgamated into large groups to deal better with government and the bureaucracy. In the 1970s, under the direction of the aggressively socialist Prime Minister, Indira Gandhi, India took further measures to bring the remaining companies under its control. This affected not only the sterling companies but also the rupee companies that had more than 40 per cent of their shares controlled by foreigners. All companies had to become rupee companies, with Indians owning a minimum of 26 per cent of the shares.

This catalogue of attacks on the British tea interest might have been expected to drive it out of India. However, it proved remarkably resilient. The companies that were sold were, in general, those with the poorer land or less successful management. The yield on the remaining British estates remained consistently higher than on the Indian-owned estates so that, although acreage fell, production was proportionately less affected. Production of tea in India trebled after independence, to reach 1,730 million lbs by the end of the second millennium. It is difficult to unravel how much of this was ultimately owned by British interests, but it was probably about half.

Furthermore, with the brands they controlled, the British captured much of the wholesale market within India. As the population rose past 1 billion there was a massive expansion of tea sales. So much so that India, which was the world's largest producer of tea, became only the third biggest exporter. Three quarters of all the tea produced in India was now drunk there. The biggest wholesaler was a subsidiary of the Anglo-Dutch corporation, Unilever, which owned the Brooke Bond and Lipton brands.

The British did not have it entirely their own way. Tata Tea, part of a huge Indian conglomerate, accumulated about sixty tea estates. On the wholesale side it worked closely with Tetley, the British company that pioneered the tea bag. In 2000, Tata bought control of Tetley with its worldwide brand.

On 26 June 2002 the Indian government, concerned that its tea estates needed rejuvenation and fresh investment, reversed its policy of Indianization. Foreign investors were once again permitted to make new investments in Indian tea plantations, and to keep a 100 per cent interest. Given the huge British involvement in the Indian wholesale market, it was expected that British companies would take advantage of this liberalization to increase their investment in India further.

At the beginning of the twentieth century, tea was the most important crop in Ceylon, responsible for more than half of all export earnings. This situation continued throughout the century. There was only a modest increase in tea acreage during the remaining years of British rule, but improved agricultural techniques doubled the crop.

When Ceylon achieved independence from Britain in 1948, there were 550,000 acres of tea on the island. Under the government of the United National Party business carried on much as before, with the British controlling most of the agency houses that managed the tea plantations and the sale and export of tea.

The impact of independence was severe for the tea estate Tamils. The United National Party was keen to restrict their citizenship, their right of residence, and particularly their right to vote, even though many had been settled in Ceylon for generations. This was partly to appease anti-Tamil sentiment among the Sinhalese, but also because the UNP feared an electoral alliance between the estate Tamils and Sinhalese socialists. Estate Tamil voting rights had been restricted even under the British, but the Tamils had still managed to elect several MPs in the tea districts. Legislation after independence took away more of their rights, so that eventually only about 10 per cent of them could vote. These moves embittered the estate Tamils, especially as the other Tamils on the island, those whose ancestors had come to Ceylon over 2,000 years before, were also suffering. Both groups of Tamils found their language marginalized by the government, and suffered discrimination in education and employment. This eventually led to a civil war, but meanwhile many estate Tamils left unwillingly for an often difficult life in India.

Ceylon's powerful neighbour, India, had originally insisted that any Tamils with five years' residence in Ceylon should be given citizenship and the vote. In the face of Ceylon's intransigence, India agreed to a deal in 1964 by which Ceylon would give citizenship to 300,000 Tamils, and India would take back 525,000 over a fifteen-year period. Another 150,000 Tamils were not covered by this agreement, but in 1974 the two governments agreed to take 75,000 each. It was a shabby end for many who had devoted their lives – and whose parents and grandparents had devoted their lives – to making tea Ceylon's biggest asset.

With the accession of a socialist government in 1956, the British tea estates came under pressure. Company taxation was increased and the export of after-tax profits back to Britain was restricted. There was also talk of outright nationalization. In response to these threats, many British estates were sold into local ownership. The proportion of foreign-owned estates, mostly British, dropped from 70 per cent to 31 per cent.

Nationalization finally arrived in the early 1970s. Small owners were allowed to keep fifty acres for each member of their immediate family, but other land was taken away. The state acquired two thirds of the total tea acreage. Although managerial staff and the workforce were generally left in place, increased bureaucracy and political interference took their toll. Production dropped and quality fell. The British companies that had been nationalized received very little compensation. Angered by this they ceased to be major buyers at the Colombo auctions.

Following land reform, there was a large increase in the proportion of tea grown on smallholdings. At the end of the century this accounted for nearly half the total acreage. There were 200,000 smallholders, the great majority growing only an acre or perhaps two of tea.

In 1993 the United National Party returned to power on a

platform of privatization. The government tea estates were initially put out to private management, and later offered for sale. Controls over the marketing and export of tea were lifted. British companies took advantage of these opportunities, but Sri Lankan companies became the dominant force. James Finlay became the biggest British owner and manager, with about 5 per cent of total production. By 2000 production of both estate and smallholder tea was rising again, and stood at a record 675 million lbs. Quality had also improved. Further expansion is being inhibited by a shortage of labour.

Ceylon (which became Sri Lanka in 1972, but retains the name Ceylon for many of its brands) exports over 90 per cent of its production, and is the world's biggest tea exporter. In the past Ceylon was very much dependent on the British tea market. In recent years there has been a policy of diversifying sales, and building up new markets. Britain now only takes a mere 3½ per cent of Ceylon's exports, putting it well behind the Russian Federation, the United Arab Emirates and Turkey. Much of this tea is not shipped in bulk, but already packeted, which brings a bigger profit to Ceylon.

Events in Ceylon, and to a much smaller extent in India, forced the British to reconsider their global tea policy. In the nineteenth century, when China had seemed an unreliable supplier, the British had established tea in India and Ceylon. Similarly, following the loss of India and Ceylon, the British turned to a part of the globe that they still controlled – Africa.

The planting of tea in Britain's African colonies had begun in Nyasaland (now Malawi) in the very late nineteenth century. It was always clear that given the amount of suitable land, tea there would never be a very large industry. The possibilities in Tanganyika (now Tanzania) and Uganda were also limited. The British therefore focused on another of their African colonies – Kenya. Tea had been grown on an experimental basis in Kenya since 1903. Some European farmers tried to plant it on a small scale, but by 1924 the country was only producing 1,000 lbs of tea a year. Two British companies – Brooke Bond and James Finlay – then transformed production.

In 1922 Brooke Bond established a branch in Kenya to market its teas. By 1925 it had captured 60 per cent of the whole East African market. In 1924 it bought 1,000 acres of land near Limuru, with the intention of both planting tea and also buying in tea for manufacture from neighbouring smallholders.

In 1925, James Finlay & Company arrived in Kenya. James Finlay was an old established firm with estates and managing agencies in India and Ceylon. It saw an opportunity to buy land cheaply. After the First World War the Kenyan government had made land available to British ex-servicemen – a highly contentious policy that was much resented, since Africans claimed ownership over much of it. The British East Africa Disabled Officers Colony was given 25,000 acres of 'surplus' land near Kericho. The scheme was badly managed, and ridiculed for its quasi-military discipline and regulation by bugle call. The arrival of fifty-five ex-officers, who intended to grow flax, coincided with the collapse of the world flax market, and there was not the necessary expertise to grow alternative crops. The scheme went into liquidation, and James Finlay was able to acquire 20,000 acres of land on a ninety-nine-year lease. The other 5,000 acres were bought by Brooke Bond, which later acquired additional acreage.

The soil and climate of Kericho and Limuru proved excellent for tea. The land was relatively high, lying between 5,000 and 7,400 feet above sea level. The nights were cool, which produced tea of good quality. Yields, too, were high. By 1947, Brooke Bond and James Finlay had planted out about 5,000 acres of tea each, and a further 6,000 acres had been planted out on smaller estates. Spurred on by events in India and Ceylon, the two British companies dramatically increased their acreage right until Kenya became independent in 1963. They continued to plant further until 1976, after which the Kenyan government blocked future expansion. As of 2000 the British companies had over 50,000 acres of tea between them, with Brooke Bond, still the leading brand in Kenya, the biggest owner.

In the 1960s there was another very significant development – the establishment of the Kenya Tea Development Authority to encourage African smallholders to grow tea. Funded by the World Bank and other international agencies, it built factories to process the leaf from small plots of tea that farmers grew alongside more traditional crops. Most of these farmers planted out less than one acre, but so many took to it that the total acreage became huge. Excellent management, hard work by the farmers and a willingness to embrace modern methods of horticulture made the project the most successful in the world. As early as 1975 smallholder tea represented a third of Kenya's overall production. By 1988, the combined production of over 150,000 smallholders had overtaken that of the big British estates. At the end of the second millennium there were 170,000 acres of smallholder tea. Much of this tea was auctioned in Mombassa by British companies, and bought and sold through old-established British brokers.

Kenya exports about 95 per cent of its tea. This, together with the phenomenal expansion of acreage, has had the extraordinary effect of making Kenya the world's second biggest tea exporter.

At the end of the twentieth century the British had a much bigger role in world tea than could have been expected after the collapse of their empire. This was despite the increase in consumption in other countries, which left the British themselves only taking 4½ per cent of world production. In 2000, British companies still owned tea estates in most of the major tea-producing countries, and British companies still traded huge volumes of tea world-wide. James Finlay, for example, grew over 100 million lbs of tea on its plantations in Kenya, Sri Lanka, Uganda and Bangladesh, and traded in double that amount. Most importantly, British brands dominated the world's markets. Unilever alone, through its Brooke Bond and Lipton brands, had sales of over 700 million lbs. This was one sixth of all the world's black tea.

The Chinese are once again a power in the world's tea trade. In the nineteenth century the British tea enterprises severely damaged the Chinese tea industry, and the Opium Wars left much of the country in anarchy. During the first half of the twentieth century China was plagued by turbulent politics and civil war. Green tea exports also suffered as many western countries took to drinking black tea. Tea production in China, which had peaked at 296 million lbs in 1886, fell to only 41 million lbs in 1920. However, in the second half of the twentieth century production and consumption of Chinese green tea rose fast. China is now the world's second largest tea producer, with an output of over 1,500 million lbs. It exports about a third of this, and could become a bigger exporter as tariffs are lowered under pressure from the World Trade Organisation. There are also new opportunities for green tea, which is seen by many as a healthier drink. Chinese tea can be expected to have a serious impact on an already saturated tea market.

The huge increase in world tea production which occurred in the second half of the twentieth century was due less to the increased acreage than to improved horticultural techniques, especially that of cloning. Traditionally, tea was grown from seed taken from specially selected seed-bearing trees. These trees took many years to mature, which made improvement by further selection a very slow process. Cross-fertilization often produced many seeds of poor quality. Cloning bypassed both these problems.

Cloning, or vegetative propagation, of tea had been pioneered by the Japanese in the nineteenth century. In essence, cloning is simple – cuttings about an inch long are taken from the shoots of freshly pruned bushes, planted in a nursery, and allowed to root. Several hundred cuttings can be taken from a single bush, and all the progeny will be identical. When developed, the small bushes are transplanted out into the fields.

Selection has become a major part of tea research. In a traditional field of tea it can be seen by a casual observer that some bushes are more vigorous than others. This enables a first selection to be made. From this selection the bushes whose cuttings root and develop faster are chosen. Selection can also be made for such characteristics as resistance to pests and disease, or response to fertilizer. Tea research institutes have even developed miniature 'factories' to process and evaluate the leaf from individual bushes. This selective propagation provides the types of tea the modern market requires, and with much higher yields. Fields that produce over 2,000 lbs of made tea an acre are now commonplace, and small acreages of experimental tea have yielded many times that. As old fields are taken out of commission and replanted with clonal tea, world tea production can be expected to rise sharply.

Tea production was founded on very cheap labour, and continues to rely on very cheap labour. For example, the wage in 2000 for India's industry's 1 million workers was equivalent to about £1 a day, in Sri Lanka it was about 90p. a day; in Malawi only 50p. In all these countries there were people worse off, otherwise it would be impossible to recruit workers. Nevertheless, these were barely living wages, and many people were better off in other industries. Why were tea wages so low? The answer was simple – oversupply.

If the output of tea were controlled, as is the output of oil, the price paid to the producer would increase. Tea is not, of course, as important as oil, but it is a luxury many would not like to do without. If sensibly pursued, an agreement between the producing countries would be unlikely to raise the retail price of tea so fast as to reduce sales drastically. The auction price of ordinary teas in the producing country is currently only about 40p. a lb. The retail price in a UK supermarket is between £1 80p. and £2 70p. Freight, packaging and distribution costs make up much of the pre-profit price. Doubling the price of auctioned tea would only increase the retail price by 50p. or 60p. This would hardly provoke a consumers' boycott. In fact, over the last decade the price of auctioned tea has fallen sharply.

There have been attempts to restrict tea production in the past. In the world recession of the 1930s, tea prices fell dramatically. This prompted the major producers – India, Ceylon and the Netherlands East Indies – to enter into International Tea Agreements, which restricted production to 85 per cent of normal. These measures were fairly successful, until rendered superfluous by the Second World War. Another agreement restricted output in 1970–1 to 94 per cent of normal, with moderate success. In spite of these precedents the producing countries have failed to reach agreement since.

There has been much talk in the last decade of 'fairtrade' tea. There have been laudable attempts to channel consumers towards fairtrade brands, which guarantee that the tea is produced on estates that have certain minimum standards for their workers. Labels such as Teadirect have been gaining in popularity, but still only have a small fraction of the market. Such schemes deserve support, and it is to be hoped they will capture more sales. However, the prices these labels charge have to be reasonably competitive, and they are unlikely to raise wages significantly in a world of overproduction.

Under pressure from consumers, and the fairtrade movement,

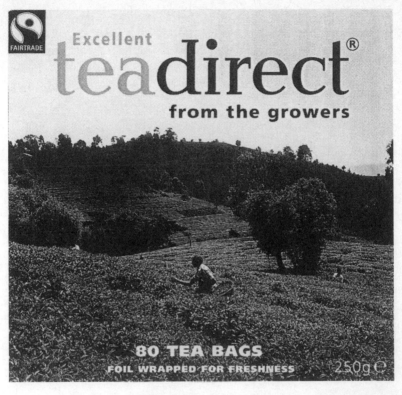

© Cafédirect Limited

some of the major packers are also monitoring the conditions on the tea estates from which they obtain their supplies. This is a welcome development. However, as many of these packers also own tea estates on which they are expanding production, it is doubtful if they are really committed to redressing overproduction and the consequent low wages.

World tea consumption is currently increasing by 1 per cent a year, but production is increasing by 2 per cent a year. In general, buyers will always try to obtain tea for as low a price as possible.

To obtain a fair deal for the tea estates and their workers, production needs to be reduced gradually, so as to bring supply and demand into equilibrium. This can only be done by inter-governmental cooperation, but there is no sign of this. Tea prices, and the wages of the estate workers, seem set to fall even further.

SEVEN

A Year in Africa

*The wind of change is blowing through this continent,
and, whether we like it or not, this growth of national
consciousness is a political fact.*

British Prime Minister, HAROLD MACMILLAN –
Cape Town, February 1960

Each day we went round George's estate, Satemwa; and mine, Mwalanthunzi. We started early. A servant arrived at my bedside with tea at five-fifteen. As the sky lightened, I would struggle out from beneath the mosquito net for a shower. The water was very cold – from the mountainside – for George was a great believer in cold showers. As soon as I was dressed – khaki shorts and shirt, up-to-the-knee socks and desert boots – we were off. Normally we went to Mwalanthunzi first, and would be there by six a.m., just as the first workers were entering the fields. Early as it was, the tea bushes were a dazzling green; the sky a deep clear blue. The crystal clear air seemed to magnify the nearby mountain, so that each tree stood out.

I had arrived in January, at the height of the rainy season. The rains normally began in November, were at their greatest in January and February, and petered out by May. Mwalanthunzi received about 90 inches of rain a year but this was not well spread out, and most of it fell in these six months. The days would start perfectly clear, then gradually huge cumulus clouds, which expanded as I looked, would fill the sky. It would rain in

219

the early afternoon, so hard that in seconds I could be soaked through. Then it would clear again, and soon it would be hot enough for the roads to steam. Ten minutes later my clothes would be dry.

Mwalanthunzi had 500 acres of tea, 400 of these were mature and 100 not fully grown. They were in separate fields of around 20 acres. There were about 500 labourers – 350 men, 50 women, and 100 teenage children. Each gang of about fifty had a foreman, called a *capito*, and there were other men who were clerks, builders, watchmen and cooks. Half the men and children and a few of the women were plucking tea. The rest were weeding.

George and I would squeeze our way gently between the tea bushes, trying not to get our legs cut by the sharply pruned lower branches, to arrive behind the row of workers as they pushed across the field. We avoided coming in from the front, for the workers would be driving any snakes before them. George would exhort the *capitos* to ensure that only 'two leaves and a bud' were plucked. Other older darker leaves on the top were broken off and discarded so as to keep the bush flat. We would look in the wicker baskets that were slung over the pluckers' backs to monitor the quality, but the main check would be when the leaf was weighed in.

A plucking basket held about 40 lbs of leaf, which would eventually produce about 8 lbs of made tea. The basic 'task' was about 40 lbs, depending on the amount of new shoots on the bushes. For plucking that quantity the worker received the basic wage, and then would be paid extra for any excess. This could double the wage of a fast plucker, but usually it was rather less. In the dry season, when the flush was not so prolific, workers made very little extra, or they might even revert to being paid the daily wage.

Weeding, pruning and many other operations were all done on a similar piecework system. It was the job of the manager, in consultation with the *capitos*, to fix the basic daily 'task'. This was the manager's trickiest job. Fortunately, I had done a fair amount of piecework myself, picking fruit in my school holidays in the Vale of Evesham, so I was conscious of the difficulties.

Weeding was much harder work than plucking, and much of this was done by women. The traditional hoes were of Portuguese origin – T shaped, with a thirty-inch wooden shaft at the end of a heavy sharpened iron plate. The women had to bend low to wield these heavy implements. The tall weeds left by the recent strike were already woody and tough. There were castor-oil plants ten feet high. Once the sun was fully up, the women were continually bathed in sweat. It was extraordinary how happy they seemed to be, always laughing and singing.

From the very first, what most struck me about the estate workers, and other Nyasas, was their cheerfulness. I assumed that this was an African characteristic, but learned later that, like so many of my generalizations about Africa, this was not the case. Certainly, it was not related to income, for this was low even for Africa. The men wore European-style shirt and trousers and the women a brightly coloured wrap-around cloth, but these were invariably torn. Some of them had bought bicycles, but usually only after working for several years. The basic wage on the tea estates was only two shillings (10p.) a day.

George drummed into me that I must repeatedly count the workers in each gang. Keeping count, and composing a muster sheet, was primarily the responsibility of the clerks. It was a favourite ruse to mark in labourers who were not there, and then split the proceeds with the phantom labourer at payday. This was made easier by the traditional system of working a thirty-day 'ticket'. As each day was worked it was ticked off, together with a note of any work done beyond the task. Payment was only made when the full thirty days had been completed, although small weekly advances against this might be made. It was quite normal for workers to take a longish time to fill their cards, for many of them took days off to work their own plots of land. This meant that the workforce was more casual than permanent, and harder to keep track of. The estate was moving on to an easier system to control the weekly wage, but this change was still in transition. It was extremely difficult to keep tabs on the hundreds of workers spread across the fields.

'Count them carefully, and count them often,' George instructed. 'In the last four years we've had to sack four Mwalanthunzi head-clerks for fiddling. The clerks need watching closely. Try not to upset them too much, though, since you'll be relying on them, as they are the only people on this estate who speak a word of English!'

Payday was on Fridays, in the late afternoon, and very stressful. It was there that disputes tended to erupt, as workers argued about the correct recording of their work, or demanded advances against future earnings. We collected the cash in coin from the Cholo agency of the Standard Bank, which was just a tin-roofed shack opened for a few hours on a Wednesday. The money was handed over in old army ammunition boxes, tied with steel bands and sealed. These were kept unopened until the Friday, when they were collected from the factory office, taken to the estate office, and counted. Any small discrepancy would be adjusted the next week.

I moved into the Mwalanthunzi bungalow at the end of my first week. It was strange to sit on the verandah by myself at dusk, and watch the night close in. In those first weeks, the sudden sound of an insect in the dark, or the weird cry of a hyena, would sometimes unnerve me. At other times, it seemed delicious just to lie in my bed, in the empty house, and listen to the murmurs of the African night.

The house was large and modern. It had been built only a few years back with the possibility of it having to house a

SATEMWA TEA ESTATES LIMITED.
MWALANTHUNZI ESTATE

_____ 6TH FEBRUARY _____ 196_

MUSTER CHIT				W	C	M	K
Native Staff				-	6	-	-
Watchmen				-	-	11	-
GARDEN BOY				-	-	4	-
MEDICAL				-	-	1	-
COOKS				1	-	3	-
MAIZE MILL				-	-	1	-
PENSIONED				-	-	2	-
COMPOST MANURE				-	-	3	-
CATTLE BOYS				-	-	2	2
PLUCKING BASKETS				-	-	1	-
" F. NO	1			9	2	-	(73)
" " "	13			-	2	(100)	-
TIPPING " "	14. 15 #16			-	5	(170)	-
(BAGGING)				-	-	10	-
WEEDING F. NO	13			-	2	79	-
" " "	14			-	1	17	-
" " "	16			63	2	-	-
" " "	18			-	1	-	46
BRIDGE UP KEEP				-	-	2	-
LINES				4	1	40	4
KHOLA				-	-	4	-
GROUND				-	-	1	15
BUNGALOWS				-	-	-	8
DAMBO SAND				-	-	4	-
GARAGE				-	-	2	-
Total	(70.4)			77	22	457	148
Not at Work TOTAL				77		479	148
Cut Wages NOT AT WORK				102		204	116
Left Estate							
Total on Check Roll				179		683	264
Arrived on Estate							

Hetherwick—609—K—58

Muster Chit – Mwalanthunzi Estate, 6 February 1962
(W stands for women, C for _capitos_, M for men and K for kids.)

manager with a big family, Unlike any of the other managers' houses it was not set amid tea, but in the middle of uncleared woodland, full of splendid large trees. It was approached by a long dirt road, lined for the last hundred yards by fruiting grapefruit, orange and lemon trees. The house was on top of a knoll, giving splendid views across the estate to Cholo Mountain. There was a large lawn, and the previous manager had planted a few flowering trees – blue jacarandas with red poinsettias and hibiscus. The bungalow was brilliant white and very long. Three bedrooms, bathroom, living room, dining room and kitchen, all lay in a straight line off one side of a long corridor, so that it was 150 feet from end to end. A large covered verandah jutted out from the centre, with steps in front, to give an entrance through French windows. Surprisingly, it had mains electricity, taken from the line that went to the factory. There was basic furniture – beds, chairs, tables, and an antiquated paraffin refrigerator – but no curtains, floor coverings, linen or cooking utensils. It was going to be expensive to furnish.

Fortunately, credit in Nyasaland (unlike in Britain at that time) was easily available. I had some crockery, cutlery and linen being shipped out from Britain, which would arrive in a month or two. The company had given me a £50 outfitting allowance before I left. In London, while I was completing contract formalities, the chairman of our managing agents had taken me on one side:

'Can I give you a spot of advice, my boy?'

'Thank you, Sir,'

'It's most important that you are properly turned out. There are plenty of tailors out there, who are cheap, but they need a pattern to work from. Get yourself down to Simpsons or Austin Reed and get yourself measured up for a really first-class bush-jacket and shorts. You won't regret it.'

I did enquire at Simpsons, but they quoted me £25, half my allowance, so I did not follow his advice. This was fortunate, since when I arrived the only man in the whole territory who wore a bush-jacket was the local manager of the same managing agents, who was considered to be a bit of a fool. Later on, I met other planters who had been given lists of what to purchase, and who had come out fully equipped with solar topees and red spine flannels.

George took me into Blantyre and introduced me to C. K. Raman, a highly respected Indian businessman, who conducted household auctions and also sold new furniture and household items.

'This is Mr Moxham,' George said. 'He's just started with us at Satemwa.'

'Welcome to Nyasaland,' he gestured towards the cluttered warehouse. 'Take whatever you need.'

'I haven't even opened a bank account yet,' I said, 'but . . .'

'Don't bother about that,' he said, 'pay whenever you like.' He laughed. 'Most people pay me a year or two later!'

Of course, he knew that if I stayed in the country and did well he would have a loyal customer. Inflation then was minimal, and interest rates were low. Most importantly, Mr Raman knew, although nothing had been formalized, that the estate would probably clear my debts if I defaulted. George and I then went to several other stores where, on George's introduction, they opened accounts for me without a piece of paper ever being signed.

George also helped me to engage servants – a cook and a houseboy who were paid by me, and a gardener and watchman paid for by the estate. They had modern, but small, houses a hundred yards behind the bungalow. None of them spoke any English.

I set about learning Chinyanja with enthusiasm. Once I had moved into the Mwalanthunzi residence, George only came over for half days. I listened to his Chinyanja, learning what I could from his conversations. In the evenings I assiduously did an hour or two of grammar. When George was not there, I always

225

travelled with one of the clerks, taking lessons as we went around the fields. I would point at things to learn vocabulary, and then write the word down to remember. This was fairly straightforward since the language had only been written in recent times, so it was in the Roman alphabet and phonetic. A few days after I began this, one of the *capitos* pointed out something beneath the tea:

'*Marvu!*' he gestured excitedly.

I bent down to look, keen to learn a new word. Suddenly I felt a pain like a hot needle stab my leg. I had been stung by a huge red hornet. The sting remained painful, and the leg was swollen for days. This gave great amusement to the labourers who as I hobbled past would shout out '*Marvu, marvu!*'

As I picked up the language, I began to deal more and more through my head *capito*, Yotum. He struck me as being far more reliable than the clerks. He had been in tea many years, and knew – far better than I – what to do. He was a Muslim, and unlike many of the clerks and other *capitos*, never drank alcohol. He could also be relied on to give sensible advice on the many personal disputes that were brought to me.

I had been absolutely flabbergasted when I had first been asked to adjudicate in a dispute between workers. There had been a fight one weekend, fuelled by illegally distilled spirit. One worker had made a pass, or so it was claimed, at another's wife, and then been violently assaulted. His arm had been broken so that he would not be able to work for some weeks. He came to me claiming compensation from his assailant.

'It's nothing to do with me,' I said. 'The whole business took place after work. Go to the chief or a magistrate.'

'But, Bwana,' he protested. 'The previous managers have always decided these cases. It will be too much time and trouble to go elsewhere. You decide, and if one of us does not want to accept your judgement, we'll go to someone else.'

Reluctantly, I decided to listen. I heard both their tales, and then consulted Yotum. He advised me to make the assaulter, who was well known as a troublemaker, pay the injured man half his wages until he was fit to work again. I told the men that it was my judgement. Both men accepted it as fair, and I adjusted their wages accordingly.

Later, I adjudicated in many cases of theft, adultery and assault. Local custom was that all but the most serious cases were settled by the payment of money. Jailing an offender, so that he was precluded from earning the money to pay compensation, was regarded as absurd. This made my role relatively easy, especially as the parties had come to me voluntarily. Only very occasionally was it necessary to send them to the police, a chief, or a magistrate.

Learning the job and the language were my main priorities. At the back of my mind, however, there was always the worry of having no driving licence, or any driving experience whatsoever. For my first fortnight I walked about the estate for half of the day, and travelled with George the other half, watching his driving carefully. Sometimes in the evening George would send a driver to take me to one of the estate managers' houses or the club. Then came the day when, while we were both at the factory office, my vehicle arrived. Fortunately it was about lunchtime, and I was able to stay in the office on some pretext until everyone had gone home to eat. Fortunately too, the Morris 1000 pick-up was pointing the right way. I climbed in and, with a clashing of gears, hesitantly moved off. I drove through the factory gates and headed for Mwalanthunzi. Driving very slowly, I made it home safely.

Mwalanthunzi estate had many miles of private road. These were of red earth, heavily potholed, and corrugated by the rains. When it was wet the tractors churned deep ruts. All this was to my advantage, for I was able to drive slowly without being

conspicuous, learning all the time. In rain the roads were treach-
erous, and it was a while before I mastered the technique of
turning into a skid. Surprisingly quickly though, I became confident enough to drive to the factory and leave again even though
everyone was standing around. I began to roam further afield –
on to the public road leading either to the club or to the little
shops in Cholo town. It was on one of these expeditions that
nemesis struck.

I was on my way to buy some groceries, when I suddenly
came to a police roadblock. The policemen checked my car and
then asked for my licence. I told them I did not have it with me.
Similarly as in Britain, I was given a note to produce it at a police
station within five days. I prevaricated for a couple of days, then
rang the district Superintendent of Police, to see how serious
things were and whether my stupidity could be kept quiet. I was
not optimistic.

'Alan? It's Roy Moxham. I don't know whether you remember
me, but we were introduced at the club and . . .'

'Yes, of course, how are you? Everything all right?'

'Well, actually, some of your men stopped me for a vehicle
check and asked for my licence and . . .'

'I know,' he interrupted me. 'Don't tell me – you've forgotten
to renew your licence, haven't you?'

'Well, actually, I . . .'

'You're not the only one,' he interrupted again. 'Make sure
you get it fixed right away. I'll get things quashed this time, but
next time you'll be for the high jump!'

'Thanks, thanks very much,' I said, but he had already put the
phone down.

I immediately booked a driving test in Blantyre. A few days
later I drove into town on my own – searching anxiously for any
sign of roadblocks. I parked just round the corner from the office,
and tied on my L-plates. The British examiner was notoriously
severe. He made me do a hill-start with his packet of cigarettes

lodged tight behind the rear wheel. The cigarettes survived, I passed, and no one ever learnt of my foolishness.

The Cholo Sports Club, where I had met the Superintendent of Police, was on land that Mr Kay had given from the edge of Mwalanthunzi. Unfortunately there was no direct road from my house, and I had to go by a roundabout route, via the main road, for three miles. Considering it only had about 100 members, men and women, the premises were palatial. There was a modern clubhouse looking down on a pitch used for rugby in the rainy season and cricket in the dry months. There were tennis courts, a snooker room and a large dance floor. Most of the activity, however, revolved around the bar. The planters and their wives were heavy drinkers, although there were few real alcoholics. It was considered reprehensible to drink whisky before sundown. Gin, however, was perfectly all right.

All beer and spirits were imported but, as the duty was low, they were much cheaper than in Britain. There was only bottled fizzy beer, which I disliked, so I took to drinking gin or whisky with lots of water. It was a much harder drinking school than I was used to. People bought rounds, so I found myself trying to drink level with hardened planters, often with years of practice in the army. The sessions could go on well after midnight, and we were all up by five-thirty. After a heavy session I would usually be all right first thing, but later as the sun strengthened I would begin to feel queasy. Once or twice in my first months I was discreetly sick while 'examining the tea bushes'.

'I don't care what you get up to,' George had told me, 'but you must be in the field at six a.m. to check your labour force. You can turn up in your dinner jacket if you want to, but be there on time.'

It was a while before I did go to work in my dinner jacket

(fashionably white), for the dances at which they were obligatory were few and far between – unlike at Zomba, the Nyasaland capital, where they wore evening dress to the club for the weekly film. Nevertheless, a couple of times in my first month I only just managed to get back to the estate in time for work. On the other hand, I never drank on my own on the many nights I stayed in, for I had been warned about planters who drank a bottle of whisky a day on their remote estates.

The club was strictly for European members, although various Indian sports clubs would visit to play cricket. The only Africans allowed in were the staff. Already, however, there was talk of what would happen if an African were appointed to Cholo as Assistant District Commissioner. Most members were opposed to any relaxation. It was only fairly recently, after all, that they had granted membership to Italians, and many thought that a mistake for one had reportedly been seen pissing in the club shower.

There was a widespread colour bar in the colony. Many hotels and bars operated a 'whites only' policy. I was told that the first African to enter the bar of the prestigious Ryall's Hotel in Blantyre had been Dr Banda. Ironically, he had been taken there by Winston Field, leader of the white Southern Rhodesian farmers, with whom he was forging an alliance to oppose the Federation, which Field saw as a threat to Rhodesian white rule.

In Nyasaland as a whole, there were few well-educated Africans. Education had been terribly neglected by the colonial government. In the entire country there were only 1,500 pupils at secondary school, and ten years previously there had only been 140. This was for a population of 3 million. (The federal government provided good schools for all the children among the less than 10,000 Europeans.) Those very few Africans who had external degrees or equivalent qualifications tended to be employed in Zomba or Blantyre, and rarely came into contact with the planters. As a result the planters regarded Africans in general as illiterate and inferior. The attitude of a planter to his labour was patrician, and he liked to behave like an English squire. There was very little brutality. Very occasionally I would hear of a planter punching someone in anger, but there was none of the systematic beating that I heard tell of in the Rhodesias (now Zimbabwe and Zambia). Most planters treated their African labour with condescending affection. The exceptions were the sons of early settlers, who thought of themselves as white Africans. Some of them would refer to the black Africans, especially politicians seeking independence, as 'rock apes', and call African women 'jungle bunnies'.

There were a few plantations that followed a more socially enlightened agenda. In Cholo the most conspicuous was Nchima Estate, owned by the Gardiner family. The manager was viewed by the other planters as sound enough, even though he constructed better housing for his workers and gave them other fringe benefits. The planters' ire was directed towards Rolf Gardiner who came out from time to time. He was viewed as dangerously sympathetic to the Africans, and liable to involve the industry in unnecessary expense if others had to follow his example. He was denounced as ridiculous when he paid for a group of African farmers to visit his estate in Dorset to study his aforestation and organic agriculture. Any wider influence he might have had was destroyed by rumours of his past involvement with the Hitler Youth. There was probably some truth in this, although perhaps not in the wilder story that he had planted trees on the Dorset Downs in the shape of a swastika.

What the Africans thought of the Europeans was hard to gauge. Naturally, if I asked, they would praise the colonial regime, and pooh-pooh the African nationalists, but I was not convinced. The elections in August would clarify that. Superstitious fear of Europeans was rife. Occasionally I would see mothers pick up their children and run off to hide when I approached. This happened more often when a neighbouring planter appeared on his horse. My clerks would laughingly explain that this was because of belief in *chifwamba* – that some Europeans or their horses ate African children. This Dracula-like myth was widespread, and encouraged by unscrupulous politicians. The 1953 troubles had been largely about land rights, but they had been sparked off by a *chifwamba* incident on an orange estate near Cholo. Two Africans, who had been stealing oranges, had been locked up to await the arrival of the police. They mysteriously escaped before the police arrived, and a gathering crowd accused the farmers of *chifwamba*. In the riots that followed many protesters were injured and eleven died.

Much of the talk at the club, or whenever the British met, was of land and political power. A crisis was looming which had its origins in the short history of the protectorate, and the tea estates were centre-stage.

British interest in Nyasaland began when the missionary and explorer, David Livingstone, reached Lake Nyasa in 1859. British churches set up missions over the next two decades, and in 1883 Captain Foot was appointed as British consul in the areas adjacent to the lake. In 1889, to forestall the nearby Portuguese, Britain declared a protectorate over the highlands to the south of the lake. In 1891 this protectorate was extended to cover a territory similar to that of Nyasaland. This was called British Central Africa. In 1904 it was renamed Nyasaland.

The first of the British to acquire land were the missionaries, and this was usually given by a local chief after he had received gifts. Whether these gifts were in payment for the land, as the missionaries often claimed later, or merely gifts of friendship, was ambiguous. The legal status of these plots of land – which might run to hundreds or even thousands of acres – was unclear. Furthermore, it was doubtful if the chief had the power to alienate

232

his people's land permanently. Nevertheless, the missionaries were usually well meaning, and not commercially minded, so few problems arose.

The trading companies and planters who followed were different. They saw the opportunity to acquire valuable agricultural land cheaply. The most important of these enterprises was the African Lakes Corporation, a Scottish company established in 1878. It was an interesting example of trade following the cross, for the company was vaguely affiliated to the Scots missions, and its employees were required to do some missionary work. At one of their trading posts they bravely gave shelter to Africans being harassed by Arab slave traders. This developed into a minor war, which was much publicized in Britain. This incident, and other encounters, together with a wish to check the Portuguese, eventually led the British government to take over the administration of the territory.

Involvement in the suppression of the slave trade did not stop the African Lakes Corporation staff themselves from exploiting the Africans. They persuaded illiterate chiefs to sign documents, which they pretended were for just enough land for a plantation, but in fact were for hugely greater acreages. In 1885 they signed 'treaties' with forty-one separate chiefs, which they later used to claim rights over millions of acres. Smaller companies and individuals, almost exclusively British, gave a few yards of cloth and trinkets to chiefs in exchange for large acreages.

The first Commissioner of the new protectorate, Sir Harry Johnston, refused to recognize some of the more outrageous claims. Of the African Lakes Corporation's applications, he observed: 'there was hardly a document put before me which was not more or less of a fraud.' Nevertheless, the African Lakes Corporation had good connections in Britain and was given the freehold of 2,734,687 acres. A further 1 million acres was split between about fifty British owners. The land that was most suitable for plantation crops, the most fertile land in the country, was mostly in the southern Shire Highlands. Fully half of all this, some 867,000 acres, was given to the British entrepreneurs. Coffee was seen as the crop that would bring rewards.

John Buchanan was the pioneer of coffee in Malawi. A gardener by training, he had been sent out in 1876 by the Church of Scotland to their mission at Blantyre in the Shire Highlands to develop horticulture. Two years later, Buchanan arranged for some coffee seedlings to be sent out from the Royal Botanic Garden Edinburgh. Only one survived, but this did well, and 1,000 beans from it were planted out. In 1883 these plants yielded 1,600 lbs of coffee.

In the meantime the Blantyre mission had been enveloped by scandal. A number of lay members had become involved in disputes with local Africans, and had assumed magisterial powers. One African was sentenced to death and shot; several others were flogged to death. The Church of Scotland eventually instituted an inquiry, and those involved were dismissed. John Buchanan, who had supervised the flogging to death of a suspected thief with a rhinoceros-hide whip, became a coffee planter.

In 1880 Buchanan, who was later joined by his brothers, acquired the 3,000-acre Michiru Estate. It cost him thirty-two yards of calico, a gun and two red hats. The first Buchanan coffee was exported in 1889. Eugene Sharrer, who owned 363,000 acres in the Shire Highlands, started planting coffee that year, as did the African Lakes Corporation. The coffee was of good quality, other planters arrived, and by 1900 exports were over 2,000,000 lbs. This, however, was the high-water mark for coffee. A collapse in prices, combined with increasing insect damage, led to the demise of what had been a promising crop. A decade later it was almost commercially extinct.

Tea arrived in Malawi in almost the same way as had coffee. Indeed there was a tea plant with the consignment of coffee and other plants that had come out from the Royal Botanic Garden Edinburgh in 1878. This, however, had soon died. In 1886 Dr

Emslie came out to the Church of Scotland mission situated at Livingstonia on the north of the lake. He brought some tea seed, which he gave to the gardener at the Blantyre mission, Jonathan Duncan. Some other seeds also came from Kew Gardens. From these consignments Duncan managed to grow two plants, one of which still survives. He tried to make tea from the mature bushes but the brew was not pleasant.

The bushes were not wasted. In 1891 a Ceylon coffee planter, Henry Brown, who had been almost ruined by the coffee fungus, moved to Malawi to take up some land at the base of Mlanje mountain. He planted some coffee, but when he saw the tea bushes at the Blantyre mission he begged twenty seeds, for he had seen the success of tea in Ceylon, and thought the climate and soil similar. Half the seeds were planted out on his Thorn-wood Estate, and half on the nearby Lauderdale Estate. They did well, and other planters followed suit. By the turn of the century some tea was being exported. Tea was also planted at Cholo, another high rainfall area around a mountain, which lay fifty miles west of Mlanje. As in Ceylon, tea planting was given impetus because of problems with coffee. The damage wrought by the coffee borer beetle pushed many Nyasaland planters into growing tea.

By 1922 tea production from the two areas in the Shire Highlands reached 800,000 lbs. By the end of the 1950s, 24,000 acres were producing about 30 million lbs of tea. Two thirds of this was exported to Britain.

When Johnston arrived to establish the protectorate, he had brought with him a very small army. This force of seventy-one Indian soldiers under a Captain Maguire had quickly defeated a number of Arab slave-trading expeditions. These victories had made the Africans keen to enter into treaties with the British. To pay for the army, and for the other costs of the administration, Johnston insisted that any chief who wished to claim protection must agree to the imposition of a hut tax. From the very beginning, the new administration also realized that this tax would encourage the Africans to work for wages on the settlers' plantations. In 1901 this became even clearer when the hut tax was doubled, but with half being remitted if the African hut-holder worked for a European for at least one month in the year. It became customary for the European settlers to pay the tax for a whole village, and then demand the labour when they required it.

Unlike in India or Ceylon, the European settlers did not usually build accommodation for their workforce. In order to work for the settlers, therefore, the Africans usually had to build themselves huts. Usually, too these were on private estate land, for the settlers had been given the freehold over huge tracts. (Any 'original tenants' were supposed to be able to stay on rent-free and secure.) The settlers then charged rent, which might involve – in addition to what was needed for the poll tax – a month's work to pay off. As all this land had originally been African common land and, moreover, was never actually farmed by the Europeans, this practice became a long-standing grievance of the Africans. The settlers fought tooth-and-nail for decades to keep this undeveloped land, for it provided them with free labour. Ironically, it was this policy of holding on to undeveloped acreages that slowed the country's development, and stopped it becoming a major British settler colony.

The extraction of labour in lieu of rent was known as *thangata*. It was temporarily abolished in 1917, but reintroduced in 1928 with an even higher rent of two or even three months' labour. Ten per cent of the entire country's population found themselves on private estate land. In the 1940s hundreds of Africans were evicted from the estates when they refused to pay *thangata*. This caused massive resentment, and was a major factor behind the disturbances that broke out in Cholo in 1953.

In 1954 the Colonial Secretary visited Nyasaland. Overriding opposition from the white planters and farmers, he decided that *thangata* should be gradually abolished. He accelerated plans for the government to purchase those parts of estates on which the Africans lived.

Land and *thangata* were emotive subjects for the planters, although many were resigned to the changes. What really incensed the planters, however, was what was happening in the constitutional arena, and what they considered was British duplicity.

Nyasaland had been federated together with Southern Rhodesia and Northern Rhodesia in 1953. It was a poor colony, unable to balance its budget, and the British government had seen economic advantages in federation with the more prosperous Rhodesias. In addition white settlers in all three countries saw the opportunity to expand white control of Southern Rhodesia across the three countries, and then to push for self-governing status under a white parliament. Ever since the idea had been first mooted in the 1930s, many Nyasas had opposed it. Throughout the 1950s there were African demonstrations against the Federation. The campaign was galvanized in 1958 by the return of Dr Hastings Kamuzu Banda – who had been abroad for forty-three years – to lead the opposition.

Dr Banda addressed huge meetings, and polarized African and European opinion. In February 1959 more disturbances, mostly caused by police dispersal of political gatherings, resulted in the death of seventy-one Africans. The government received information (never authenticated) that a massacre of Europeans and African 'collaborators' was planned. Further clashes occurred, and in March 1959 a State of Emergency was declared. Dr Banda and many of his supporters were sent to prisons in Southern Rhodesia.

A British judicial report that followed these events labelled Nyasaland 'a police state.' This prompted the establishment of a Royal Commission to consider the future of the Federation. The commission's report was issued in October 1960, and it recommended that Nyasaland could, if the Africans wanted, secede from the Federation.

Meanwhile in April 1960, the British government released Dr Banda from prison, and the State of Emergency was lifted. A constitution was devised, which set up a Legislative Council with an elected African majority. Real power would reside with an Executive Council of ministers under the chairmanship of the Governor, but some of the ministers would be Africans. Elections, with a much wider franchise than previously, would be held in August 1961.

This then was the maelstrom into which I had arrived. At the time I had very little knowledge of the history of the country, and how it had led to conflict. I only knew about the current tension. The owner of a tea estate adjacent to Mwalanthunzi was Sir Malcolm Barrow, who was a minister in the Federation's cabinet, and unofficial spokesman for the tea planters. He had warned that 10,000 people would be killed in riots if Dr Banda were released from jail. This had not yet happened, but many planters feared the worst. In particular, they dreaded the prospect of the elections scheduled for August.

I had already absorbed many of the colonial values of the planters and was opposed to African rule in the near future. However, the majority of the tea planters who thought of themselves as expatriates, including myself, were less upset by the prospect of an overwhelming victory by Dr Banda than the settlers, who were mostly federal citizens. This led to some ill feeling, and jibes from the settlers about expatriates who would retire to Cheltenham to live on their fat pensions. However, almost everyone became agitated, and vociferously anti-nationalist when illegal roadblocks were set up at night. In fact, those who suffered most from the rise in African nationalism were the

Africans who had supported colonialism and the Federation. Many of these 'collaborators' were attacked, severely beaten or even killed.

I left a neighbouring planter's house late one evening after dinner, and drove slowly home. It was raining heavily. Suddenly, I saw a eucalyptus tree lying across the road. I braked hard, and gave a sigh of relief as I managed to stop just before I hit the massive trunk. Then the windscreen shattered. Another brick bounced off the bonnet. I reversed at speed. As I turned into the eucalyptus plantation, my headlights caught a group of men running away. I drove fast between the trees until I regained the road. Then I sped home, and downed a large whisky. Around the same time a neighbouring planter was robbed in his house and badly beaten. The company had issued me with a Beretta pistol to carry when I collected money from the bank. I took to keeping it on my bedside table as I slept. Once a week I ostentatiously did target practice on the lawn, and became proficient enough to hit a cigarette packet at twenty-five paces.

In addition to a pistol, I also bought a second-hand rifle. I used it to shoot rabbits and guinea fowl to supplement the rather poor local meat. Occasionally I saw bushbuck on Mwalanthunzi, but I thought them too attractive to shoot. I loved to watch the African birds – bishops, sunbirds, whydahs, bee-eaters and rollers – all so much brighter than the birds of Britain. I fished on the estate's dams, which had been stocked with black bass and the delicious Lake Nyasa *chambo*. Every evening a flight of what I thought were ducks flew straight over my house. Only when I borrowed a shotgun did I discover that they were giant fruit bats.

Coming back from the factory office one night, a hare became trapped in my vehicle's headlights. When I turned into a bend, a leopard suddenly reached out with its paw and scooped it up. Next week, I went home for breakfast one morning to find a rabid dog in the dining room. It had all the classic symptoms – it dripped saliva, and snapped at imaginary flies. I edged my way out of the room, collected my rifle, and shot it. Thinking the veterinary officer might be interested to examine the dead dog, I put on protective gloves and placed it high up in a garden tree for safekeeping. I saw the vet at the club that evening, and we arranged for him to come out next morning. However, during the night the dog disappeared, presumably carried away by a leopard. In all probability this was now rabid. The veterinary officer put it succinctly: 'Moxham – you're a bloody fool!'

The temperature rarely rose much above 90°F (32°C), but the humidity was high, so that it felt hotter. The latitude and altitude meant that the sun was full of ultra-violet radiation. Without protection a white newcomer could burn severely in less than an hour. I managed to do this, on and off, throughout my first months, and was always applying ointments. More uncomfortable though, were my 'tea sores'. Every few years the tea bushes were severely pruned, which left the lower branches with sharp edges. Despite wearing knee-length socks, my legs became badly cut. The humidity discouraged these cuts from healing, so that my inflamed legs had to be smeared with ointments too. All in all, it was fairly obvious to anyone I met that I was new.

My very name, when I was introduced, would give people a jolt. I would see them recoil.

'Moxham,' I would hurriedly say, 'm – o – x – h – a – m – nothing to do with Moxon.'

Major Moxon had created quite a stir in the colony. A small farmer, he was famous for having paid his poll tax under protest – for he thought the annual tax of £4 for Europeans, but £1½ for Africans, was discriminatory – by writing his cheque out on the back of a young pig. He had delivered the cheque to the district commissioner at the last possible moment – late on a Saturday morning. The DC had accepted it with insouciance, and taken it on a lead to the nearby bank. The bank had put it through the system, and stamped it 'paid'. Then came a problem, for in those days banks returned paid cheques to the issuer. As the bank was about to close, some of the bank's young British employees volunteered to take the pig back to their shared lodging for the weekend. Unfortunately, their dog then killed it. Major Moxon had been incensed when all he got back from the bank was a photograph of his dead pig. One of the bank clerks later told me that the pork had been delicious.

Major Moxon had been considered eccentric but amusing. Recently, however, he had gone too far. He had, I was told, abandoned his wife and family, and run off with the African nanny. This was totally unacceptable behaviour in the British community, and he had left the country. Small wonder, then, that people initially viewed me with suspicion.

At the beginning of the rainy season the tea flushed with extra-ordinary vigour. Everywhere the rate of growth was phenomenal – I measured a castor-oil plant growing at five inches a day. Even though we were only picking the new tea shoots when two leaves and a bud had fully developed – otherwise the yield would have been depressed – the fields had to be plucked every five days. The factory worked day and night to keep up with the harvest.

The daily 'task' for plucking was kept low, so that there was plenty of scope for the workers to enhance their wages. This seeming anomaly was because we never had enough labour. Not only were the exceptionally heavy rains good for the tea, they were also good for the Africans' own crops – maize, beans and peanuts. Most of the labourers had their own smallholding, and these took priority. Even those workers who were near to being paid at the end of their thirty-day tickets were reluctant to devote all their days to the estate. Plucking was not the only concern, for weeds grew rampantly, and I was still trying to get on top of the messy aftermath of the strike that had occurred before my arrival. That strike, I had discovered, had been caused by an over-zealous manager setting the daily task too high. Within the limits of my budget, I always made sure to err on the soft side when setting these. We were in no position to weather another strike.

I tried to boost the Sunday workforce. On Sundays work stopped at two p.m., and then the labourers were paid for the day, irrespective of whether they had other tickets to complete. I attracted some labourers from nearby estates for this Sunday work, since I paid well. This could cause friction with neighbouring planters and could not be overdone. When tackled at the club, I would plead a newcomer's ignorance of the 'right' wage. My ploys worked well, and on several Sundays the workforce – men, women and children – totalled over 1,000.

The estate's labour had originally come from nearby villages. Some of these were on our land, and the inhabitants came to work off the *thangata* rent. Over the past decade this source of labour had diminished as the government compulsorily purchased land and gave it to the Africans. Nevertheless, many of these Africans still worked for us for some of the year since they still had to pay their poll tax, and this had recently been increased. Other, more regular workers lived in accommodation provided by the estate. There were about 150 thatched white huts, in neat lines on the edge of the tea fields. The conditions were basic – one or two rooms, depending on the size of the family – but they were clean and well maintained. They had outside latrines and water. They were very similar to the houses the workers had in their own villages.

During the week, even though there were never less than 500 employees, we were short-staffed. George sent lorries into Portuguese East Africa, and recruited labour with the promise of generous cash advances. This worked quite well, but we were constrained by the lack of surplus accommodation, even though some recruits were willing to share huts for the few remaining months of the busy season.

The rains came to an end in April. Already, however, the tea flushed less prolifically – as if it were exhausted by the prodigious growth at the beginning of the season. The weather, especially at night, became colder as we approached the winter of the southern hemisphere. The plucking cycle lengthened from five, to seven, and then to ten days. The workforce stabilized at about 500, and Sunday work ended.

A quick look at the rainfall figures would convince most tea planters around the world that tea in Cholo was not a viable crop. The rains ended in April and only resumed in November. This six-month gap might have been fatal for tea, had it not been for the *chiperone*. At the height of the cold weather, in June and July and hopefully for longer, the *chiperone*, Chinyanja for 'blanket', descended. The district became enveloped in a thick Scotch mist for days on end. There was very little precipitation, but it was enough to control water loss. The *chiperone* was particularly thick at night and, aided by the condensation as the air cooled, it would cover everything in thick dew. At daybreak the tea bushes would be soaking. Even on the days when the sun did break through, the leaves would still be wet late into the morning. At night the mist was so thick that it made driving almost impossible, and several times I found myself off the road, driving between trees. During the day the mist was still so thick that I could watch it curl over the window-ledge of an open window and drop swirling to the floor.

Morning work in the *chiperone* was unpleasant. As we squeezed between the bushes we got soaked through. The sharply pruned branches made any waterproofing of the lower body impractical. We were cold and wet. The labourers normally had a free midday meal of red beans and maize porridge – the Nyasas' staple diet. In the *chiperone* I supplemented this with generous helpings of tea, brewed for the huge labour force in forty-gallon oil drums, each drum sweetened with a twenty-lb sack of sugar.

As the rains came to an end, pruning began. It was a skilled job, usually left to men who had been on the estate for years, and was paid for at a higher rate. The wooden-handled, curved knives they used were a foot long and very sharp. The youngest tea on Mwalanthunzi had been planted four years before. This had already been pruned two years before when the plants had been cut across horizontally to eighteen inches high. The following year the bushes had been plucked for the first time. The bushes had spread wide, and we cut them to a height of thirty inches, so that over the next year they would fan out further to meet the adjacent bushes. Fields of mature tea also needed pruning in some years to stop falling yields and promote new vigorous growth. When and how to prune were subjects on which planters had very different views, and there were heated arguments. On Satemwa we pruned the mature bushes every two years – a heavy prune every four years, interspersed with a light prune two years later. The heavy prune left the plants a bare skeleton, but the vast root system of what was actually meant to be a tall tree soon brought them back into full leaf.

In August the *chiperone* disappeared, and the weather grew warmer. There followed three months of unbroken sunshine, each month hotter than the last. At first it was extremely pleasant. After the cold damp of the *chiperone*, it was good to feel the sun. The air was fresh; the vegetation vibrant, washed clean by rain and mist. Soon, however, it began to feel uncomfortably hot. The grass turned brown; the sky grew milky with haze; dust covered the landscape.

It should have been the slack season but Mr Kay, who had remained in Europe during my first months, wanted to expand the Mwalanthunzi tea acreage. There were plenty of seedlings in a Satemwa nursery, but there had been some doubt as to whether these would be planted out, until I was given the go-ahead for Mwalanthunzi. The delay was unfortunate since it meant the land was not prepared. In Nyasaland, tea had few pests or diseases. The only serious problem was with a root fungus, which came from decayed tree roots on land that had not been properly cleared. If the trees had a strip of bark removed from around their trunks a year or two before clearing this greatly reduced the risk, but this had not been done. Furthermore, because of the exceptionally long dry season in Nyasaland, tea there tended to have exceptionally deep roots. A taproot might go down twenty feet. We therefore had to ensure that the ground was well cleared to that depth.

Felling the trees was easy, for the land selected was more bush than heavy forest, although there were some big trees. We had no power tools, but the men were good with axes, and in a few weeks all the bushes and trees on twenty acres had been felled. Then the difficult work began – men and women dug out huge stumps and roots right down to twenty feet. This was hard labour, made all the harder by the steadily increasing ferocity of the sun. Some of the timber was cut into planks and firewood. What remained was burnt, for the potash this produced was good for the tea. The holes were filled in, and then made ready for the tea seedlings for when the rains broke. The land was fairly flat so, rather than plant on the contour, we intended to plant up, four feet by four feet, in straight rows.

Twenty acres of land planted in that way takes 54,450 seedlings. These plants were already two years old, and had a considerable taproot. They needed holes cut six inches square and eighteen inches deep. Much of the land was hard. A hoe blade was attached to a heavy vertical pole, and then raised and lowered repeatedly. Although the weight of the implement did some of the work, it also needed a good deal of extra effort. Then the loose earth had to be scooped out by hand, and left in a pile beside the hole ready for the planting. Women did much of this work, for the method used was very similar to that which they used at home to pound grain. It was tough work, and I would often find the workers had been in the field since four-thirty a.m., hoping to finish their task before it became too hot.

There were other plantings to prepare for, too. Many of the fields needed 'supplying' – that was filling in the gaps left by plants that had died. It was essential for the land to have a full umbrella of plant cover. Otherwise, apart from not using the full potential of the expensively cleared land, there would be rampant weeds and soil erosion. In a well-planted tea field the impact of the rain was softened and there was very little erosion. Indeed, you could see from the level of the roads that the older fields had risen as the prunings and dead leaves had mulched down, so that they were five or six feet higher than when they had been planted.

A few of the older fields had small-leaved tea bushes, of a predominantly Chinese variety. The other fields had the larger leaf Assam type of plant. In the warm climate of Cholo the Assam plants did much better, and yielded up to 2,000 lbs an acre. Eventually it was expected that the China tea would be ripped out and replanted. This, however, would be an expensive business, for the long taproots would have to be fully removed to prevent fungus developing. Meanwhile, as spare land was available, it was more economic to open up new fields.

Mr Maclean Kay came to look at the new clearing from time to time, driving extremely slowly in a massive old American car. He seemed pleased with the progress we were making.

'I put managers into two categories,' he said, 'the savers, and the spenders. When you're opening out new land the savers are useless, for they're so busy watching the pennies that nothing gets done on schedule. You strike me as a spender, so I'll tell George to let you establish a nursery of your own to plant up another 100 acres.'

'Thank you very much, sir.' I was excited at the prospect; I could see the possibility of a bonus.

'That's all right.' As the huge car began to glide off, he turned to me and smiled. 'Of course once the land's been planted, it's best to get rid of the spender, and put in a penny-pinching Scotsman.'

We cleared three acres of land for a huge nursery, with raised seedbeds of finely tilthed earth for the quarter of a million plants that would be needed. There were only a few seed bearers – old thirty-foot-high tea trees – on Satemwa, so seed had to be ordered from estates that specialized in providing it. It would be delivered just before the rains. The Tea Research Station at Mlanje was very active. We went to an open day and were very impressed with the clonal teas they had grown from cuttings. The techniques needed refining to be practicable on a commercial scale, but we were all convinced that clonal tea would eventually replace tea grown from seed.

By far the most important event that August was the election. Given the recent history of Nyasaland most of us expected trouble. In July there had been violent incidents, when Dr Banda's supporters burnt down several houses belonging to members of the United Federal Party. Dr Banda had decided, however, that August would be peaceful. A week before the election he gave instructions that all manufacture and consumption of alcohol by Africans was to stop. These commands were enforced by his Youth League, who destroyed any liquor that contravened the ban. Election day was 15 August. Dr Banda told the electors that they had the choice of 'slavery within federation, or freedom and independence outside the federation'.

I was called up by the Colonial Police Reserve to assist in the running of Cholo police station, while the regular officers went out to supervise the polling stations. A queue of voters stretched all the way along the road to the government offices and polling station. Many had obviously camped out all night. It was eerily quiet, for Dr Banda wanted to show the British that he could control the country effectively. If anyone so much as raised their voice, a youth leaguer would pounce on them. There was no trouble, and I had a very boring day.

The turnout of voters on the all-important lower electoral roll was 95 per cent, with Dr Banda's Malawi Congress Party getting 99 per cent of the votes and all twenty seats. Even on the small upper roll the MCP did well, taking two seats against the UFP's five. Dr Banda took the most important Ministry of Natural Resources and Local Government, and seven of his colleagues received other ministries. The new ministers announced that they would be broadening the franchise for elections to local government, and that penalties that had been imposed on poor African farming practice would be replaced by persuasion. Otherwise there were no radical new measures. The change of government brought no revolution, for under the new constitution the Governor was still in ultimate control. In any case, Banda wanted to present a moderate image in order to improve the argument for independence. I noticed that personal cases no longer came to me for adjudication, but were dealt with by officials of the Malawi Congress Party. I had seen the very last months of an old custom.

As September progressed, the weather became unpleasantly hot. During the day the back of my shirt was always damp with sweat;

at night it was difficult to sleep. Fortunately, there was very little tea to pluck, and even the weeds were struggling to survive. There were out of season tasks to do. Sulphate of ammonia was sprinkled around the tea roots to await the rains; huts were replastered and rethatched; roads and bridges were mended. Nevertheless, there was much less work than in the season, and we went on to a four-day week.

In the middle of the month, I handed the estate over to George, and went on a fortnight's holiday. I drove with a couple of other bachelor planters to Cape Maclear on Lake Nyasa. It was my twenty-second birthday, so we stopped on the way at Zomba and Fort Johnston clubs for drinks. It was hot, for the lake was 1,500 feet lower than Cholo. The water was wonderful – clear and deep and full of luminous blue fish. The hotel on the promontory had been built for the great flying boats of Imperial Airways, which had spent the night anchored there en route between Southampton and Cape Town. The owner was an eccentric widow who liked to display her status by putting a jar with her husband's ashes on the bar. We swam, sailed, drank a great deal, met up with some nurses, and made a lot of noise. I left fully refreshed.

My mother sent out a cookery book for my birthday. I had become bored with Ali's small round of 'school-dinner' food. Meat and two veg had been the usual offering, with the occasional chilli-spiced *piri-piri* chicken or basic curry. He set about the new modern recipes with enthusiasm, and I began to realize that he had a much wider expertise than I had imagined. He had been giving me what other planters he had worked for had wanted, and what he thought that I too wanted. I ran through an exotic pudding recipe from the new book, painstakingly translating it into Chinyanja. When I had finished, he said:

'Oh, you mean you'd like a soufflé! Do you like it with brandy?'

It turned out that he had worked in a smart South African hotel for many years. My meals improved considerably. I raised his wages.

October was a deadly month. Much of the grass in Cholo caught fire, and the sky was thick with smoke haze. In the heat of the day some cloud would build up, but it would then dissipate in the afternoon without raining. Tempers became short. In the club there were heated arguments over such trivialities as to whether the balls on the snooker table had been correctly placed. Everyone drank too much.

We went into November, and at last it rained. I rushed out of the office during the first downpour and deliberately got soaked. The smell of the wet earth was wonderful.

A week later the landscape was green and vibrant, as if it had never been brown. Once again the air was crystal clear, so clear that I could see the water cascading down Mlanje Mountain, which was thirty miles away. We put the tea seedlings into their pits. By the middle of the month the tea fields were in flush once more, and we were back on a six-day week. Everyone became good-natured again. The Planters' Ball, the highlight of the Cholo social calendar, was a great success. The musicians of the police band got drunk and lost the rhythm, but no one minded. I weaved my way home at five-thirty a.m.

Then it was December, and the estate was at full stretch. We started to work on Sundays again. It was a constant battle to keep on top of the weeds and the plucking. The labour force went up to over 700. Once again I had to rush around, counting workers as I went, to minimize the amount that the clerks were stealing. I worked late into some evenings balancing the books. Nevertheless, it was not all work, for Christmas was approaching and there was a plethora of parties.

Christmas Eve was a Sunday. We started work at six a.m. as usual, but finished at noon. I gave my servants their Christmas boxes, and my head *capito*, Yotum, a chicken for all the help he had given me. I went for drinks at the Superintendent of Police's house, and then went home for a quick doze before going to the club to play football against a ladies' team. I left the club just before midnight, in order to reach Mrs Kay's private chapel in time for midnight mass. Afterwards, we stayed for a drink with Mr and Mrs Kay, and I reached home at two a.m. On Christmas morning I worked from six to twelve again, and then went to a neighbouring planter's house for Christmas dinner of turkey with all the trimmings and three helpings of Christmas pudding. I had been invited to go on to George's afterwards, but never quite made it, and later told him I had drunk too much to drive. He gave me a quizzical look, but soon forgave me.

It was obvious from George's manner that he thought I had got through my first year in tea with flying colours. In January, in the week of my first anniversary in Nyasaland, there was a dispute over the weeding task. I had fixed the task at 100 bushes, and some of the women thought this too much. There was talk of bringing in the newly formed National Union of Plantation and Agricultural Workers. To resolve the matter, I took up a hoe and weeded a row myself. It was not easy, and later my hands blistered, but I forged ahead to finish the task by mid morning. In fact, the task had not been set too severely, and the women were looking for an excuse in a newly militant atmosphere. However, they were impressed by my performance, and accepted the task with good grace. George was impressed too. He bestowed his ultimate accolade:

'By Jove, Roy,' he said. 'We could have done with you in the Gurkhas!'

I had enjoyed my first year as a planter enormously. The beautiful country, the life and the job had exceeded all my expectations. I had received a bonus of £100. Nevertheless, storm clouds were gathering. The union was threatening a strike over wages. It had just been announced that the Secretary of State for Commonwealth Relations would be coming out to discuss the future of the Federation. To the planters' fury there was even talk of giving Nyasaland total independence. In the local paper there was an obituary for Chief Changata. The old chief, who had ruled over the people on Cholo Mountain for many decades, had been born before the country had become a colony. He was famous as a *nsembe*, a rainmaker, and only a year ago had brought rains to break the drought. Everything seemed to be changing. The country was heading to an uncertain future, and so was I.

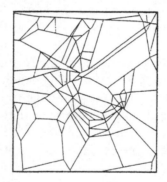

Types and Grades of Tea

GREEN TEA	Unfermented tea, in which heat has been used to kill the enzymes that would cause the leaf to ferment (oxidize) and blacken
BLACK TEA	Fermented tea, in which fermentation has been encouraged to blacken the tea before firing
SEMI-FERMENTED TEA	Tea that has been partly fermented before firing

The grading of tea has altered considerably since the first British imports. The original Chinese teas were loosely categorized, often under names that were derived from the districts the tea supposedly came from. They included:

Singo	Green tea from wild or semi-wild bushes
Twankay	Superior grade of *Singo*
Hyson	High-class green tea from cultivated bushes. *Young Hyson* was the superior tea from the early flushes, whereas *Hyson Skin* was the dregs
Gunpowder	Superior tightly rolled small leaf green tea, resembling lead shot
Bohea	Coarse black tea
Congou	Good quality black tea
Souchong	Superior *Congou*

Pekoe	Very superior black tea made from young leaves with downy hair

The first teas from India were given variants of the old Chinese grading names, such as *Assam Hyson*. Later in the nineteenth century, as black teas became dominant, a new grading system evolved, with categories for whole leaves and for broken leaves:

WHOLE LEAVES

Orange Pekoe	Long thin leaves
Pekoe	Shorter thin leaves
Souchong	Broader leaves

BROKEN LEAVES   (descending size)

Broken Orange Pekoe

Broken Pekoe

Broken Pekoe Souchong

Broken Orange Pekoe Fannings (small particles)

Dust

In addition, these grades were prefixed *Flowery* if they were high quality and had an abundance of buds or *tips* – for example *Flowery Broken Orange Pekoe*. These teas were also sometimes described as being *Golden* or *Tippy*, or both. These grades are still in use for loose teas. A much simpler system of size grading is now used in the trade for the teas destined for common teabags.

Specialist teas that are now widely available often carry the names of well-known tea districts such as *Assam, Ceylon, Darjeeling and Kenya*. Other names used include:

254

Earl Grey	A black high quality blend, flavoured with oil of bergamot, supposedly copied from a blend given to Earl Grey in the 1830s
Jasmine	Green China tea scented with jasmine flowers
Keemun	Fine black tea from the Anhui province of east China
Lapsang Souchong	Black *Souchong* flavoured with pinewood smoke
Oolong	A semi-fermented China tea
Pouchong	China tea scented with the petals of flowers, such as roses
Russian Caravan	Strong black China tea with a slight smoky aroma
Yunnan	A black tea from the Yunnan province of west China

Glossary

arkatti	Indian labour-recruiting agent
capito	African foreman
chifwamba	African myth that Europeans eat African children
chiperone	heavy mist
cohong	guild of Chinese merchants allowed to deal with foreigners
coolie	oriental labourer
cumbly	coarse cotton shawl
diwani	the right to collect revenue in the Mughal Empire
kangany	south Indian labour contractor and foreman
korahl	Ceylonese elephant stockade
mahout	elephant driver or keeper
nawab	prince of the Mughal Empire
palkee	palanquin
punkah	large manually operated fan
sardar	headman or foreman
thangata	work in lieu of rent
-walla	suffix for person – i.e. a palanquin bearer is a *palkee-wallah*

Weights and Measures
Approximate Equivalents

£1 sterling	=	10 Indian Rupees
1 s. (shilling)	=	5p.
2½d. (pennies)	=	1p.
1 oz. (ounce)	=	28 grams
1 lb. (pound)	=	454 grams
1 ton	=	1,016 kilograms
1 foot	=	0.3 metre
1 yard (3 feet)	=	0.9 metre
1 mile (1,760 yards)	=	1.6 kilometres
1 acre (4,840 square yards)	=	0.40 hectare
1 square mile (640 acres)	=	2.49 square kilometres

Select Bibliography

H. A. Antrobus, *A History of the Assam Company, 1839–1953* (Edinburgh: Constable, 1957)

Samuel Baildon, *The Tea Industry in India* (London: Allen, 1882)

Colin Baker, *Seeds of Trouble: Government Policy and Land Rights in Nyasaland, 1946–64* (London: British Academic Press, 1993)

George Barker, *A Tea Planter's Life in Assam* (Calcutta: Thacker, Spink, 1884)

H. K. Barpujari, *Assam in the Days of the Company, 1826–1858* (Gauhati: Lawyer's Book Stall, 1963)

Rana P. Behal and Prabhu P. Mohapatra, 'Tea and Money versus Human Life' in *Plantations, Proletarians and Peasants in Colonial Asia* (London: Frank Cass, 1992)

Zhang Binglun, 'Tea', in *Ancient China's Technology and Science* (Beijing: Foreign Languages Press, 1983)

John Blofeld, *The Chinese Art of Tea* (London: Allen & Unwin, 1985)

Edward Bramah, *Tea & Coffee* (London: Hutchinson, 1972)

C. A. Bruce, *Report on the Manufacture of Tea* (Edinburgh: Adam & Charles Black, 1840)

H. W. Cave, *Golden Tips* (London: Low, Marston, 1900)

K. N. Chaudhri, *The Trading World of Asia and the English East India Company, 1660–1760* (Cambridge: Cambridge U. P., 1978)

Maurice Corina, *Pile it High, Sell it Cheap* (London: Weidenfeld & Nicolson, 1971)

Sir Henry Cotton, *India and Home Memories* (London: Fisher, Unwin, 1911)

David Crole, *Tea* (London: Crosby Lockwood, 1897)

Select Bibliography

A. J. Dash, *Bengal District Gazeteers – Darjeeling* (Alipore, Bengal: 1947)

K. M. De Silva, *A History of Sri Lanka* (London: Hurst, 1981)

Stephen Dowell, *A History of Taxation and Taxes in England* (London: Longmans, Green, 1888)

Sir Frederick Morton Eden, *The State of the Poor* (London: J. Davis for B. and J. White, 1797)

J. C. Evans, *Tea in China* (New York; London: Greenwood Press, 1992)

John K. Fairbank, *The Cambridge History of China*, vol. 10, part 1 (London: Cambridge U. P., 1978)

Peter Ward Fay, *The Opium War, 1840–1842* (New York: Norton, 1976)

Denys Forrest, *Tea for the British* (London: Chatto & Windus, 1973)

Denys Forrest, *A Hundred Years of Ceylon Tea, 1867–1967* (London: Chatto & Windus, 1967)

Robert Fortune, *Two Visits to the Tea Countries of China and the British Tea Plantations in the Himalayas* (London: John Murray, 1853)

Sir Edward Gait, *A History of Assam* (Calcutta: Thacker, Spink, 1926)

Sir Percival Griffiths, *The History of the Indian Tea Industry* (London: Weidenfeld & Nicolson, 1967)

W. S. Griswold, *The Boston Tea Party* (Tunbridge Wells: Abacus, 1973)

A. B. Guha, *Planter-Raj to Swaraj* (Delhi: Indian Council of Historical Research, 1977)

Ranajit Das Gupta, 'Plantation Labour in Colonial India' in *Plantations, Proletarians and Peasants in Colonial Asia* (London: Frank Cass, 1992)

V. M. Hamilton and S. M. Fasson, *Scenes in Ceylon* (London: Chapman & Hall, 1881)

Jonas Hanway, *An Essay on Tea* (London: H. Woodfall, 1756)

Henry Hobhouse, *Seeds of Change* (London: Macmillan, 1992)

Sir Joseph Hooker, *Himalayan Journals* (London: Ward, Lock, 1905)

M. M. Inamdar, *Bombay GPO* (Hubli, Karnataka: Philatelic Association, 1988)

Sir Harry Johnston, *British Central Africa* (London: Methuen, 1897)

B. W. Labaree, *The Boston Tea Party* (London: Oxford U. P., 1964)

Bryant Lillywhite, *London Coffee Houses* (London: George Allen & Unwin, 1963)

Oscar Lindgren, *The Trials of a Planter* (Kalimpong: Lindgren, 1933)

Jan Huygen van Linschoten, *Discours of Voyages into y East & West Indies* (London: 1598)

H. H. Mann, *The Early History of the Tea Industry in North-East India* (1918)

W. Milburn, *Oriental Commerce* (London: Black, Parry, 1813)

P. D. Millie, *Thirty Years Ago: Or Reminiscences of the Early Days of Coffee Planting in Ceylon* (Colombo: Ferguson, 1878)

H. B. Morse, *The Chronicles of the East India Company Trading to China 1635–1834* (London: Oxford U. P., 1926)

Hoh-cheung Mui and Lorna H. Mui, *Shops and Shopkeeping in Eighteenth-Century England* (Kingston, Ontario: McGill-Queen's U. P., 1989)

Hoh-cheung Mui and Lorna H. Mui, 'Smuggling and the British Tea Trade before 1784', *American Historical Review*, 74(1) (1968), 44–73

R. B. Nye and J. E. Morpurgo, *The History of the United States* (London: Penguin, 1964)

B. Pachai, *Land and Politics in Malawi, 1875–1975* (Kingston, Ontario: Limestone Press, 1978)

B. Pachai, *Malawi: The History of the Nation* (London: Longman, 1973)

Simon Paulli, *A Treatise on Tobacco, Tea, Coffee, and Chocolate* translated by Dr James (London: T. Osborne, 1746)

Patrick Peebles, *Sri Lanka: A Handbook of Historical Statistics* (Boston, Mass: G. K. Hall, 1982)

Jane Pettigrew, *A Social History of Tea* (London: National Trust, 2001)

R. K. Renford, *The Non-Official British in India to 1920* (Delhi: Oxford U. P., 1987)

G. B. Ramusio, *Navigazioni e Viaggi* (Amsterdam: Theatrum Orbis Terrarum, 1967–70)

W. A. Sabonadière, *The Coffee Planter of Ceylon* (Guernsey: Mackenzie, Son & Le Patourel, 1866)

J. Sainsbury Ltd, *JS 100: The Story of Sainsbury's* (London: Sainsbury, 1969)

Nicola Swainson, *The Development of Corporate Capitalism in Kenya, 1918–77* (Berkeley: University of California, 1980)

Tea Association (Central Africa) Ltd, *Tea in Malawi* (Zomba: Tea Association [Central Africa], 1967)

Stephen H. Twining, *The House of Twining 1706–1956* (London: Twining, 1956)

W. H. Ukers, *All about Tea* (New York: Tea and Coffee Trade Journal, 1935)

John Weatherstone, *The Pioneers 1825–1900: The Early British Tea and Coffee Planters and their Way of Life* (London: Quiller Press, 1986)

Bennett Alan Weinberg and Bonnie K. Bealer, *The World of Caffeine* (New York: Routledge, 2001)

Dharmapriya Wesumperuma, *The Migration and Conditions of Immigrant Labour in Ceylon* (unpublished Ph.D. thesis, University of London, 1974)

T. David Williams, *Malawi: The Politics of Despair* (Ithaca: Cornell U. P., 1978)

Warwick Wroth, *The London Pleasure Gardens of the Eighteenth Century* (London: Macmillan, 1896)

Lu Yü, *The Classic of Tea*, translated by Francis Ross Carpenter (Boston, Mass: Little, Brown, 1974)

Anonymous, *An Essay on the Nature, Use and Abuse of Tea* (London: J. Bettenham for James Lacy, 1722)

Anonymous, *Deadly Adulteration and Slow Poisoning* (London: Sherwood, Gilbert & Piper, 1830?)

Anonymous, *The Genuine History of the Inhuman and Unparalell'd Murders committed on the Bodies of Mr. W. G. . . .* (London: 1749)

Anonymous, *The History of the Tea Plant* (London: London Genuine Tea Co., 1820)

A collection of reports, letters, advices, tables, etc., related to trade in the East, 1691–1732 (University of London Library, MS 56):

— *Instructions for Chooseing of Tea Fitt for London*

— *Observations of ye Sorts of Tea & the Methods used in Dryeing & Cureing Tea in China*

Official Publications (British Library, Oriental and India Office Collections)

Report of the Committee Appointed to Enquire into the Causes of Mortality Amongst Labourers Proceeding to the Tea Districts, 1867

Report of the Commissioners Appointed to Enquire into the State and Prospects of Tea Cultivation in Assam, Cachar, and Sylhet, 1868

Papers Regarding the Tea Industry in Bengal, 1873 (Including a Note by J. Ware Edgar)

Report of the Labour Enquiry Commission of Bengal, 1896

Report of the Assam Labour Enquiry Committee, 1906

Report of the Assam Labour Enquiry Committee, 1921–2

Report of the Royal Commission on Labour in India, 1931

Reports on the Administration of the Province of Assam, 1880–1900

Emmigration Letters from Bengal and India, 1880–1910

Index

Page numbers in italics refer to illustrations.

Index

Index

Index

Index

270

Index

Acknowledgements

I should like to thank D. Hegde, Krishn Dev, Richard Illingworth, Malik Fernado and Stephen Kitchen for updating my knowledge of the tea industry.

My researches in Britain were made much easier by the help I received from the staff of the British Library, the libraries of the Royal Botanic Garden Edinburgh, the Royal Horticultural Society, and of the School of African and Oriental Studies and the Institute of Historical Research in the University of London. Once again, my colleagues at the University of London Library have given me much assistance. The tea tree and tea bud drawings were by Gabriel Sempill.

The idea for this book came from Mel Yarker. My agent, Carole Blake, and my editor, Carol O'Brien, helped shape it. Helen Armitage, Maria Lord and Nerina de Silva gave me much useful advice. I am very grateful to them all.